Englischer Wortschatz
Geographie

Englischer Wortschatz Geographie

von
Margitta Eckhardt
Peter Metschar
Christian Moser

Ernst Klett Sprachen
Stuttgart

Bildquellennachweis:
Umschlag Fotosearch Stock Photography, Waukesha, WI; **9** shutterstock (Angela Jones), New York, NY; **33** Klett-Archiv (Wolfgang Schaar, Grafing nach Globus Infografik, dpa 6730), Stuttgart; **252** Avenue Images GmbH RF (Geoatlas), Hamburg; **252** shutterstock (AridOcean), New York, NY; **252** Fotolia LLC (Flavijus Piliponis), New York; **252** Fotolia LLC (cpauschert), New York; **252** Klett-Archiv (Klett-Archiv), Stuttgart; **253** NASA (PD), Washington, D.C.; **253** shutterstock (Sam DCruz), New York, NY; **253** Fotosearch Stock Photography, Waukesha, WI; **255** Fotolia LLC (Renato Francia), New York; **255** Klett-Archiv (www.klett-gis.de), Stuttgart; **261** Klett-Archiv (Wolfgang Schaar, Grafing), Stuttgart; **261** shutterstock (Evskaya Daria Igorevna), New York, NY; **262** Klett-Archiv (Aribert Jung), Stuttgart; **262** Fotolia LLC (Otto Durst), New York; **262** Klett-Archiv (Rausch-Linsenhofen), Stuttgart; **262** iStockphoto (Denis Selivanov), Calgary, Alberta; **262** DEBRIV, Köln; **262** Fotolia LLC (myfoto), New York; **262** shutterstock (Markus Gann), New York, NY; **262** MEV Verlag GmbH, Augsburg; **262** Klett-Archiv (Marion Rausch, Frickenhausen-Linsenhofen), Stuttgart; **262** Bayerische Landesanstalt für Landwirtschaft (LfL). **263** (http://www.lfl.bayern.de/(umfangreiches Internetangebot)), Freising
Nicht in allen Fällen war es uns möglich, den Rechteinhaber der Abbildungen ausfindig zu machen. Berechtigte Ansprüche werden selbstverständlich im Rahmen der üblichen Vereinbarungen abgegolten.

1. Auflage   1 $^{10\ 9\ 8}$ | 2024 23 22

Alle Drucke dieser Auflage sind unverändert und können im Unterricht nebeneinander verwendet werden.
Die letzte Zahl bezeichnet das Jahr des Druckes. Das Werk und seine Teile sind urheberrechtlich geschützt. Jede Nutzung in anderen als den gesetzlich zugelassenen Fällen bedarf der vorherigen schriftlichen Einwilligung des Verlags.

© Ernst Klett Sprachen GmbH, Stuttgart 2009. Alle Rechte vorbehalten.
Internetadresse: www.klett.de

Autoren: Margitta Eckhardt, Peter Metschar, Christian Moser

Redaktion: Bettina Höfels
Fachkorrektorat: Rob Bowden, EASI-Educational Resourcing, UK
Layoutkonzeption: Eva Mokhlis, Ulrike Wollenberg
Illustrationen: Sven Palmowski, Barcelona
Gestaltung und Satz: Dörr + Schiller GmbH, Stuttgart
Umschlaggestaltung: Elmar Feuerbach
Titelbild: Fotosearch Stock Photography, Waukesha, WI
Druck und Bindung: Elanders GmbH, Waiblingen

Printed in Germany

ISBN 978-3-12-580102-8

Inhaltsverzeichnis

Einführung	7

I. In the geography classroom ... 9

1 General classroom phrases . 10
1.1 In the classroom ... 10

2 Geographic disciplines ... 12
2.1 Physical geography ... 12
2.2 Human geography ... 12
2.3 Climatology ... 13
2.4 Geomorphology ... 14
2.5 Pedology ... 15
2.6 Economic geography ... 15

3 Working with 16
3.1 Atlas and maps ... 16
    Physical maps ... 17
    Talking about topographic maps ... 19
    Thematic maps ... 20
    Comparisons ... 21
3.2 Illustrations and presentations ... 21
    Illustrations and visuals ... 21
3.3 Numbers ... 26
3.4 GIS ... 31

II. Thematic vocabulary ... 33

1 Planet earth ... 34
1.1 Topography ... 34
1.2 Continents and countries ... 36
    General ... 36
    Continents and oceans ... 37
    Straits and gulfs ... 39
    Rivers ... 39
    Lakes ... 40
    Deserts ... 40
    Mountains ... 41
    Glaciers and more ice ... 41
    Europe ... 41
    Northwestern Uplands ... 42
    North European Lowlands ... 42
    Central Plateaus ... 43
    The Alpine system ... 43
    Germany ... 44
    Asia ... 46
    North America: physiographic regions ... 48
    A brief geography of North America ... 49

2 Physical environment ... 51
2.1 Tectonics ... 51
    Earth's interior ... 51
    Plate tectonics ... 52
    Volcanism and earthquakes . 53
2.2 Lithosphere ... 57
    Rock types ... 57
    Weathering ... 59
    Soils ... 60
2.3 Climate ... 63
    Weather ... 63
    Climate ... 65
    Atmospheric circulation ... 69
    Wind systems ... 70
    Climate and vegetation zones ... 71
2.4 Landforms ... 76
    Mountains, hills and valleys . 76
    Rivers, streams and swamps 78
    Oceans and the sea ... 79
    Glacial ... 79
    Fluvial ... 81
    Wind ... 84
    Coastal ... 84
2.5 Hydrology ... 87
    Resource water ... 87
    Marine ecosystems ... 90
2.6 Endangered environments ... 93
    Natural hazards ... 93
    Man-made hazards ... 95
    Sustainability ... 98

3 Human environment ... 100
3.1 Industry ... 100

Natural resources 103
Industries 108
3.2 Agriculture 113
    Agricultural products 118
    Agricultural systems 123
    Food industry 126
    Ecological agriculture 127
3.3 Population 129
    Characteristics 129
    Development 133
    Migration 135
3.4 Trade, services and consumer 138
    Trade 138
    Services 146
    Growth of services 147
    Service sectors 148
    Distribution of services 149
    Consumer and market 151
3.5 Ecology and economy 155
    The social question 155
    Economic background 156
    Energy demand 157
    Ecology and the environment 159
    Environmental protection 161
3.6 Urban areas and urbanisation 162
    Urban areas – rural areas 162
    Indicators for cities 166
    Dwellings 168
    Traffic 168
    Infrastructure 169

Cities in different historical
and cultural environments ... 170
Central-place theory 174
Stages in urbanisation 176
Effects of urbanisation 176
Regional planning and spatial
development 177
Spatial analysis: indicators ... 178
3.7 World development: stages
    and indicators 178
    Stages 178
    Indices 180
    Factors 183
    Explaining inequalities 188
    Aid 190
    Examples 192
3.8 Globalisation 194
    Multinational corporations ... 194
    Consequences of globalisation 195
    Economic 196
    Geographical 197
    Communication and Internet 199

Appendix
Englisches Stichwortregister 201
Deutsches Stichwortregister 225
Übersicht über die Infoboxen 249
Phonetische Umschrift 249
Verwendete Abkürzungen 250

Illustrations 251

Einführung

Der vorliegende Wortschatz wurde für den bilingualen Sachfachunterricht konzipiert und ist aus der Unterrichtspraxis heraus entstanden. Entsprechend ist der Wortschatz auf die Themen der aktuellen Lehrpläne für das Fach Erdkunde ausgerichtet. Dabei wurden die thematischen Ansätze der gängigen Lehrwerke für den deutschsprachigen Erdkundeunterricht ebenso berücksichtigt, wie auch die Ansätze von Werken, die speziell für den englischsprachigen Unterricht entwickelt wurden.
Darüber hinaus bilden Lehrwerke aus dem angelsächsischen Sprachraum, englischsprachige Fachzeitschriften, Quellen aus dem Internet sowie ein- und zweisprachige Wörterbücher eine wichtige Grundlage für den vorliegenden Wortschatz.

Ziel des Wortschatzes ist es, Lehrenden und Lernenden schnell Zugang zur relevanten Lexik, die für eine reibungslose Kommunikation im Erdkundeunterricht unabdingbar ist, zu verschaffen. Dabei werden nicht allein geographische Fachtermini im thematischen Zusammenhang gelistet. Vielmehr ermöglicht die Kombination aus Fachbegriffen und zahlreichen Redemitteln, Textbausteinen und Beispielsätzen den korrekten Einsatz der Fachbegriffe in schriftlicher und mündlicher Kommunikation.

Der *Englische Wortschatz Geographie* gliedert sich in zwei große Teilbereiche sowie einen umfangreichen Anhang mit Stichwortregistern und illustriertem Wortschatz.

Der erste Teil **In the Geography Classroom** ist der schriftlichen und mündlichen Kommunikation gewidmet. Hier finden sich neben grundlegendem Klassenzimmervokabular, Kernbegriffe des Sachfachs und – in Form von Sprachbausteinen und Redemitteln – umfangreicher Wortschatz für alle aktiven Bereiche des Erdkundeunterrichts. So geht es um die Arbeit mit Atlas und Karten genauso wie um den Einsatz von GIS. Der Umgang mit Tabellen, Charts und Grafiken wird ebenso dargestellt wie die Präsentation von Arbeitsergebnissen.

Im Zentrum des Wortschatzes steht der zweite Teil des Buches: **Thematic Vocabulary**. Dieser Teil vermittelt den thematisch geordneten Wortschatz zu den Kernthemen des Erdkundeunterrichts. Dabei ist jedes Kernthema in Unterthemen gegliedert, in denen der Wortschatz in lernerfreundlichen, übersichtlichen Lerneinheiten präsentiert wird. Die Gliederung in Haupteinträge und davon abgeleitete Untereinträge ermöglicht einen schnellen Überblick über einen Themenbereich sowie eine gründliche Vertiefung. Zahlreiche Fachbegriffe werden mit ihren gängigen Synonymen dargestellt. Zusatzinformationen, die einer Vielzahl von Begriffen zugeordnet werden, erleichtern darüber hinaus das Verständnis des komplexen Fachwortschatzes.
Natürlich werden auch im **Thematic Vocabulary** die Fachbegriffe durch Redemittel und Beispielsätze so angereichert, dass die individuelle Sprachproduktion

leicht fällt. Schwierig auszusprechende Wörter werden mit der phonetischen Umschrift wiedergegeben.

Um größere Dopplungen im Wortschatz zu umgehen, finden sich bei einzelnen Kapiteln Querverweise auf engverwandte Themenbereiche.

Beide Bereiche, **In the Geography Classroom** und **Thematic Vocabulary**, enthalten zahlreiche **Infoboxen** zu verschiedenen Themen, die Wortschatz und kontextuelle Informationen fokussiert darstellen. Eine Liste der Infoboxen findet sich im **Anhang**.

Der *Englische Wortschatz Geographie* versteht sich als Lernwortschatz. Seine thematische Aufbereitung ist darauf ausgerichtet, den Wortschatz in leicht zu verarbeitenden Lernportionen zu präsentieren. Dabei können das Pensum und die Vorgehensweise ganz individuell gehandhabt werden. Natürlich empfiehlt es sich hier, wie bei Wortschatzarbeit generell, regelmäßig und in kleinen Einheiten zu lernen. Dazu bietet die vorliegende Zusammenstellung eine ideale Grundlage.

Darüber hinaus ermöglicht der umfangreiche **Anhang** mit **deutschem und englischem Stichwortregister**, das schnelle Nachschlagen des hochspezialisierten Fachwortschatzes in beide Sprachrichtungen. Der Verweis auf die entsprechenden Seiten ordnet das Wort jeweils in den spezifischen Kontext ein. Dabei kann ein Begriff mehr als einem Kontext zugeordnet sein.

In Kombination mit dem Inhaltsverzeichnis, ist der richtige Zusammenhang schnell gefunden.

Schließlich enthält der Anhang einen umfangreichen, vierfarbigen **Abbildungsteil**, der ausgewähltes Kernvokabular visualisiert und so den Lernerfolg unterstützt.

Wir wünschen viel Erfolg und Spaß
mit dem *Englischen Wortschatz Geographie*!

Das Autorenteam

I. In the Geography Classroom

1 General classroom phrases

1.1 In the classroom

»

Take out your ...	exercise book. notebook. pencil case.	Nimm dein ... Nehmen Sie Ihr ... Nehmt euer ...	Heft, Schulheft Federmäppchen	heraus.

Keep your books closed.	Lasst die Bücher zu / geschlossen.
copy sth	etw. abschreiben / etw. übertragen
trace sth	etw. nachmalen / etw. durchpausen
chart	Diagramm / Schaubild / Tabelle / Tafel

Describe ... Look at ... Study ... Think about ... Point at ... Explain ...	the picture the text the exercise the map the graph the table the climate graph the diagram the chart the line the contour the elevation profile the following	Beschreibt ... Schaut ... an Untersucht ... Denkt über ... nach Zeigt auf ... Erklärt ...	das Bild » Abb. 3 den Text die Aufgabe die Karte das Diagramm die Tabelle das Klimadiagramm das Diagramm das Schaubild die Linie die Kontur / den Umriss das Höhenprofil das Folgende / Folgendes
Examine ... List ...	reasons for sth reasons against sth arguments for sth arguments against sth	Untersucht ... Führt ... auf.	Gründe für etw. Gründe gegen etw. Argumente für etw. Argumente gegen etw.
Use evidence from (the text)	to explain ...	Verwendet Hinweise aus (dem Text)	um zu erklären ...
Find out ... Show ... Investigate ... Examine ...	when / where / why / how much ...	Findet heraus ... Zeigt ... Untersucht ... Untersucht ...	wann / wo / warum / wie viel ...

Give examples of sth	Gebt Beispiele von / für etw.
Find evidence of / for sth	Findet Anhaltspunkte für etw.
What evidence can you find to show ...?	Welche Anhaltspunkte könnt ihr finden, um ... zu zeigen?

What reasons are there for …?		Welche Gründe gibt es für …?	
What evidence is there that …?		Welche Anhaltspunkte gibt es dafür, dass …?	
What indicates that …?		Was deutet darauf hin, dass …?	
What proves that …?		Was beweist, dass …?	
Give reasons	for your answer. for your view.	Gebt Gründe	für eure Antwort. für eure Ansicht.
Interpret … Discuss …	the text. the sources. the material.	Interpretiert … Diskutiert …	den Text. die Quellen. das Material.

What conclusion do you draw / reach from …? | Welchen Schluss / Welche Schlussfolgerung zieht ihr aus …?

What is your opinion on …?
What do you think of … / about …?
What is your impression of …?
What impression do you get from …? | Was denkt ihr über …?
Was ist eure Meinung über …?
Was ist euer Eindruck von …?
Welchen Eindruck bekommt ihr von …?

What were (could/might have been) (the) reasons for …?
What were (could/might have been) the results of …? | Was waren (könnten gewesen sein) die Gründe für …?
Was waren (könnten gewesen sein) die Ergebnisse von …?

Why do you think this happened? | Warum glaubst du / glaubt ihr ist dies passiert?

What were the reasons this happened?
Where (When, Why, How) can you find …?
When (Where, Why, How) did it happen? | Aus welchen Gründen geschah dies?
Wo (Wann, Warum, Wie) findet man …?
Wann (Wo, Warum, Wie) geschah es?

Let's compare X and Y. | Lasst uns X und Y vergleichen.

Let's examine the development of X and Y. | Lasst uns die Entwicklung von X und Y untersuchen.

Let's draw a parallel between … | Lasst uns eine Parallele zwischen … ziehen.

Let's contrast X with Y. | Lasst uns einen Vergleich zwischen X und Y anstellen.

The major (central) differences (similarities) between X and Y are … | Die wichtigsten (zentralen) Unterschiede (Ähnlichkeiten) zwischen X und Y sind …

What differences (similarities) can you find between X and Y?
Welche Unterschiede (Ähnlichkeiten) könnt ihr zwischen X und Y finden?
What are the main differences (similarities) between X and Y?
Was sind die Hauptunterschiede (Hauptähnlichkeiten) zwischen X und Y?

2 Geographic disciplines

geography [ʤiˈɒgrəfi] n   Geografie
physical geography [ˈfɪzɪkəlʤiˈɒgrəfi] n   Physische Geografie
human geography n   Humangeografie / Anthropogeografie
discipline [ˈdɪsəplɪn] n   wissenschaftliche Disziplin

2.1 Physical geography

biogeography [baɪəʊ ʤiˈɒgrəfi] n   Biogeografie
climatology [klaɪməˈtɒləʤi] n   Klimageografie / Klimatologie
coastal geography n   Küstengeografie
environmental geography [ɪnˌvaɪrənˈmentl ʤiˈɒgrəfi] n   Umweltgeografie
geodesy [ʤiˈɒdɪsi] n   Geodäsie / Vermessungswesen
geomorphology [ˌʤiːəʊmɔːˈfɒləʤi] n   Geomorphologie
glaciology [ˈgleɪsiɒləʤi] [glæfiɒləʤi] (Aussprache AE) n   Glaziologie
hydrology [haɪˈdrɒləʤi] n   Hydrologie
landscape ecology n   Landschaftsökologie / Geoökologie
oceanography [ˌəʊʃənˈɒgrəfi] n   Ozeanografie
palaeogeography [ˌpæliɒʤiˈɒgrəfi] n   Paläogeografie
palaeoclimatology [ˌpæliɒklaɪməˈtɒləʤi] n   Paläoklimatologie
pedology [ˌpedɒˈləʤi] n   Pedologie / Bodengeografie

2.2 Human geography

agricultural geography n   Agrargeografie
behavioural geography [bɪˈheɪvjərəlʤiˌɒgrəfi] n   Verhaltensgeografie
cognitive geography n   Wahrnehmungsgeografie
cultural geography n   Kulturgeografie
development geography n   Entwicklungsgeografie
economic geography n   Wirtschaftsgeografie
health geography n   Gesundheitsgeografie
historical geography n   Historische Geografie
political geography n   Politische Geografie
population geography n   Bevölkerungsgeografie
demography [dɪˈmɒgrəfi] n   Demografie / Bevölkerungswissenschaft

geography of religion / religious geography n — Religionsgeografie
rural geography ['rʊərl͵dʒi'ɒgrəfi] n — Geografie des ländlichen Raumes
settlement geography n — Siedlungsgeografie
social geography n — Sozialgeografie
transportation geography n — Verkehrsgeografie
tourism geography n — Fremdenverkehrsgeografie
urban geography ['ɜːbndʒi͵ɒgrəfi] n — Stadtgeografie

2.3 Climatology » II 2.3 Climate

climatology [͵klaɪmə'tɒlədʒi] n	Klimatologie
climate ['klaɪmət] n	Klima
element n	Element
factor n	Faktor
natural environment / environment n	Umwelt

weather n	Wetter
weather record n	Wetteraufzeichnung
weather conditions n	Witterungsverhältnisse
average ['ævrɪdʒ] n	Durchschnitt
average ['ævrɪdʒ] adj	durchschnittlich
long-term adj	Langzeit~
atmosphere ['ætməsfɪə] n	Atmosphäre
composition n	Zusammensetzung
ocean n	Ozean
land surface [lænd 'sɜːfɪs] n	Landfläche
weather forecast n	Wettervorhersage

pollution [pə'luːʃn] n	Verschmutzung
man-made pollution / anthropogenic pollution [͵ænθrəpəʊ'dʒenɪk pə'luːʃn]	anthropogene Verschmutzung
atmospheric boundary layer n	atmosphärische Grenzschicht
circulation pattern n	Zirkulationsmuster
heat transfer n	Wärmeaustausch
radiative adj	Strahlungs~ / radioaktiv
convective adj	konvektive
latent ['leɪtnt] adj	latent

climate ['klaɪmət] n	Klima
climate zone ['klaɪmət ˌzəʊn]	Klimazone
polar climate [ˌpəʊlə'klaɪmət]	polares Klima
temperate climate [ˌtempret'klaɪmət]	gemäßigtes Klima
subtropical climate [sʌb'trɒpɪkl ˌklaɪmət]	subtropisches Klima
tropical climate	tropisches Klima
global warming n	globale Erwärmung
CO_2 emission n	CO_2-Emission

» anthropogenic greenhouse effect | anthropogener Treibhauseffekt

» Climatology focuses on long-term observations of atmospheric processes, whereas meteorology observes the short-term weather systems.
Die Klimatologie befasst sich mit Langzeitbeobachtungen atmosphärischer Prozesse, wohingegen sich die Meteorologie mit der Beobachtung von kurzzeitigen Wettersystemen beschäftigt.

2.4 Geomorphology » II 2.4 Landforms

geomorphology [ˌdʒiːəʊmɔː'fɒlədʒi] n	Geomorphologie
physiography [ˌfɪzi'ɒgrəfi] n	Physiografie *(Morphologie der Erdoberfläche)*
shape n	Form / Gestalt
shape of the earth	Form der Erde
geology [dʒi'ɒlədʒi] n	Geologie
geological structure	geologische Struktur
surface ['sɜːfɪs] n	Oberfläche
landscape n	Landschaft

process n	Prozess
erosion [ɪ'rəʊʒn] n	Erosion / Abtrag
weathering ['weðərɪŋ] n	Verwitterung
deposition n	Ablagerung / Deposition
sediment ['sedɪmənt] n	Sediment
denudation [ˌdiːnjuː'deɪʃn] n	Abtragung / Denudation
eolian denudation [iˌəʊliəndiːnjuː'deɪʃn] / wind erosion	Winderosion
abrasion [ə'breɪʒn] n	Abrasion / Abrieb / Abschleifung
ablation [ə'bleɪʃn] n	Ablation / Ablösung / Abtragung

river n	Fluss » Abb. 7
coastline n	Küstenlinie
rock type n	Gesteinsart
slope n	Hang
slope formation n	Hangbildung
ice n	Eis

» Geomorphology is the study of landforms and the processes by which the surface of the Earth is shaped.
Geomorphologie ist die wissenschaftliche Untersuchung der Landformen und der Prozesse, die die Erdoberfläche formen.

2.5 Pedology » II 2.2 Lithosphere

pedology [ˌpedɒˈlədʒi] n	Pedologie / Bodengeografie
soil n	Boden
composition n	Zusammensetzung
layer n	Schicht
soil layer	Bodenschicht
topsoil n	Oberboden
organic matter n	organisches Material
biomass [ˌbaɪəʊˈmæs] n	Biomasse
cultivation n	Anbau / Bestellung *(von Land)*
eluviate v	auswaschen
substance n	Substanz
mineral n	Mineral / Mineralstoff
subsoil n	Unterboden
illuviate v	anreichern

» Pedology is the study of soils in their natural environment.
Pedologie ist die Wissenschaft der Böden in ihrer natürlichen Umgebung.

2.6 Economic geography » II 3.4; 3.5; 3.6; 3.8

economic geography n	Wirtschaftsgeografie
analysis, *pl* analyses n	Analyse
spatial distribution [ˌspeɪʃldɪstrɪˈbjuːʃn] n	räumliche Verteilung
consumption n	Konsum / Verbrauch
resource n	Ressource
goods n pl	Güter / Waren

15

service n	Dienstleistung
produce v	produzieren
economic activity n	wirtschaftliche Aktivität
optimise *BE* / optimize *AE* v	optimieren
development n	Entwicklung
underdevelopment n	Unterentwicklung
interrelationship n	Wechselbeziehung
industrial adj	industriell / Industrie~
spatial analysis [ˌspeɪʃləˈnæləsɪs] n	Raumanalyse

» Economic geography analyses the spatial distribution of the production, transportation and consumption of services, resources and goods and their effects.
Wirtschaftgeografie analysiert die räumliche Verteilung von Produktion, Transport und Konsum von Dienstleistungen, Ressourcen und Gütern und deren Auswirkungen.

3 Working with ...

3.1 Atlas and maps

atlas [ˈætləs], *pl* atlases n	Atlas *(Pl. Atlasse)*
historical atlas	Geschichtsatlas
road atlas	Straßenatlas
school atlas	Schulatlas

projection [prəʊˈdʒekʃn] n	Projektion / Darstellung » Abb. 1
map projection	Kartendarstellung
plane projection	Azimutalprojektion
conic projection [ˈkɒnɪkprəʊˌdʒekʃn]	Kegelprojektion
cylindrical projection [səˈlɪndrɪklprəʊˌdʒekʃn]	Zylinderprojektion
interrupted projection	zerlappte Projektion

table of contents n	Inhaltsverzeichnis
index [ˈɪndeks] n	Stichwortverzeichnis / Index / Register
index of maps	Kartenübersicht
register [ˈredʒɪstə] n	Register
legend [ˈledʒənd] / key n	Legende » Abb. 2

scale [skeɪl] n	Maßstab
scale line	Maßstabsbalken
large scale	großmaßstäblich (groß dargestellter, detaillierter Karteninhalt)
small scale	kleinmaßstäblich (klein dargestellter Karteninhalt)
section n	Abschnitt / Absatz / Kapitel
data ['deɪtə] n pl	Daten
data set	Datensatz
gazetteer [ˌgæzə'tɪə] n	alphabetisches Ortsverzeichnis (mit geografischen Angaben)
physical map n	physische Karte
thematic map [θɪ'mætɪkˌmæp] n	thematische Karte

What scale is this map? It's one to five thousand.		Welchen Maßstab hat diese Karte? Sie ist eins zu fünftausend.	
1:1,000,000	1/1,000,000	1:1.000.000	1/1.0000.000
one centimetre to one million metres		eins zu einer Million	

Physical maps » Abb. 2

feature ['fiːtʃə] n	Merkmal / Bestandteil
orientation [ˌɔːrien'teɪʃn] n	Orientierung
colouring BE / coloring AE n	Farbgebung
shade n	Farbton / Schattierung
physical features n pl	physische Merkmale / Kennzeichen
relief [rɪ'liːf] n	Oberflächenform / Relief
mountain n	Berg » Abb. 9
mountainous ['maʊntɪnəs] adj	gebirgig
mountain range n	Gebirgskette / Gebirgszug
valley n	Tal
lowland n	Tiefland
drainage system ['dreɪnɪdʒˌsɪstəm] n	Abflusssystem
river n	Fluss » Abb. 7
lake n	See » Abb. 8
reservoir ['rezəvwɑː] n	Stausee » Abb. 8

3 Working with ... › 3.1 Atlas and maps

» Different colours are used in topographic maps for mountains, lowlands, rivers and lakes or towns and cities.
In topographischen Karten werden für Berge, Tiefländer, Flüsse und Seen oder Städte und Großstädte verschiedene Farben verwendet.

road n	Straße
road network	Straßennetz
transportation route n	Transportweg
railway line *BE* / rail road *AE* n	Bahnlinie / Eisenbahnlinie / Bahngleis
railway network / railway system *BE*	Bahnnetz
line / track *AE*	Gleis
border ['bɔːdə] n	Grenze

height n	Höhe
high adj	hoch
depth [depθ] n	Tiefe
deep adj	tief
width [wɪtθ] n	Breite
wide adj	breit
length [leŋkθ] n	Länge
long adj	lang
elevation [ˌelɪ'veɪʃn] n	Höhe / Erhebung
extension n	Ausdehnung
extend v	sich erstrecken / sich ausdehnen
size n	Größe

region n	Region
map title n	Kartentitel
locate v	verorten / lokalisieren
grid square [ˌgrɪd'skweə] n	Planquadrat
global grid n	Gradnetz der Erde » Abb. 2
longitude ['lɒndʒɪtjuːd] n	(geographische) Länge
latitude ['lætɪtjuːd] n	(geographische) Breite
meridian [mə'rɪdiən] n	Meridian / Längengrad
prime meridian	Null-Meridian
equator [ɪ'kweɪtə] n	Äquator
sea level n	Normalnull / Meeresspiegel
above sea level	über dem Meeresspiegel
below sea level	unter Normalnull

Talking about topographic maps

A place is ...	located situated lies	in a country ... in a region ... east of ... west of ... south of ... north of ... in the west of ... on a river. in the Pacific Ocean. at about 49°N and 9°E.	Ein Ort liegt ...	in einem Land ... in einer Region ... östlich von ... westlich von ... südlich von ... nördlich von ... im Westen von ... an einem Fluss. im Pazifik. bei ca. 49°N und 9° Ost.
The road The railway line		runs from Paris to Lyon. runs along the river. follows the course of a river.	Die Straße Die Bahnlinie	führt von Paris nach Lyon. verläuft am Fluss entlang. folgt dem Flusslauf.
The river		flows from north to south. joins another river. drains into a lake.	Der Fluss	fließt von Norden nach Süden. mündet in einen anderen Fluss. fließt in einen See ab.
The National Park		is 20 km wide and 30 km long. covers an area of 45 sq km. extends for 50 miles into the desert.	Der Nationalpark	ist 20 km breit und 30 km lang. bedeckt eine Fläche von 45 qkm. erstreckt sich 50 Meilen in die Wüste hinein.
The peak of the mountain		is 2000 m high. reaches a height of 2963 m.	Der Gipfel des Berges	ist 2000 m hoch. erreicht eine Höhe von 2963 m.
The elevation of the mountain range		is between 1000 and 1500 m. reaches up to 4000 m.	Die Höhe der Gebirgskette	ist zwischen 1000 und 1500 m. erreicht bis zu 4000 m.

3 Working with ... › 3.1 Atlas and maps

Thematic maps » Abb. 2

thematic map n	thematische Karte
theme [θiːm] n	Thema
main topic n	Gegenstand / Thematik / Thema
nature n	Natur
agriculture [ˈægrɪkʌltʃə] n	Landwirtschaft
industry n	Industrie
economy [ɪˈkɒnəmi] n	Wirtschaft
environment [ɪnˈvaɪrnmənt] n	Umwelt
population n	Bevölkerung
location n	Ort / Lage
distribution n	Verteilung
comparison [kəmˈpærɪsn] n	Vergleich
relation n	Bezug / Beziehung
connection n	Verbindung / Zusammenhang
usage [ˈjuːsɪdʒ] n	Verbrauch / Verwendung

» Most thematic maps use a great variety of symbols which are explained in the key.
Die meisten thematischen Karten verwenden eine große Vielfalt an Zeichen, die in der Legende erklärt sind.

symbol n	Symbol / Zeichen
abstract sign n	abstraktes Zeichen
shading [ˈʃeɪdɪŋ] n	Farbgebung
texture [ˈtekstʃə] n	Aufbau / Struktur

»
location and distribution	Lage und Verteilung
The floor of the valley is used for ...	Die Talsohle wird für ... genutzt.
Agriculture is dominated by ... in ...	In ... wird die Landwirtschaft wird von ... dominiert.
The production of tomatoes is concentrated in the south of ...	Der Anbau von Tomaten konzentriert sich im Süden von ...
Vineyards stretch along ...	Weinberge erstrecken sich entlang ...
Reservoirs are mainly located in / along ...	Stauseen liegen hauptsächlich in / entlang ...
Wheat fields are scattered all over ...	Weizenfelder sind überall in ... verstreut.

Comparisons

comparison n — Vergleich

The production of ... is	higher than ...
	lower than ...
	of higher value than ...
	of lower value than ...
	dominates in ...

Die Produktion von ... ist	höher als ...
	niedriger als ...
	von höherem Wert als ...
	von niedrigerem Wert als ...
	dominiert in ...

Most of the north is used for ...	Der größte Teil des Nordens wird für ... genutzt.
Rice is grown to a greater / smaller extent in the north.	Reis wird im Norden in großem / geringem Ausmaß angebaut.
The range of crops is wider in ...	Die Palette der Feldfrüchte ist in ... größer.
connections and relations	Verbindungen und Beziehungen
The settlements are loosely / directly connected to ...	Die Siedlungen sind lose / direkt verbunden mit ...
Regions are linked with each other by ...	Regionen sind durch ... miteinander verbunden.
A road network / railway network links ...	Ein Straßennetz / Bahnnetz verbindet ...

3.2 Illustrations and presentations

Illustrations and visuals » Abb. 3

visual ['vɪʒuəl] n	Bildmaterial
picture n	Bild
photograph n	Fotografie
aerial photograph [ˌeərɪəl'fəʊtəgrɑːf] n	Luftbild / Luftaufnahme
vertical aerial photograph ['vɜːtɪkl]	Senkrechtluftbild
oblique aerial photograph [ə'bliːk]	Schrägluftbild
satellite image [ˌsætlaɪt'ɪmɪdʒ] n	Satellitenbild
cartoon [kɑː'tuːn] n	Karikatur / Cartoon

3 Working with ... › 3.2 Illustrations and presentations

»

Let's have a look at		Lasst uns ... ansehen.	das Foto
Describe	the photograph	Beschreibt	das Bild
Interpret	the picture	Interpretiert	das Satellitenbild
Discuss	the satellite image	Diskutiert	die Karikatur / den Cartoon
Investige / Examine / Study	the cartoon	Untersucht	

| Use evidence from the picture / satellite image to explain ... | Verwendet Hinweise aus dem Bild / Satellitenbild, um zu erklären ... |

description n — Beschreibung
theme [θiːm] n — Thema
subject n — Gegenstand
issue ['ɪʃuː] n — Sache / Thema
deal with v — behandeln / handeln von
consider [kənˈsɪdə] v — beachten / berücksichtigen
study v — untersuchen / erforschen / prüfen

detail n — Detail / Ausschnitt / Einzelheit
foreground [ˈfɔːgraʊnd] n — Vordergrund
background n — Hintergrund
centre *BE* / center *AE* n — Zentrum / Mitte
bottom n — unterer Rand / unterer Teil
bottom adv — unten
top n — oberer Rand / oberer Teil
top adv — oben
right / right-hand adj — rechte(r; s)
  on the right / on the right-hand side — rechts / auf der rechten Seite
left / left-hand adj — linke(r; s)
  on the left / on the left-hand side — links / auf der linken Seite
in the distance adv — in der Ferne
further away adv — weiter weg
in front of adv — vor
at a right angle adv — im rechten Winkel
near / nearby adv — nahe / in der Nähe
along adv — entlang
alongside adv — längsseits / daneben
on the horizon adv — am Horizont
caption [ˈkæpʃn] n — Bildunterschrift / Bildüberschrift / Beschriftung

» Name the theme or subject of the illustrations.
Benenne das Thema oder den Gegenstand der Illustrationen.

Describe the details.
Beschreibe die Einzelheiten.

Proceed systematically from one side to another or from foreground to background.
Gehe systematisch von einer zur anderen Seite oder vom Vordergrund zum Hintergrund vor.

Consider possible artistic techniques.
Berücksichtige mögliche künstlerische Stilmittel.

Study the words in captions, speech bubbles or labels.
Untersuche die Wörter in Bildüber-/-unterschriften, Sprechblasen oder Beschriftungen.

The … shows …	Das/der … zeigt …
In the picture …	Auf dem Bild …
In the foreground / background…	Im Vordergrund / Hintergrund…
In the top left-hand corner …	In der linken oberen Ecke …
In the bottom right-hand corner …	In der rechten unteren Ecke …
… you can see …	… ist … zu sehen.
The … uses / employs …	Der/die/das …benutzt / setzt … ein.
The caption says …	Die Bildüber-/-unterschrift besagt …
To the right of …	Rechts von …
To the left of …	Links von …

source [sɔːs] n — Quelle
reliable source [rɪˈlaɪəbl] — verlässliche Quelle
title n — Titel / Überschrift
author n — Autor(in)
cartoonist [kɑːtuːnɪst] n — Karikaturist(in)
name v — nennen
publish [ˈpʌblɪʃ] v — veröffentlichen
published adj — veröffentlicht

setting n — Schauplatz
action n — Handlung
device [dɪˈvaɪs] n — Hilfsmittel / Instrument
 rhetorical device [rɪˈtɒrɪkl] — rhetorisches Mittel

3 Working with ... › 3.2 Illustrations and presentations

irony ['aɪrəni] n	Ironie
satire ['sætaɪə] n	Satire
symbolism n	Symbolik
symbol n	Symbol / Bild / Sinnbild
feature n	Kennzeichen / Merkmal
facial expression [ˌfeɪʃlɪk'spreʃn] n	Gesichtsausdruck
body language n	Körpersprache
exaggerate [ɪg'zædʒreɪt] v	übertreiben
exaggerated adj	übertrieben
positioning n	Platzierung
emphasise BE / emphasize AE ['emfəsaɪz] v	betonen / hervorheben
meaning n	Bedeutung
topical event n	aktuelles Ereignis / aktueller Anlass
context n	Zusammenhang / Kontext
refer [rɪ'fɜː] v	(sich) beziehen auf
discuss v	behandeln / erörtern / diskutieren
explain v	erklären / erläutern
positive adj	positiv
negative adj	negativ
neutral adj	neutral
intention n	Absicht / Intention
message n	Botschaft / Mitteilung / Nachricht
effect n	Wirkung / Effekt
aspect n	Gesichtspunkt / Aspekt
reflect v	reflektieren / nachdenken

»

make a point in favour of sth	ein Argument für etw. anbringen
raise a point against sth	ein Argument gegen etw. einbringen

Name the source of the visual.
Nenne die Quelle des Bildmediums.

State what the illustration refers to.
Stelle dar, auf was sich die Illustration bezieht.

Discuss how the figures are presented – in a positive, negative or neutral light.
Erörtere, wie die Figuren dargestellt sind – in einem positiven, negativen oder neutralen Licht.

Analyse the form and function of rhetorical devices, e.g. irony or symbolism.
Analysiere Art und Funktion von rhetorischen Mitteln, z. B. Ironie oder Symbolik.

Explain the intention of the visual.
Erkläre die Absicht des Bildmediums.

»

The ... has to do with / deals with ...	Der/die/das ... hat zu tun mit / handelt von ...
This symbolises / stands for ...	Dies symbolisiert / steht für ...
... refers to ...	... bezieht sich auf / deutet auf ...
... stands for / represents ...	... steht für / ist stellvertretend für ...
The message of ... is ...	Die Botschaft ... ist ...
The ... emphasises ...	Der/die/das ... betont / hebt hervor
The ... wants to express ...	Der/die/das ... möchte ausdrücken ...
... is meant to criticise / satirise ...	... soll kritisieren / persiflieren / satirisch darstellen

»

Explain the effect the visual has on you.
Erkläre, welche Wirkung das Bildmedium auf dich hat.

State your opinion about the topic portrayed in the illustration.
Äußere deine Meinung zu dem Thema, das in der Illustration dargestellt wird.

State why you (do not) like it.
Sage, warum es dir (nicht) gefällt.

agree [əˈgriː] v   zustimmen / einer Meinung sein
disagree v   nicht zustimmen / anderer Meinung sein
in principle adv   prinzipiell / grundsätzlich
opinion / view n   Meinung
point of view n   Ansicht / Sichtweise / Standpunkt
judge [dʒʌdʒ] v   beurteilen / richten

»

I agree / disagree in principle.	Ich stimme dem grundsätzlich zu / nicht zu.
I can't share this point of view.	Ich kann diesen Standpunkt nicht teilen.
In my opinion ...	Meiner Meinung nach ...
From my point of view ...	Aus meiner Sicht ...
As far as I can judge ...	Soweit ich das beurteilen kann ...
The ... touches me / leaves me cold.	Der/die/das ... berührt mich / lässt mich kalt.
I like / dislike ...	Mir gefällt / missfällt ...

3.3 Numbers » Abb. 4

number n	Zahl
data ['deɪtə] n pl	Daten
raw data [rɔː'deɪtə]	Rohdaten / Ausgangsdaten / Ursprungsdaten
process v	aufbereiten / verarbeiten
process data	Daten aufbereiten
data processing	Datenverarbeitung
electronic data processing (EDP)	elektronische Datenverarbeitung (EDV)
graphics ['græfɪks] n pl	Grafik / grafische Darstellung
chart [tʃɑːt] n	Auflistung / Tabelle
table n	Tabelle
graph [grɑːf] n	Diagramm / Schaubild
grid system n	Gittersystem / Rastersystem
axis ['æksɪs], pl axes n	Achse » Abb. 4
horizontal axis	waagerechte Achse
x-axis ['eks͵æksɪs]	X-Achse
vertical axis	senkrechte Achse
y-axis ['waɪ͵æksɪs]	Y-Achse
caption ['kæpʃn] n	Überschrift / Titel
label ['leɪbl] n	Beschriftung
axis label	Achsenbeschriftung
specific label [spə'sɪfɪk͵leɪbl]	spezifische Beschriftung
visualise BE / visualize AE ['vɪʒulaɪz] v	veranschaulichen / sichtbar machen
visualise comparisons	Vergleiche veranschaulichen
visualisation [͵vɪʒulaɪ'zeɪʃn] n	Visualisierung / Veranschaulichung
illustrate v	veranschaulichen / bildlich darstellen

study category n	Untersuchungskategorie
measurement ['meʒəmənt] n	Abmessung
amount [ə'maʊnt] n	Betrag
percentage [pə'sentɪdʒ] n	Prozentsatz

decrease ['diːkriːs] n	Abnahme
decrease [dɪ'kriːs] v	abnehmen
increase ['ɪnkriːs] n	Zunahme
increase [ɪn'kriːs] v	zunehmen
drop n	Fall
drop v	fallen
rise n	Anstieg
rise v	ansteigen
low n	Tief

low adj	tief
peak [piːk] n	Spitze / Gipfel

line graph n	Liniendiagramm » Abb. 4
maximum data / maximum value [ˌmæksɪməmˈvæljuː] n	Höchstwert(e) / Maximalwert(e)
minimum data / minimum value [ˌmɪnɪməmˈvæljuː] n	Minimalwert(e)
unit [ˈjuːnɪt] n	Einheit
scale [skeɪl] n	Maßeinteilung / Skala
value [ˈvæljuː] n	Wert
variable [ˈveəriəbl] n	Variable
independent variable	unabhängige Variable *(unabhängig von der Datengrundlage)*
dependent variable	abhängige Variable *(abhängig von der Datengrundlage)*
increment [ˈɪnkrəmənt] n	Erhöhung / Zuwachs / Schrittgröße

» Draw a grid with straight lines.
Zeichne ein Gitternetz mit geraden Linien.
Use all the space available for clarity.
Verwende für die Übersichtlichkeit den gesamten zur Verfügung stehenden Platz.
Assign the horizontal axis to the independent variable (independent scale, e.g. years), and the vertical axis to the dependent variable (dep. on the data set).
Ordne der waagerechten Achse die unabhängige Variable (unabhängige Maßeinheit, z. B. Jahre) zu, und der senkrechten Achse die abhängige Variable (abhängig von der Datengrundlage).
Use increments which are regularly spaced and mark the values.
Verwende Schrittgrößen mit regelmäßigem Abstand und markiere die Werte.
Add a key if more than one data set is portrayed.
Füge eine Legende hinzu, wenn mehr als eine Datenreihe dargestellt ist.
Plot the data clearly and connect them with lines.
Zeichne die Daten deutlich ein und verbinde sie mit Linien.

A line graph is used to show the development of something over a period of time.
Ein Liniendiagramm wird gebraucht, um eine bestimmte Entwicklung über einen bestimmten Zeitraum zu zeigen.
It shows tendencies or trends very clearly, and can be used to compare different developments.
Es zeigt Tendenzen oder Trends sehr deutlich und kann auch benutzt werden, um verschiedene Entwicklungen zu vergleichen.

3 Working with ... › 3.3 Numbers

bar chart [ˈbɑːˌtʃɑːt] / bar graph
[ˈbɑːˌgrɑːf] n
vertical bar chart

horizontal bar chart
[ˌhɒrɪˈzɒntlˈbɑːtʃɑːt]
stacking bar chart [ˌstækɪŋˈbɑːtʃɑːt]

Balkendiagramm /
Säulendiagramm » Abb. 4
senkrechtes
Balkendiagramm » Abb. 4
waagerechtes
Balkendiagramm » Abb. 4
Stapel-Balkendiagramm

»
Decide which data to put on each axis.
Entscheide, welche Daten auf welche Achse gehören.
Study categories are usually placed on the horizontal axis.
Die Untersuchungskategorien sind normalerweise auf der waagerechten Achse platziert.
Measurements, amounts and percentages are placed on the vertical axis.
Abmessungen, Beträge und Prozentsätze sind auf der senkrechten Achse platziert.
Label the axes and decide the scale.
Beschrifte die Achsen und lege die Maßeinteilung fest.
Add a key if there is more than one data set.
Füge eine Legende hinzu, wenn es mehr als einen Datensatz gibt.

A bar chart is used to compare the amounts, quantities, sizes, etc of two or more different things.
Ein Balken-/Säulendiagramm wird verwendet, um Beträge, Mengen, Größen usw. von zwei oder mehr Dingen zu vergleichen.
It also can visualise change from one point in time to another.
Es kann auch den Wandel von einem zum anderen Zeitpunkt veranschaulichen.

pie chart [ˈpaɪˌtʃɑːt] n
circle graph [ˈsɜːklˌgrɑːf] n

Tortendiagramm / Kuchendiagramm
Kreisdiagramm » Abb. 4

consist of v
percentage [pəˈsentɪdʒ] n
segment [ˈsegmənt] n
piece n
sector n

bestehen aus
Prozentsatz / Prozent
Segment
Stück
Sektor / Bereich / Zone

»
A pie chart consists of a circle divided into different sections / sectors / segments that represent parts of a whole – usually in the form of percentages.
Ein Torten-, Kuchendiagramm besteht aus einem Kreis, der in verschiedene Stücke/Sektoren/Segmente unterteilt ist, die für einen Teil des Ganzen stehen – normalerweise in Prozentanteilen.

protractor [prəˈtræktə] n	Winkelmesser » Abb. 6
compasses n pl	Zirkel
plot v	einzeichnen
colour *BE* / color *AE* v	färben
shade v	schattieren

»

Draw a circle with a protractor.
Zeichne einen Kreis mithilfe eines Winkelmessers.

Then plot the sectors from largest to smallest.
Dann zeichne die Sektoren vom größten zum kleinsten hin ein.

If sectors are too small, group them into one sector called 'Others'.
Wenn die Segmente zu klein sind, gruppiere sie in einen Sektor mit dem Titel 'Sonstige'.

Colour or shade the sectors.
Färbe oder schattiere die Segmente.

Add a title, labels and a key.
Füge einen Titel, Beschriftungen und eine Legende hinzu.

present v	präsentieren / vorstellen
component n	Komponente / Bestandteil
formal component	formaler Bestandteil
period of time n	Zeitspanne
column [ˈkɒləm] n	Spalte
curve [kɜːv] n	Kurve
absolute numbers n pl	absolute Zahlen
relative numbers n pl	relative Zahlen
quantity [ˈkwɒntəti] n	Menge / Größe

»

Mention the source of the numbers and the topic, included in the title and the legend.
Führe die Quelle der Zahlen und das Sachthema an, das im Titel und der Legende steht.

Explain the formal components, table, graph or chart.
Erläutere die formalen Komponenten, die Tabelle, das Schaubild oder die Aufstellung.

Describe the contents and details, e.g. changes and developments over time, peak and low points or relationships.
Beschreibe die Inhalte und Einzelheiten, z. B. Veränderungen und Entwicklungen im Laufe der Zeit, Spitzen- und Tiefpunkte oder Beziehungen.

3 Working with ... › 3.3 Numbers

»

Draw a conclusion from the data, and also be critical about the form of presentation:	Ziehe eine Schlussfolgerung aus den Daten und betrachte auch die Art der Präsentation kritisch:
Biased representation or objective information?	Voreingenommene Darstellung oder objektive Information?
Clear / comprehensible?	Verständlich?
Reliable source?	Verlässliche Quelle?
Well-chosen form?	Gut gewählte Form?
Up-to-date numbers?	Aktuelle Zahlen?
Manipulation and speculation?	Manipulation und Spekulation?
This table shows / is about / provides information about ...	Diese Tabelle zeigt / handelt von / gibt Informationen über ...
In the first column, ...	In der ersten Spalte ...
In 2004 there were ...	Im Jahre 2004 gab es ...
On the horizontal line, there is ...	Auf der waagerechten Linie ist ...
The vertical line represents ...	Die senkrechte Linie steht für ...
The chart consists of ...	Die Tabelle besteht aus ...
64 per cent of ...	64 Prozent von ...
The percentage of ... is very small / large.	Der Prozentsatz von ... ist sehr klein / groß.
The majority of ...	Die Mehrheit von ...
Nearly half of ...	Nahezu die Hälfte von ...
Compared to ...	Verglichen mit ...
You can see a huge decrease / increase ...	Man kann eine riesige Zunahme / Abnahme ...
There is a slight rise ...	Es gibt eine geringfügige Zunahme ...
The development ...	Die Entwicklung ...
... remained constant.	... blieb konstant.
... reached a peak.	... erreichte eine Spitze.
... reached an all-time high.	... erreichte einen Höchststand.
It clearly indicates ...	Es deutet eindeutig darauf hin ...

3.4 GIS » Abb. 5

Geographic Information System (GIS) n	Geografisches Informationssystem
computer software n	Computerprogramme
capture ['kæptʃə] v	erfassen
store v	speichern
analyse BE / analyze AE ['ænlaɪz] v	analysieren
display v	zeigen / darstellen
data set n	Datensatz
digital data n	digitale Daten
digitally enhanced data ['dɪdʒɪtliɪnˌhɑːnst'deɪtə]	digital aufgearbeitete Daten
data-based information n	datengestützte Information
geographically referenced information	geografiebezogene Informationen

» Analysing geographically referenced information allows a better understanding of natural and human processes on earth.
Geografiebezogene Informationen zu analysieren, ermöglicht ein besseres Verständnis von natürlichen und menschlichen Abläufen auf der Erde.

scientific investigation n	wissenschaftliche Untersuchung
geography n	Geografie
geology [dʒiˈɒlədʒi] n	Geologie
resource management n	Rohstoffmanagement
business marketing n	Vermarktung
development planning n	Entwicklungsplanung
politics n pl	Politik
layer [leɪə] n	Ebene / Schicht

» GIS combines various components such as different layers of maps, digital data and digitally enhanced photographs.
Ein GIS verbindet verschiedene Komponenten wie unterschiedliche Kartenebenen, Daten in digitaler Form und digital aufbereitete Fotografien.

contain v	enthalten / beinhalten
individual information n	individuelle Information
activate v	aktivieren
insert [ɪnˈsɜːt] v	einfügen
create v	erstellen / entwerfen
enhance [ɪnˈhɑːns] v	anreichern / aufbereiten / weiterentwickeln

31

tabular data [ˌtæbjələ'deɪtə] n
  attribute table ['ætrɪbjuːtˌteɪbl]
simulation [ˌsɪmjə'leɪʃn] n
superimpose [ˌsuːprɪm'pəʊz] v
orthophoto [ɔː'θəʊˌfəʊtəʊ] n
orthorectify [ɔː'θəʊˌrektɪfaɪ] v

tabellarische Daten *(in Tabellenform)*
  Attributtabelle
Simulation
übereinander lagern / einkopieren
Orthofoto
orthorektifizieren

» An orthophoto is an aerial photograph geometrically corrected ("orthorectified") such that the scale is uniform.
Ein Orthofoto ist eine derart geometrisch korrigierte (orthorektifizierte) Luftaufnahme, dass der Maßstab gleichförmig ist.

spatial ['speɪʃl] adj
  spatial context
insight n

räumlich
  räumlicher Zusammenhang
Einblick

» The biggest asset of a GIS is that it produces visuals to convey the results of complex analyses.
Die größte Stärke von GIS liegt darin, dass es Grafiken erstellt, mit denen die Ergebnisse vielschichtiger Analysen dargestellt werden können.

II. Thematic Vocabulary

1 Planet earth

1.1 Topography » II 2.4 Landforms

atlas ['ætləs], *pl* atlases n	Atlas *(Pl. Atlasse)*
projection [prəʊ'dʒekʃn] n	Projektion / Darstellung » Abb. 1
map projection	Kartendarstellung
plane projection	Azimutalprojektion
conic projection ['kɒnɪkprəʊˌdʒekʃn]	Kegelprojektion
cylindrical projection [sə'lɪndrɪklprəʊˌdʒekʃn]	Zylinderprojektion
interrupted projection	zerlappte Projektion

river n	Fluss » Abb. 7
spring n	Quelle
brook n	Bach
waterfall n	Wasserfall
estuary ['estjʊəri] / river mouth n	Mündung
delta n	Delta
delta distributary	Delta-Arm
alluvial deposits [ə'luːvɪəldɪˌpɒzɪts] n pl	Alluvion *(fluviale Aufschüttungen)*
floodplain n	Überschwemmungsebene
valley n	Tal
canyon n	Canyon / Schlucht
gorge [gɔːdʒ] n	Schlucht / Klamm
tributary ['trɪbjətri] n	Zufluss
confluence n	Zusammenfluss
receiving water / receiving stream n	Vorfluter

lake n	See » Abb. 8
glacial lake ['gleɪsɪəlˌleɪk]	Gletschersee
volcanic lake	vulkanischer See
crater lake	Kratersee
artificial lake	künstlicher See
oxbow lake ['ɒksbəʊˌleɪk]	Altarm
tectonic lake	tektonischer See
reservoir ['rezəvwaː] n	Stausee / Speichersee
oasis [əʊ'eɪsɪs] n	Oase

mountain n	Berg » Abb. 9
mountains n pl	Gebirge
mountain range	Gebirgskette
mountain slope	Berghang
massif [mæs'iːf] n	Massiv

isthmus ['ısməs] n	Landenge
summit n	Gipfel
peak [piːk] n	Gipfel / Spitze
ridge [rıdʒ] n	Grat
pass n	Pass
crest n	Kamm
cliff n	Steilhang
face n	Wand
north face n	Nordwand
spur [spɜː] n	Vorsprung
plateau ['plætəʊ] n	Hochebene
plain n	Ebene

sea n	Meer » Abb. 11–12
sea level	Meeresspiegel
ocean n	Ozean
ocean floor	Meeresboden
ocean bay	Meeresbucht
gulf [gʌlf] n	Golf
strait n	Meerenge

coast n	Küste » Abb. 11
coastal plain	Küstenebene
shore n	Küste / Meeresufer
bay n	Bucht
cape n	Kap
headland n	Landspitze
spit n	Landzunge
tombolo [tɒm'bəʊləʊ] n	Nehrung
beach n	Strand
dune [djuːn] n	Düne
lagoon [lə'guːn] n	Lagune
surf / surge n	Brandung
natural arch [ˌnætʃrl'ɑːtʃ] n	Brandungstor
stack n	Brandungspfeiler
skerry n	Felssäule
cliff n	Klippe
shoreline n	Küstenform
barrier beach ['bæriəˌbiːtʃ] n	Riffküste
fjord [fjɔːd] / fiord n	Fjord(-küste) *(glazial übertiefte Meeresbucht)*
shore cliff n	Steilküste
rias ['riːəz] n	Riasküste *(ertrunkenes Flusstal)*

1 Planet earth › 1.2 Continents and countries

island n	Insel » Abb. 12
island arc ['aɪlənd‿ɑːk]	Inselkette
volcanic island	Vulkaninsel » II 2.1 Tectonics
peninsula [pə'nɪnsjələ] n	Halbinsel
archipelago [ˌɑːkɪ'peləgəʊ] n	Archipel / Inselgruppe
atoll ['ætɒl] n	Atoll
coral reef [ˌkɒrəl'riːf] n	Korallenriff

1.2 Continents and countries

General

landscape ['lænskeɪp] n	Landschaft
ordinary landscape	vorherrschende Landschaft(-sform)
vernacular landscape [vəˌnækjələ'lænskeɪp]	(landes-)typische Landschaft
political landscape	politische Landschaft
glaciated landscape [ˌglæsijeɪtɪd'lænskeɪp]	glazial überformte Landschaft
region n	Region
formal region	homogene Region
physical-geographical region	physiogeografische Region
area n	Fläche
delimited area [dɪ'lɪmɪtɪd‿eəriə]	begrenzte Fläche
language n	Sprache
culture n	Kultur
areal unit	Flächeneinheit
functional region	funktionale Region

pattern n	Struktur / Muster
spatial ['speɪʃl] adj	räumlich / den Raum betreffend
spatial interaction	räumliche Interaktion / räumliche Wechselwirkung
spatial organisation BE / spatial organization AE	räumliche Organisation
spatial modelling	Raummodellierung
spatial structure	Raumstruktur
coherence [kəʊ'hɪərns] n	Kohärenz / Zusammenhang
coherent adj	kohärent / zusammenhängend
mosaic [məʊ'zeɪɪk] n	Mosaik
cluster ['klʌstə] n	Cluster / Haufen / Gruppe

boundary ['baʊndri] n	Grenze » Abb. 2
administrative boundary	Verwaltungsgrenze
[əd͵mɪnɪstrətɪv'baʊndri]	
formal boundary	formelle Grenze
national boundary	Staatsgrenze
natural boundary	natürliche Grenze
zoning boundary [͵zəʊnɪŋ'baʊndri]	Zonierungsgrenze
field boundary	Feldgrenze

the Iron Curtain n	der Eiserne Vorhang

divide [dɪ'vaɪd] n	Wasserscheide / Grenze
restrict access [rɪ͵strɪkt'ækses] v	Zugang begrenzen
restrict contact v	Kontakt unterbinden
permeable ['pɜːmiəbl] adj	durchlässig / passierbar
permeability [͵pɜːmiə'bɪləti] n	Durchlässigkeit / Passierbarkeit
territory ['terɪtri] n	Staatsgebiet / Hoheitsgebiet / Gebiet
turf [tɜːf] n	Revier
regionalism n	Regionalismus
sectionalism ['sekʃənəlɪzm] n	Partikularismus
coexistence [͵kəʊɪg'zɪstəns] n	Koexistenz / Miteinander
coexist v	koexistieren / nebeneinander existieren
identity n	Identität
interest n	Interesse
custom n	Gewohnheit

world n	Welt
world region	Weltregion
nation n	Staat / Nation
nation-state n	Nationalstaat
settlement n	Siedlung
community n	Kommune / Gemeinschaft

Continents and oceans

Pangaea [͵pæŋ'geɪə] n	Pangaea / Pangäa » Abb. 16
supercontinent [suːpə'kɒntɪnənt] n	Superkontinent
Laurasia [lɔː'reɪʒə] n	Laurasien
Gondwanaland [͵gɒndwænə'lænd] n	Gondwanaland
North America n	Nordamerika
South America n	Südamerika
subcontinent [sʌb'kɒntɪnənt] n	Subkontinent

1 Planet earth › 1.2 Continents and countries

Europe ['jʊərəp] n
Asia n
Africa n
Australia n
Antarctica [æn'tɑːktɪkə] n

Europa
Asien
Afrika
Australien
Antarktis

» North and South America can be regarded as subcontinents of the American continent.
Nord- und Südamerika können als Subkontinente Amerikas betrachtet werden.

Pacific Ocean [pəˌsɪfɪk'əʊʃn] n
Atlantic Ocean n
Indian Ocean n
Arctic Ocean [ˌɑːktɪk'əʊʃn] n
North Sea n
Baltic Sea [ˌbɔːltɪk'siː] n
Mediterranean Sea [ˌmedɪtrˌeɪniən'siː] n
Adriatic Sea [ˌeɪdriˌætik'siː] n
Sea of Marmara [ˌsiːəvmɑː'mərə] n
Black Sea n
Sea of Azov [ˌsiːəv'ɑːsɒv] n
Caspian Sea [ˌkæspiən'siː] n
Red Sea n
Arabian Sea n
Sea of Okhotsk [ˌsiːəvəʊ'kɒtsk] n
Sea of Japan n
Yellow Sea n
East China Sea n
South China Sea n
Coral Sea n
Tasman Sea n
Andaman Sea [ˌændəmæn'siː] n
Philippine Sea [ˌfɪlɪpiːn'siː] n
Sulu Sea [ˌsuːluː'siː] n
Celebes Sea [selˌiːbiz'siː] n
Java Sea [ˌdʒɑːvə'siː] n
Flores Sea [ˌflɔːrɪz'siː] n
Timor Sea [ˌtiːmɔː'siː] n
Banda Sea [ˌbændə'siː] n
Arafura Sea [ærəˌfʊərə'siː] n
Caribbean Sea [krɪˌbiːən'siː] n
Barents Sea [ˌbærənts'siː] n
Kara Sea [ˌkɑːrə'siː] n

Pazifik / Pazifischer Ozean
Atlantik / Atlantischer Ozean
Indischer Ozean
Arktisches Meer
Nordsee
Ostsee
Mittelmeer
Adriatisches Meer / Adria
Marmarameer
Schwarzes Meer
Asowsches Meer
Kaspisches Meer
Rotes Meer
Arabisches Meer
Ochotskisches Meer
Japanisches Meer
Gelbes Meer
Ostchinesisches Meer
Südchinesisches Meer
Korallensee
Tasmanisches Meer
Andamanensee
Philippinensee
Sulusee
Celebessee
Javasee
Floressee
Timorsee
Bandasee
Arafurasee
Karibisches Meer / Karibik
Barentssee
Karasee

Straits and gulfs

Mozambique Channel [ˌməʊzæmˈbiːkˌtʃænl] n	Straße von Mosambik
Bering Strait [ˌbeərɪŋˈstreɪt] n	Beringstraße
Luzon Strait [luːˌzɒnˈstreɪt] n	Luzon Straße
Makassar Strait [məˌkæssarˈstreɪt] n	Makassarstraße
Strait of Malacca [ˌstreɪtəvməˈlækə] n	Malakka Straße
Hudson Strait [ˌhʌdsnˈstreɪt] n	Hudsonstraße

Bay of Biscay [ˌbeɪəvˈbɪskeɪ] n	Golf von Biscaya
Bay of Bengal [ˌbeɪəvˌbeŋˈgɔːl] n	Golf von Bengalen
Hudson Bay [ˌhʌdsnˈbeɪ] n	Hudson Bay
Baffin Bay [ˌbæfɪnˈbeɪ] n	Baffin Bay
Gulf of Tonkin [gʌlfevˈtɒŋkɪŋ] n	Golf von Tonking
Gulf of Thailand [gʌlfevˈtaɪlænd] n	Golf von Siam
Persian Gulf [ˌpɜːʒənˈgʌlf] n	Persischer Golf / Arabischer Golf
Gulf of Aden [ˌgʌlfəvˈeɪdn] n	Golf von Aden
Gulf of Guinea [ˌgʌlfəvˈgɪni] n	Golf von Guinea
Gulf of Sidra [ˌgʌlfəvˈsaɪdrə] n	Kleine Syrte *(im Westen)*
Gulf of Sidra n	Große Sytre *(im Osten)*
Gulf of Mexico n	Golf von Mexiko

Rivers

Thames n	Themse
Danube [ˈdænjuːb] n	Donau
Rhine [raɪn] n	Rhein
Volga [ˈvɒlgə] n	Wolga
Dnieper [ˈdniːpə] n	Dnjepr
Euphrates [juːˈfreɪtiːz] n	Euphrat
Nile [naɪl] n	Nil
Amazon [ˈæməzn] n	Amazonas
Chang Jiang (Yangtze) [ˌtʃæŋdʒiˈæŋ] n	Jangtsekiang
Huang Ho (Yellow River) [ˌhwæŋˈheʊ] n	Huang He
Ob-Irtysh [ɒbˈɜːtɪʃ] n	Ob-Irtysch
Amur [əˈmʊə] n	Amut
Lena [ˈleɪnə] n	Lena
Congo [ˈkɒŋgəʊ] n	Kongo
MacKenzie [məˈkenzi] n	MacKenzie
Mekong [ˌmiːˈkɒŋ] n	Mekong
Niger [ˈnaɪdʒə] n	Niger
Yenisey [ˈjenɪzi] n	Jenissej

1 Planet earth › 1.2 Continents and countries

» There are some rivers which have different names in German and English, for example the Danube.
Es gibt manche Flüsse, die im Deutschen und Englischen unterschiedliche Namen haben, wie zum Beispiel die Donau.
However, most of the rivers' names remain unchanged like the Seine, the Mississippi or the Elbe.
Jedoch bleiben die meisten Flussnamen unverändert, wie die Seine, der Mississippi oder die Elbe.

Lakes

Lake Baikal [ˌleɪk'baɪkæl] n	Baikalsee
Aral Sea ['ɑːrəlsiː] n	Aralsee
Lake Balaton [ˌleɪkbæl'ætən] n	Plattensee
Lake Garda [ˌleɪk'gɑːdə] n	Gardasee
Lake Constance [ˌleɪk'kɒnstəns] n	Bodensee
Lake Geneva [ˌleɪk dʒə'niːvə] n	Genfer See
Lake Victoria [ˌleɪkvɪk'tɔːriə] n	Viktoriasee
Lake Tanganyika [ˌleɪkˌtæŋgə'njiːkə] n	Tanganyikasee
Lake Nyasa [ˌleɪknaɪ'æsə] n	Malawisee
Great Bear Lake [ˌgreɪt'beəˌleɪk] n	Großer Bärensee
Great Slave Lake [ˌgreɪt'sleɪvˌleɪk] n	Großer Sklavensee
Lake Superior [ˌleɪksuː'pɪəriə] n	Oberer See
Lake Michigan [ˌleɪk'mɪʃɪgən] n	Michigansee
Lake Huron [ˌleɪk'hjʊərn] n	Huronsee
Lake Erie [ˌleɪk'ɪəri] n	Eriesee
Lake Ontario [ˌleɪkɒn'teəriəʊ] n	Ontariosee

Deserts

Sahara Desert [se'hɑːre] n	Sahara
Kalahari Desert [ˌkælə'hɑːri] n	Kalahari
Great Sandy Desert n	Große Sandwüste
Great Victoria Desert n	Große Viktoriawüste
Gobi Desert ['gəʊbi] n	Wüste Gobi
Atacama Desert [ˌætə'kɑːmə] n	Atakama Wüste
Arabian Desert n	Arabische Wüste
Namib ['nɑːmɪb] n	Namib
Sonora ['sɒnɒrə] / Sonoran Desert n	Sonora (Wüste)

Mountains

Zugspitze n	Zugspitze
Matterhorn n	Matterhorn
Mount Everest n	Mount Everest
Uluru [uːˈluːruː] / Ayers Rock [ˌeəzˈrɒk] n	Uluru / Ayers Rock
(Cerro) Aconcagua [ˌækɒnˈkagwə] n	(Cerro) Aconcagua
Kilimanjaro [ˌkɪlɪmənˈdʒɑːrəʊ] n	Kilimandscharo
Mount Cameroon [maʊntˌkæməˈruːn] n	Kamerunberg

Glaciers and more ice » II 2.4 Landforms

Antarctica [ænˈtɑːktɪkə] n	Antarktis
Lambert Glacier [ˈlæmbətˌglæsiə] n	Lambertgletscher
Perito Moreno Glacier [perɪtəʊˌməˈriːnəʊtˌglæsiə] n	Perito-Moreno-Gletscher
Glacier Bay [ˌglæsiəˈbeɪ] n	Glacier Bay
Furtwängler Glacier n	Furtwängler-Gletscher
Pasterze Glacier n	die Pasterze
(Great) Aletsch Glacier [ˈælɪtʃˌglæsiə] n	(Großer) Aletschgletscher
Vatnajökull n	Vatnajökull
Athabasca Glacier [ˌæθəˈbæskəˌglæsiə] n	Athabasca-Gletscher
Ross Ice Shelf n	Ross-Schelfeis
Filchner-Ronne Ice Shelf n	Filchner-Ronne-Schelfeis

Europe

Europe [ˈjʊərəp] n	Europa
European Union (EU) n	Europäische Union (EU)
political landscape n	politische Landschaft
physical-geographical region n	physiogeografische Region
geology n	Geologie
relief [rɪˈliːf] n	Relief / Oberflächenform
glacial relief	glaziales Relief
landform n	Landform
soil n	Boden
vegetation [vədʒɪteɪʃn] n	Vegetation

Northwestern Uplands

Northwestern Uplands n	Nordwestliches Hochland
Caledonian mountain-building episode n	kaledonische Gebirgsbildung
erode [ɪˈrəʊd] v	erodieren / abtragen
uplift v	heben
ice sheet n	Eisschild
glacier [ˈglæsiə] n	Gletscher » Abb. 10
valley n	Tal
deepened valley	eingetieftes Tal
glaciation [ˌgleɪsiˈeɪʃn] n	Vergletscherung / Vereisung
glaciated landscape	glazial überformte Landschaft
fjord [fjɔːd] / fiord n	Fjord
fjord landscape n	Fjordlandschaft
Lapland [ˈlæplænd] n	Lappland
Scandinavian Peninsula [ˌskændɪˌneɪvənpəˈninsjələ] n	Skandinavische Halbinsel / Skandinavien
Lofoten [ləʊˈfəʊtn] n	Lofoten
The Pennines [ðəˈpenaɪnz] n	Pennines

North European Lowlands

lowlands n	Tiefland
North European Plain n	Nordeuropäisches Tiefland
topography [tɒpˈɒgrəfi] n	Topografie / Oberflächengestalt
flat topography	flache Oberflächengestalt / flache Topografie
undulating [ˈʌndjəleitɪŋ] adj	auf und ab verlaufend / wellig
Skagerrak [ˈskægəræk] n	Skagerrak
Skagerrak Strait	Skaggerakstraße
Kattegat [ˌkætiˈgæt] n	Kattegat
The Great Belt n	Großer Belt
The Little Belt n	Kleiner Belt
Gulf of Finland n	Finnischer Meerbusen
Gulf of Riga n	Rigaischer Meerbusen
Gulf of Bothnia [gʌlfəvˈbɒθniə] n	Bottnischer Meerbusen
West Frisian Islands [ˌwestˈfrɪziənˌaɪləndz] n	Westfriesische Inseln
English Channel n	Ärmelkanal
Strait of Dover n	Straße von Dover
Paris Basin [ˈpærɪsˌbeɪsn] n	Pariser Becken
North European Plain n	Norddeutsches Tiefland

East European Plain n   Osteuropäische Ebene
Polish Plain n   Mittelpolnisches Tiefland
Baltic Ridge n   Baltischer Landrücken

Central Plateaus

Central Plateaus [ˌsentrl'plætəʊz] n pl   zentrale Plateaus
erosion [ɪ'rəʊʒn] n   Erosion / Abtrag
tract n   Gebiet
forest-clad adj   waldbedeckt
slope n   Hang
  steep slopes   steile Hänge
fertile adj   fruchtbar
rolling hill n   sanfter Hügel
valley n   Tal

dipping	eingetieftes Tal
river valley	Flusstal
deeply carved river	tief eingeschnittenes Flusstal

Iberian Peninsula [aɪˌbɪəriənpə'nɪnsjələ] n   Iberische Halbinsel
Massif Central [ˌmæsiːfsɑːn'trɑːl] n   Zentralmassiv
Ardennes [aː'den] n   Ardennen
Eifel n   Eifel
Hunsrück n   Hunsrück
Taunus n   Taunus
Vosges [vəʊʒ] n pl   Vogesen
Black Forest [ˌblæk'fɒrɪst] n   Schwarzwald
Swabian Alps [ˌsweɪbiən'ælps] n pl   Schwäbische Alb
Thuringian Forest n   Thüringer Wald
Bohemian Forest [bəʊˌhiːmiən'fɒrɪst] n   Böhmerwald
Ore Mountains [ˌɔː'maʊntɪnz] n pl   Erzgebirge
Sudeten Mountains n pl   Sudeten

The Alpine system

Alpine system n   alpines System
Alps ['ælps] n pl   Alpen
Dolomites ['dɒləmaɪts] n pl   Dolomiten
Carpathian Mountains   Karpaten
  ['kɑː'peɪθiənˌmaʊntɪnz] n pl

1 Planet earth › 1.2 Continents and countries

Hungarian Plain n	Ungarische Tiefebene
Transylvanian Alps [trænsɪlˌveɪniən'ælps] n pl	Südkarpaten
Balkan Mountains n pl	Hoher Balkan
Rhodope Mountains n pl	Rhodopen
Pindus Mountains n pl	Pindos
Apennines ['æpənaɪnz] n pl	Apenninen
Sierra Nevada [siˌerənə'vɑːdə] n	Sierra Nevada / Betische Kordillere
Pyrenees [ˌpɪrə'niːz] n pl	Pyrenäen

Germany

Alps ['ælps] n pl	Alpen
limestone ['laɪmstəʊn] n	Kalkstein
Northern Limestone Alps n pl	Nördliche Kalkalpen
Alpine Foreland n	Alpenvorland
Bavarian Alpine Foreland	Bayerisches Alpenvorland
orogenesis ['ɒrəʊ'dʒenəsɪs] n	Gebirgsbildung
weathering ['weðərɪŋ] n	Verwitterung
glacier ['glæsiə] n	Gletscher
moraine [mɒ'reɪn] / till n	Moräne » Abb. 10
Ice Age / glacial period ['gleɪsiəlˌpɪəriəd] n	Eiszeit
green landscape n	Grünlandschaft
agriculture ['ægrɪkʌltʃə] n	Landwirtschaft
tourism n	Tourismus
Munich ['mjuːnɪk] n	München
Constance [ˌkɒnstəns] n	Konstanz
Lake Constance [ˌleɪk 'kɒnstəns] n	Bodensee

mountain threshold [ˌmaʊntɪn'θreʃhəʊld] n	Mittelgebirgsschwelle
Central German Uplands n pl	Deutsches Mittelgebirge
Variscian Folding n	variszische Orogenese / herzynische Faltung
Black Forest [ˌblæk'fɒrɪst] n	Schwarzwald
Swabian Alps [ˌsweɪbiən'ælps] n pl	Schwäbische Alb
scenic hilly area in Franconia n	Fränkische Alb
Bavarian Forest n	Bayrischer Wald
Harz Mountains n pl	Harz
Ore Mountains [ˌɔː'maʊntɪnz] n pl	Erzgebirge
Fichtel Hills n pl	Fichtelwald
Palatine Forest ['pælətaɪnˌfɒrɪst] n	Pfälzer Wald

Rheinish Massif ['renɪʃmæs'iːf] / Rhenish Slate Range n	Rheinisches Schiefergebirge
Rhön / Rhoen n	Rhön
Thuringian Basin n	Thüringer Becken
Thuringian Forest n	Thüringer Wald
Cologne n	Köln
North German Plain n	Norddeutsche / Ebene / Norddeutsches Tiefland
North Sea n	Nordsee
North Friesland [ˌnɔːθ'friːzlənd] n	Nordfriesland
East Friesland n	Ostfriesland
Baltic Sea [ˌbɔːltɪk'siː] n	Ostsee
Mecklenburg Lake District n	Mecklenburgische Seenplatte
wetland n	Sumpfgebiet
Berlin n	Berlin
East Frisian Islands [ˌeastˌfrɪziən'aɪləndz]	Ostfriesische Inseln
North Frisian Islands [ˌnɔːθˌfrɪziən'aɪləndz]	nordfriesische Inseln
Heligoland ['helɪgəʊlænd']	Helgoland
Heligoland Bay n	Helgoländer Bucht
Kiel Bay n	Kieler Bucht
Kiel Canal n	Nord-Ostsee-Kanal
Bavaria n	Bayern
Baden-Wurttemberg n	Baden-Württemberg
Saarland n	Saarland
Rhineland-Palatinate [ˌraɪnlændpe'lætɪnɪt] n	Rheinland-Pfalz
Hesse ['hesə] n	Hessen
Thuringia n	Thüringen
North Rhine-Westphalia n	Nordrhein-Westfalen
Saxony ['sæksni] n	Sachsen
Lower Saxony n	Niedersachsen
Saxony-Anhalt n	Sachsen-Anhalt
Brandenburg n	Brandenburg
Berlin n	Berlin
Bremen n	Bremen
Hamburg	Hamburg
Mecklenburg-Western Pomerania n	Mecklenburg-Vorpommern
Schleswig-Holstein n	Schleswig-Holstein
temperate climate n	gemäßigtes Klima
maritime climate ['mærɪtaɪmˌklaɪmət] n	meritimes Klima

1 Planet earth › 1.2 Continents and countries

Gulf Stream ['gʌlfˌstriːm] n	Golfstrom
mild adj	mild
precipitation [prɪˌsɪpɪ'teɪʃn] n	Niederschlag
snowfall n	Schneefall
flood n	Überschwemmung / Flut
drought [draʊt] n	Dürre
foehn / föhn [fɜːn] n	Föhn

» during a foehn wind | bei Föhn

Rhine [raɪn] n	Rhein
Moselle [məʊ'zəl] n	Mosel
Danube ['dænjuːb] n	Donau
Main n	Main
Weser n	Weser
Neckar n	Neckar

Zugspitze n	Zugspitze
Feldberg n	Feldberg
Wasserkuppe n	Wasserkuppe

Asia

Russian Federation n	Russische Föderation
Commonwealth of Independent States / CIS n *(former Soviet Union; USSR)*	Gemeinschaft unabhängiger Staaten / GUS *(ehemalige Sowjetunion; UdSSR)*
CIS [ˌsiːaɪ'es] n	GUS
European Plain n	Europäisches Flachland
West Siberian Plain [ˌwestsaɪˌbɪərɪən'pleɪn] n	Westsibirisches Tiefland
Central Siberian Plateau [ˌsentrlsaɪˌbɪərɪənplæ'təʊ] n	Mittelsibirisches Bergland

shield n	Schild
crystalline rock ['krɪstlaɪnˌrɒk] n	kristallines Gestein
sedimentary material ['sedɪmentrɪməˌtɪərɪəl] / sediment ['sedɪmənt] n	Sediment
sedimentary rock	Sedimentgestein
sedimentary deposit	Sedimentablagerung
glacial debris ['gleɪsɪəlˌdebriː] n	glazialer Schutt

glacial deposit n	Glazialablagerung
physiographic subregion [ˌfɪziəʊˈgræfɪksʌbˌriːʤn] n	physiografische Subregion
bog [bɒg] / marsh [mɑːʃ] n	Moor
boggy	moorig
bog landscape	Moorlandschaft
marshy	versumpft
wetland n	Feuchtgebiet
upland n	Hochland
hilly upland	bergiges Hochland
river gorge [ˈrɪvəˌgɔːʤ] n	Flussschlucht » Abb. 7
settlement n	Siedlung
oil reserves n pl	Ölvorräte
oil deposit n	Ölvorkommen
natural gas reserves n pl	Erdgasvorräte
gas deposit n	Gasvorkommen
chromite n	Chromit / Chromeisen
copper n	Kupfer
gold n	Gold
graphite [ˈgræfaɪt] n	Graphit
ore [ɔː] n	Erz
iron ore [aɪənˈɔː]	Eisenerz
nickel [ˈnɪkl] n	Nickel
volcano [vɒlˈkeɪnəʊ] n	Vulkan
active volcano	aktiver Vulkan
extinct volcano	erloschener Vulkan

» inhospitable for settlement | ungeeignet für Siedlungszwecke

Ural Mountains [ˌjʊərlˈmaʊntɪnz] n pl	Uralgebirge
Yablonovy Range [ˌjɑːblənəviˈreɪnʤ] n	Jablonowy Gebirge
Khingan Mountains [ˌkɪŋænˈmaʊntɪnz] n pl	Großer Hinggan
Altai Mountains [ˌaltaɪˈmaʊntɪnz] n pl	Altai Gebirge
Sayan Mountains [ˌsejənˈmaʊntɪnz] n pl	Sajan Gebirge
Tien Shan [ˌtiːn ˈʃɑːn] n	Tian Shan
Pamir Mountains [pəˌmɪəˈmaʊntɪnz] n pl	Pamirgebirge
Transcaucasus [trænsˈkɔːkəsəs] n	Kaukasus
Caspian Depression [ˈkæspiəndɪˈpreʃn] n	Kaspische Senke
Kola Peninsula [ˈkəʊləˌpənɪnsjələ] n	Halbinsel Kola
Taymyr Peninsula [ˈtaɪmɪrˌpənɪnsjələ] n	Halbinsel Taimyr

1 Planet earth › 1.2 Continents and countries

Chuckchi Peninsula [ˈtʃuktʃɪˌpənɪnsjələ] n	Tschuktschen Halbinsel
Kamchatka Peninsula [ˈkæmtʃætkəˌpənɪnsjələ] n	Kamtschatka Halbinsel

Lake Ladoga [ˌleɪkˈlædəʊgə] n	Ladogasee
Lake Baikal [ˌleɪkˈbaɪkæl] n	Baikalsee
Aral Sea n	Aralsee
Don River n	Don
Oka River n	Oka
Volga River [ˈvɒlgəˌrɪvə] n	Wolga
Ob River n	Ob
Irtysh River [ˈɜːtɪʃˌrɪvə] n	Irtysch
Yenisey River n	Jenissei
Lena River [ˈleɪnəˌrɪvə] n	Lena
Amur River [əˈmʊəˌrɪvə] n	Amur
Kolyma River [kəˈlɪməˌrɪvə] n	Kolyma

North America: physiographic regions

physical-geographical region n	physiogeografische Region
Appalachian Highlands [ˌæpəˈleɪʃenˌhaɪləndz] n pl	Appalachen-Plateau
Canadian Shield n	Kanadischer Schild
Great Plains n pl	Präriegebiete im Westen der USA
Gulf-Atlantic Coastal Plain n	Golf-Atlantische Küstenebene
Hudson Bay Lowlands n pl	Hudsonbai / Hudson-Bucht
Piedmont n	Pediment
Pacific Coast Ranges n pl	Gebirgsketten der nordamerikanischen Pazifikküste
Rocky Mountains n pl	Rocky Mountains

»

the Intermontane Basins and Plateaus region	die Intermontane Becken und Ebenen Region

A brief geography of North America

extraordinary adj	außergewöhnlich
desert ['dezət] n	Wüste
desertification [dɪˌzɜːtɪfɪ'keɪʃn] n	Wüstenbildung / Desertifikation
mountain range n	Gebirgskette
basin ['beɪsn] n	Becken
plateau ['plætəʊ] n	Hochebene
deciduous forest [dɪ'sɪdjuəsˌfɒrɪst] n	Laubwald
temperate rainforest [ˌtemprət'reɪnfɒrɪst] n	gemäßigter Regenwald *(im Gegensatz zu tropischem Regenwald)*
tropical climate ['trɒpɪkəlˌklaɪmət] n	tropisches Klima
prairie ['preəri] n	nordamerikanische Langgrassteppe / Prärie
swamp [swɒmp] n	Sumpf
tundra ['tʌndrə] n	Tundra
glacier ['glæsiə] n	Gletscher
peninsula [pə'nɪnsjələ] n	Halbinsel
gulf [gʌlf] n	Golf
delta ['deltə] n	Delta
canyon ['kænjən] n	Canyon / Schlucht
peak ['piːk] n	Gipfel
mainland n	Festland

» The North American continent has a huge variety of geographical landscapes, climatic zones and vegetation zones.
Der nordamerikanische Kontinent besitzt eine große Vielfalt an geographischen Landschaften, Klimazonen und Vegetationszonen.

arid			trockene	
bare			karge	
barren			karge /	
bleak	... landscape		unfruchtbare	... Landschaft
flat	... place		öde	... Stelle / Ort
inhospitable	... plain		flache	... Ebene
lush	... region		unwirtliche	... Region
gentle			üppige	
steep			sanfte	
			steile	

1 Planet earth › 1.2 Continents and countries

frontier [frʌn'tɪə] n	Grenze
frontier spirit	Pioniergeist
wilderness ['wɪldənəs] n	Wildnis
adventure n	Abenteuer
exploration [ˌekspləˈreɪʃn] n	Erkundung
exploitation [ˌeksplɔɪˈteɪʃn] n	Ausbeutung
discovery n	Entdeckung

National Park n	Nationalpark
Grand Canyon n	Grand Canyon
Death Valley n	Tal des Todes
Appalachian Mountains [ˌæpəˈleɪʃenˌmaʊntɪnz] n pl	Appalachen
Great Salt Lake n	Großer Salzsee
Niagara Falls [naɪˌægərəˈfɔːlz] n pl	Niagarafälle
Everglades [ˈevəɡleɪdz] n pl	Everglades
Great Lakes n pl	die Großen Seen
Mississippi n	Mississippi
Wheeler Peak n	Wheeler Peak
Columbia River n	Columbia River
Colorado River [ˌkɒlərˈɑːdəʊˌrɪvə] n	Colorado
Rio Grande [ˌriːəʊˈɡrænd] n	Rio Grande
St. Lawrence [sntˈlɒrnts] n	Sankt-Lorenz-Strom

2 Physical environment

2.1 Tectonics

Earth's interior » Abb. 13

interior of the earth / bowels of the earth [ˌbaʊəlzəvðiˈɜːθ] n	Erdinneres
earth structure n	Erdaufbau
layer [ˈleɪə] n	Schale
crust [krʌst] n	Erdkruste
continental crust	kontinentale Kruste
oceanic crust	ozeanische Kruste
sial [ˈsaɪəl] n	Sialschicht *(obere Schicht der Erdkruste, bildet Kontinente, besteht aus Silicium und Aluminium)*
sima [ˈsaɪmə] n	Simaschicht *(untere Schicht unter dem Pazifik, besteht aus Silicium und Magnesium)*
Mohorovičić discontinuity [məʊhəˈrɒvətʃitʃdɪsˌkɒntɪˈnjuːəti] / Moho [ˈməʊhəʊ] n	Mohorovičić-Diskontinuität *(Schwächezone)*
mantle [mæntl] n	Erdmantel
upper mantle	oberer Erdmantel
lower mantle	unterer Erdmantel
lithosphere [ˈliθəʊˌsfɪə] n	Lithosphäre / Gesteinshülle
asthenosphere [ˈæsθenɔˌsfɪə] n	Asthenosphäre / Fließzone
core n	Erdkern
outer core	äußerer Erdkern
inner core	innerer Erdkern
molten [ˈməʊltn] adj	flüssig / geschmolzen
semi-molten [ˌsemɪˈməʊltn]	zähflüssig / plastisch
solid adj	fest
rigid [ˈrɪdʒɪd] adj	starr / fest
consist of v	bestehen aus
composed of adj	zusammengesetzt aus
deform [dɪˈfɔːm] v	(sich) verformen
fracture [ˈfræktʃə] v	(zer)brechen

2 Physical environment › 2.1 Tectonics

» The Earth is divided into three main layers: the core, the mantle and the crust.
Die Erde wird in drei grundlegende Schalen aufgeteilt: den Erdkern, den Erdmantel und die Erdkruste.

Plate tectonics » Abb. 15

tectonics [tek'tɒnɪks] n pl	Tektonik *(Lehre vom Aufbau und der Veränderung der Erdkruste)*
plate n	Platte / Erdplatte
plate tectonics n pl	Plattentektonik
crustal movement / plate movement n	Bewegung der Erdkruste / Plattenbewegung

» The theory of Plate Tectonics describes the movement of plates across the Earth's surface.
Die Theorie der Plattentektonik beschreibt die Plattenbewegung der Erdoberfläche.

Two tectonic plates slide by laterally at the San Andreas fault.
Am San-Andreas-Graben (San-Andreas-Verwerfung) schieben sich zwei Erdplatten seitlich aneinander vorbei.

Plates	… drift.	Erdplatten	… driften.
	… float.		… schweben.
	… collide.		… kollidieren / stoßen zusammen.
	… diverge.		… divergieren / gehen auseinander.
	… spread.		… dehnen sich aus.
	… slide by laterally.		… gleiten seitlich aneinander vorbei.
	… subduct.		… tauchen ab.

convection current [kən'vekʃn̩ˌkʌrnt] n	Konvektionsstrom
sea-floor spreading n	Sea-floor-spreading *(Auseinanderrücken zweier Platten im Bereich der Ozeane)*
rifting n	Rifting *(Auseinanderrücken von kontinentalen Platten innerhalb eines Kontinents)*

faulting ['fɔːltɪŋ] / fault n
  fault line ['fɔːltˌlaɪn]
	Verwerfung
	  Verwerfungslinie

folding n	Faltung
uplift n	Hebung
depression [dɪ'preʃn] n	Senkung
geosyncline [ˌdʒiːəʊˌsɪŋ'klaɪn] n	Geosynklinale

anticline ['æntıklaın] n	Sattel / Antiklinale
syncline ['sıŋklaın] n	Mulde / Synklinale

plate boundary n	Plattenrand
divergent plate [daɪ'vɜːdʒənt‚pleɪt] n	divergierende Platte
subduction zone [sʌb'dʌkʃən‚zəʊn] n	Subduktionszone / Abtauchzone
collision zone [kə'lıʒn‚zəʊn] n	Kollisionszone
slip zone n	Scherungszone

conservative margin n	Erdkruste bewahrender Rand (einer Platte)
constructive margin n	Erdkruste bildender Rand (einer Platte)
destructive margin n	Erdkruste verbrauchender Rand
collision margin n	Erdkruste aufschiebender Rand

continental shelf n	Kontinentalschelf
continental slope n	Kontinentalabhang
Mid-Ocean Ridge [mıdəʊʃn'rıʤ] n	Mittelozeanischer Rücken
Mid-Atlantic Ridge [mıdət'læntik‚rıʤ] n	Mittelatlantischer Rücken
deep-sea trench [‚diːpsiː'trenʃ] n	Tiefseegraben
fold mountains n pl	Faltengebirge
Alpine folding ['ælpaın‚fʊʊldıŋ] n	Alpidische Faltung
Caledonian folding [‚kælı'dəʊnıən‚fʊʊldıŋ] n	Kaledonische Faltung
rift valley n	Grabenbruch
island arc ['aılənd‚ɑːk] n	Inselbogen
shield n	Schild / Plateau

continental drift n	Kontinentalverschiebung
Pangaea [pæŋ'ʤıə] n	Pangaea / Pangäa »Abb. 16
Laurasia [lɔː'reıʒə] n	Laurasia
Gondwanaland [‚gɒnd'wænəlænd] n	Gondwanaland

geological era [‚ʤiəʊlɒʤıkl'ıərə] n	Erdzeitalter
Ice Age n	Eiszeit
interglacial [‚ıntə'gleısıəl] n	Zwischeneiszeit / Warmzeit

Volcanism and earthquakes »Abb. 14

volcano, pl volcanoes n	Vulkan
shield volcano	Schildvulkan
stratovolcano [‚strɑtəʊvɒl'keınəʊ]	Schichtvulkan / Stratovulkan
volcanism n	Vulkanismus

53

2 Physical environment › 2.1 Tectonics

volcanology n	Vulkanologie
volcanic adj	vulkanisch

crater ['kreɪtə] n	Krater
lateral crater	Nebenkrater
crater lake	Kratersee
maar [mɑː] / volcanic lake n	Maar
atoll ['ætɒl] n	Atoll
fissure ['fɪʃə] n	Spalte
vent [vent] n	Schlot
cone [kəʊn] n	Kegel
cone-shaped adj	kegelförmig
slope [sləʊp] n	Abhang / Bergflanke
caldera [kæl'deərə] n	Caldera *(Einbruchstrichter)*
magma n	Magma *(Gesteinsschmelze)*
magma chamber	Magmakammer / Magmaherd
volcanic plug n	Quellkuppe

eruption [ɪ'rʌpʃn] / blast [blɑːst] n	Ausbruch
erupt v	ausbrechen
eject v	herausschleudern
solidify [sə'lɪdɪfaɪ] v	fest werden / erhärten

lava ['lɑːvə] n	Lava
lava flow n	Lavastrom
outpouring ['aʊtˌpɔːrɪŋ] n	Ausströmen
cool v	abkühlen
solidify v	erhärten
mudflow ['mʌdˌfləʊ] / lahar ['lɑhɑː] n	Schlammlawine / Lahar
flow v	sich wälzen / fließen
liquid adj	flüssig / dünnflüssig
viscous ['vɪskəs] adj	zähflüssig
gaseous ['gæsɪəs] adj	Gas~ / aus Gas bestehend
volcanic ash / ash n	Vulkanasche / Asche
cinders ['sɪndəs] n pl	Schlacke
smoke n	Rauch
gas n	Gas
sulphurous gas ['sʌlfrəsˌgæs] n	Schwefelgas
porous ['pɔːrəs] adj	porös

pyroclastic fall [ˌpaɪərəʊ'klæstɪkˌfɔːl] n	Auswurfmaterial
bomb n	Gesteinsbrocken / „Bombe"
lapilli ['læpɪli] n pl	Lapilli *(kleinere Steinbrocken)*

igneous rock ['ɪgnɪəsˌrɒk] n	vulkanisches Gestein / Eruptivgestein
basalt ['bæsɔːlt] n	Basalt
tuff [tʌf] n	Tuff / Tuffstein
pumice ['pʌmɪs] n	Bims
mineral water spring n	Mineralquelle
solfatara ['sʌlfətæːrə], pl solfataras n	Solfatar *(Austritt schwefelhaltiger Gase)*
fumarole ['fjuːmərəl] n	Fumarole *(Ausströmen von Wasserdampf)*
geyser ['giːzə; 'gaɪzə] n	Geysir
geothermal power station [dʒɪːəʊ'θɜːmlˌpaʊəsteɪʃn] n	geothermisches Kraftwerk
hot spot / plume [pluːm] n	Hot Spot *(ortsfester Schlot)*
Ring of Fire n	Zirkumpazifischer Feuergürtel

» Volcanism explains the processes and forms that happen when semi-solid magma from the Earth's mantle is forced into the crust due to the pressure exerted upon it.
Vulkanismus erklärt die Prozesse und Formen, die entstehen, wenn halbflüssiges Magma aus dem Erdmantel durch den Druck, der auf ihm lastet, in die Kruste gedrückt wird.

The molten rock is called magma when it is below the surface; when on the surface, it is called lava.
Das flüssige Gestein wird Magma genannt, wenn es unter der Erdoberfläche ist; an der Oberfläche heißt es Lava.

declining volcanic activity	nachlassende vulkanische Aktivität
lava flows out of a central vent ...	Lava fließt aus einem zentralen Schlot ...
lava solidifies ...	Lava erhärtet ...
lava spreads ...	Lava breitet sich aus ...

seismology [saɪz'mɒlədʒi] n	Seismologie *(Erdbebenkunde)*
earthquake / quake [kweik] n	Erdbeben / Beben
tremor ['tremə] / earth tremor n	Beben / Erdbeben / Erschütterung
shock / seismic shock [saɪz'mɪkˌʃɒk] n	Erdstoß
seismic wave n	Erdbebenwelle
pressure wave n	Druckwelle
P-wave / primary wave n	Primärwelle / Longitudinalwelle
S-wave / secondary wave n	Sekundärwelle / Transversalwelle
shear wave ['ʃɪəˌweɪv] n	Scherwelle

2 Physical environment › 2.1 Tectonics

focus / seismic centre *BE* / seismic center *AE* n	Erdbebenherd / Hypozentrum *(Ausgangspunkt des Erdbebens im Erdinneren)*
epicentre ['epɪsentə] n	Epizentrum *(über dem Herd liegendes, am stärksten betroffenes Gebiet)*
aftershock n	Nachbeben
tsunami n	Tsunami
liquefaction [ˌlɪkwɪ'fækʃn] n	Verflüssigung *(hier: loses Gesteinsmaterial, wie z. B. Sand, das sich bei Erdbeben wie eine Flüssigkeit verhält)*

earthquake area n	Erdbebengebiet
earthquake-prone adj	erdbebengefährdet
earthquake belt / earthquake zone n	Erdbebengürtel
fault line n	Bruchlinie
San Andreas fault [sæn'ændrɪəsˌfɔːlt] n	San-Andreas-Linie / San-Andreas-Verwerfung / San-Andreas-Graben
pressure ['preʃə] n	Druck
tension ['tenʃn] n	Spannung
accumulate [ə'kjuːmjəleit] v	sich aufbauen / ansammeln

»

at risk from earthquakes	erdbebengefährdet
move sideways	(sich) seitwärts bewegen

seismograph ['saɪzməgrɑːf] n	Seismograph / Erdbebenmesser
seismometre n	Erdbebenmessgerät
magnitude ['mægnɪtjuːd] n	Magnitude / Erdbebenstärke / Erdbebenausmaß
Richter scale ['rɪktəˌskeɪl] n	Richter-Skala
Mercalli scale ['mɜːkælɪˌskeɪl] n	Mercalli-Skala

seismological station n	Erdbebenwarte
advance warning n	Vorwarnung
resistance to earthquakes n	Erdbebensicherheit *(Bauwerke)*
earthquake-proof n	erdbebensicher *(Bauwerke)*
earthquake victim / earthquake casualty ['kæʒjuəltɪ] n	Erdbebenopfer

» Earthquakes are caused by colliding tectonic plates.
Erdbeben werden verursacht durch zusammenstoßende tektonische Platten.
Aftershocks often cause buildings to collapse.
Nachbeben führen häufig zum Einsturz von Gebäuden.
An earthquake struck Japan's capital last night. The 6.1 magnitude quake is classified as "strong", but it doesn't pose a tsunami threat.
Letzte Nacht traf ein Erdbeben Japans Hauptstadt. Das Beben der Stärke 6.1 gehört zur Kategorie „stark", aber es zieht keine Tsunami-Warnung nach sich.

2.2 Lithosphere

Rock types » Abb. 17

rock n	Gestein
bedrock n	anstehendes Gestein / Grundgestein
lithology [lɪˈθɒlədʒi] n	Gesteinskunde / Lithologie
mineral n	Mineral
crystal n	Kristall
crystalline [ˈkrɪstlaɪn] adj	kristallin
quartz [ˈkwɔːts] n	Quarz
feldspar [ˈfeldspɑː] n	Feldspat
mica [ˈmaɪkə] n	Glimmer
silicon n	Silicium
oxygen [ˈɒksɪdʒən] n	Sauerstoff
calcium [ˈkælsiəm] n	Calcium

» Rocks consist of different minerals such as quartz, feldspar and mica.
Gesteine bestehen aus verschiedenen Mineralien wie z. B. Quarz, Feldspat und Glimmer.
Minerals consist of molecules and atoms arranged in a special order and are therefore classified as crystalline solids.
Mineralien bestehen aus Molekülen und Atomen in einer bestimmten Anordnung und werden deshalb als kristalline Feststoffe klassifiziert.

rock type n	Gesteinsart
igneous rock [ˈɪgniəsˌrɒk] / magmatite [ˈmæɡˈmætaɪt] n	Erstarrungsgestein / Magmatit
plutonite [ˈpluːtəʊnaɪt] n	Tiefengestein / Plutonit
extrusive rock [ɪkˈstruːsɪvˌrɒk] / volcanic rock n	Ergussgestein / Vulkanit
effusive rock [ɪˈfjuːsɪvˌrɒk] n	Ganggestein / Subvulkanit
granite [ˈɡrænɪt] n	Granit

2 Physical environment › 2.2 Lithosphere

basalt ['bæsɒlt] n   Basalt

» Granite was formed when magma intruded into the upper crust cooling slowly and under pressure.
Granit bildete sich durch Eindringen von Magma in die obere Kruste, wobei es langsam und unter Druck abkühlte.
Basalt is formed on the Earth's surface when lava rapidly cools and solidifies.
Basalt bildet sich an der Erdoberfläche, wenn Lava schnell abkühlt und sich verfestigt.

sedimentary rock [ˌsedɪˈmentriˌrɒk] n	Ablagerungsgestein / Sedimentgestein
loess [ˈləʊes] n	Löss
sandstone n	Sandstein
limestone [ˈlaɪmstəʊn] n	Kalkstein
chalk [tʃɔːk] n	Kreide
shale [ʃeɪl] / schist [ʃɪst] n	Schiefer
(mineral) coal n	Steinkohle
lignite [ˈlɪgnaɪt] / brown coal n	Braunkohle
peat [piːt] n	Torf
rock salt / halite [ˈhalaɪt] n	Steinsalz
marl [mɑːl] n	Mergel
conglomerate [kənˈglɒmrət] n	Konglomerat *(Gestein aus abgerundetem Geröll)*
breccia [ˈbrætʃɪə] n	Breccie *(Gestein aus eckigem Gesteinsschutt)*

» Sedimentary rocks are formed by deposition of layers of sands and other materials that are compacted by pressure.
Ablagerungsgesteine werden durch Ablagerung von Sandschichten und anderen Materialien gebildet, die durch Druck zusammengepresst werden.

metamorphic rock [ˌmetəˈmɔːfɪkˌrɒk] n	Umwandlungsgestein / Metamorphit
slate [sleɪt] n	Schiefer / Tonschiefer
marble n	Marmor
gneiss [naɪs] n	Gneis
quarzite [ˈkwɔːsite] n	Quarzit

» Metamorphosed rocks consist of sedimentary rocks or magmatites that have been transformed by high pressure and high temperatures after sinking into the mantle.
Metamorphe Gesteine bestehen aus Ablagerungs- oder Erstarrungsgesteinen, die durch hohen Druck und hohe Temperaturen nach dem Absinken in den Erdmantel umgewandelt werden.

Weathering

weathering n	Verwitterung
weather v	verwittern
mechanical weathering	mechanische Verwitterung
physical weathering	physikalische Verwitterung

frost shattering [frɒst'ʃætrɪŋ] / freeze-thaw process [friːzθɔː'prəʊses] n	Frostsprengung
heating n	Erwärmung
cooling n	Abkühlung
shatter v	zertrümmern
pressure release n	Druckentlastung
exfoliation [eks'fəʊli'eɪʃn] n	Exfoliation / Schalenverwitterung
crevice ['krevɪs] n	Spalte
fissure ['fɪʃə] n	Spalt / Kluft / Riss
rock joint n	Gesteinsspalte
expand v	(sich) ausdehnen
contract v	(sich) zusammenziehen
insolation weathering [ˌɪnsə'leɪʃn] n	Insolationsverwitterung / thermische Verwitterung

» Rocks are shattered by the freeze-thaw process.
Felsen werden durch die Frostsprengung zertrümmert.
Heating during the day makes the material expand, and cooling during the night makes it contract – the result is shattering.
Die Erwärmung während des Tages führt dazu, dass das Material sich ausdehnt; die Abkühlung während der Nacht führt dazu, dass es sich zusammenzieht – das Resultat ist die Zertrümmerung.

chemical weathering n	chemische Verwitterung
solution n	Lösung
oxidation [ˌɑksɪ'deɪʃn] n	Oxidation
hydration [haɪ'dreɪʃn] n	Hydration / Hydratation *(Verwitterung durch Wassereinlagerung)*
hydrolysis [haɪ'drɒləsɪs] n	Hydrolyse
carbonation [ˌkɑːbə'neɪʃən] n	Karbonisierung
solution n	Lösung / Auflösung
dissolve v	(sich) auflösen
soluble ['sɒljəbl] adj	löslich
acid ['æsɪd] adj	sauer
acid n	Säure

2 Physical environment › 2.2 Lithosphere

biological weathering n	biologische Verwitterung
weathering by root pressure n	Wurzelsprengung
organic weathering n	organische Verwitterung / biochemische Verwitterung
karst weathering ['kɑːrstˌweðərɪŋ] n	Karstverwitterung
metabolism [məˈtæbəlɪzm] n	Stoffwechsel

Soils

soil n	Boden
edaphic [ɪˈdæfɪk] adj	boden~
deep adj	tiefgründig
shallow adj	flach / flachgründig
topsoil n	Mutterboden
humus ['hjuːməs] n	Humus
humification [hjuːˌmɪfɪˈkeɪʃn] n	Humifizierung *(Zersetzung von organischem Material)*
humic acid [ˌhjuːmɪkˈæsɪd] n	Huminsäure
soil organism n	Bodenorganismus

fertile [ˈfɜːtaɪl] adj	fruchtbar
infertile [ɪnˈfɜːtaɪl] adj	unfruchtbar
soil formation [ˈsɔɪlfɔːˌmeɪʃn] n	Bodenbildung
soil fertility [ˈsɔɪlfəˌtɪləti] n	Bodenfruchtbarkeit / Bodengüte
acid soil n	saurer Boden
nutrient [ˈnjuːtriənt] n	Nährstoff
rich in nutrients	nährstoffhaltig / nährstoffreich
low in nutrients	nährstoffarm
nutrient cycle	Nährstoffkreislauf
organic material n	organische Substanz
mineral substance [ˌmɪnrlˈsʌbstns] n	mineralische Substanz
clay mineral [ˈkleɪˌmɪnrl] n	Tonmineral
iron oxide [ˈaɪənˌɒksaɪd] n	Eisenoxid
aluminium oxide [ˌæljəˈmɪniəmˌɒksaɪd] n	Aluminiumoxid
pH value n	ph-Wert
acidic [əˈsɪdɪk] adj	sauer
alkaline [ˈælklaɪn] adj	basisch

»

A soil can be	fertile. infertile. rich in nutrients. low in nutrients.	Ein Boden kann	fruchtbar unfruchtbar nährstoffreich nährstoffarm	sein.

soil structure [sɔɪl'strʌktʃə] n	Bodenstruktur
soil texture [sɔɪl'tekstʃə] n	Bodentextur / Körnung / Bodenart
drainage ['dreɪnɪʤ] / permeability [ˌpɜːmɪə'bɪləɪti] n	Durchlässigkeit
waterlogging [wɔːtəlɒgɪŋ] n	Staunässe
aeration [eə'reɪʃn] n	Durchlüftung
rooting depth ['ruːtɪŋˌdepθ] n	Durchwurzelung
aerate [eə'reɪt] v	belüften
anaerobic [ˌænə'rəʊbɪk] adj	anaerob / unter Luftabschluss
water retention capacity [ˌwɔːtərɪ'tenʃnkəˌpæsəti] n	Wasserhaltekapazität
sand n	Sand
silt n	Schluff
clay n	Ton
scree [skriː] n	Geröll
gravel ['grævl] n	Kies
loam [ləʊm] n	Lehm
loamy	lehmig
calcareous [kæl'keərɪəs] adj	kalkhaltig
porous ['pɔːrəs] adj	porös
crumb structure ['krʌmˌstrʌktʃə] n	Krümelstruktur
soil type n	Bodentyp
intrazonal soil [ˌɪntrə'zəʊnlˌsɔɪl] n	zonaler Boden
azonal soil [eɪ'zəʊnlˌsɔɪl] n	azonaler Boden
podzol / podsol ['pɒdzɔːl] n	Podsol / Bleicherde
peat [piːt] n	Moorboden
marsh [mɑːʃ] n	Marschboden
brown earth n	Braunerde
lessivé n	Parabraunerde
Chernozem [tʃənə'zəm] / black earth n	Schwarzerde / Tschernosem
loess ['ləʊes] n	Löss
ferralitic soil [ˌferə'lɪtɪkˌsɔɪl] / latosol ['lætəsɒl] n	ferralitischer Boden / Latosol
laterite ['lætəraɪt] n	Laterit
terra rossa ['terəˌrɒsə] n	Roterde
gley [glæɪː] n	Pseudogley
rendzina ['rænʤɪnə] n	Rendzina
gleying ['glæɪːɪŋ] n	Vergleyung
podzolization / podsolisation / podsolisation / podsolization [ˌpɒdzɔːlɪ'seɪʃn] n	Podsolierung
calcification [ˌkælsɪfɪ'keɪʃn] n	Verkalkung

2 Physical environment › 2.2 Lithosphere

salinisation *BE* / salinization *AE* [ˌsælɪnaɪˈseɪʃn] n	Versalzung
surface crusting n	Verkrustung
degradation [ˌdegrəˈdeɪʃn] n	Degradierung *(negative Veränderung)*
soil profile n	Bodenprofil
soil horizon / horizon n	Bodenhorizont / Horizont
illuviation [ˌɪluːviˈeɪʃn] n	Anreicherung
leaching [ˈliːtʃɪŋ] / eluviation [ˌɪluːviˈeɪʃn] n	Auswaschung
decomposition [ˌdiːkɒmpəˈzɪʃn] n	Zersetzung
capillary action [kəˌpɪləriˈækʃn] n	Kapillarwirkung
A horizon n	A-Horizont »Abb. 18
topsoil n	Oberboden
zone of eluviation / zone of outwashing n	Auswaschungshorizont
litter n	Humusauflage
B horizon n	B-Horizont
subsoil n	Unterboden
zone of illuviation / zone of inwashing n	Anreicherungshorizont
iron pan / hardpan n	Ortstein *(feste, kaum durchlässige Schicht)*
C horizon n	C-Horizont
regolith [ˈrægəˌlɪθ] n	Gesteinshorizont
parent material / bedrock n	Ausgangsgestein

» Soil formation is dependent on the parent material, topography, climate, vegetation, water and human action.
Die Bodenbildung ist abhängig von Ausgangsgestein, Relief, Klima, Vegetation, Wasser und menschlicher Nutzung.
Humus forms the uppermost layer in the A horizon. It is made up of decomposed organic matter and is rich in minerals.
Humus bildet die oberste Schicht im A-Horizont. Er besteht aus zersetztem organischem Material und ist reich an Mineralien.
Podzol is the predominant type of soil in Northern Europe.
Podsol ist der vorherrschende Bodentyp in Nordeuropa.

2.3 Climate

Weather

weather n	Wetter / Witterung
meteorology [ˌmiːtirˈɒlədʒi] n	Wetterkunde / Meteorologie

»

calm		ruhiges	
cloudy	weather	bewölktes	Wetter
windy		windiges	
wet		nasses	

Weather is the day to day condition or short-term state of the atmosphere.
Wetter beschreibt den täglichen oder kurzzeitigen Zustand der Atmosphäre.

weather report n	Wetterbericht
weather forecast n	Wettervorhersage
weather map n	Wetterkarte
general weather situation	Großwetterlage
temperature n	Temperatur
average temperature [ˈavrɪdʒˌtemprətʃə]	Durchschnittstemperatur

high adj	hoch
low adj	tief
rise, rose, risen v	steigen *(Temperatur)*
fall, fell, fallen v	abfallen *(Temperatur)*
sink, sank, sunk v	sinken *(Temperatur)*
increase v	steigen / ansteigen / zunehmen
decrease v	fallen / abnehmen
stable [ˈsteɪbl] adj	stabil

frost n	Frost
hoar frost / white frost n	Raureif
freeze, froze, frozen v	gefrieren
heatwave n	Hitzewelle
sultry [ˈsʌltri] adj	schwül

»

freeze into ice	zu Eis gefrieren

wind n	Wind
wind speed n	Windgeschwindigkeit
wind direction n	Windrichtung

2 Physical environment › 2.3 Climate

prevailing wind [prɪˌveɪlɪŋˈwɪnd] n	vorherrschender Wind / vorherrschende Windrichtung
wind force / strength of the wind n	Windstärke
gust [gʌst] n	Böe
squall [skwɔːl] n	Böe / Gewitterböe
foehn / föhn [fɜːn] n	Föhn
storm n	Sturm
gale n	stürmischer Wind / Sturm
hurricane [ˈhʌrɪkən] n	Hurrikan

»   be hit by a hurricane | von einem Hurrikan getroffen werden

breeze n	Brise
cloud n	Wolke
cloud type n	Wolkenart
cumulus [ˈkjuːmjələs] n	Quellwolke / Haufenwolke / Cumulus
stratus [ˈstreɪtəs] n	Schichtwolke / Stratus
cirrus [ˈsɪrəs] n	Zirren / Cirruswolke
nimbus [ˈnɪmbəs] n	Regenwolke
cumulonimbus [ˌkjuːmjələʊˈnɪmbəs] n	Gewitterwolke / Cumulonimbus
cloud cover n	Wolkendecke
cloud formation n	Wolkenformation
cloudy adj	bewölkt
sunny intervals n pl	Aufheiterung / sonnige Abschnitte
overcast adj	bedeckt

dew [djuː] n	Tau
rainfall / precipitation [prɪˌsɪpɪˈteɪʃn] n	Niederschlag
shower n	Schauer
rain n	Regen
rainstorm n	schwere Niederschläge
rainy adj	regnerisch
rainless	niederschlagsfrei

snow n	Schnee
fresh snow	Neuschnee
heavy snow	heftige Schneefälle
snowdrift n	Schneewehe
snow storm n	Schneesturm
driving snow	Schneetreiben
snow flurry [snəʊˈflʌri]	Schneegestöber
sleet [sliːt] n	Graupel
hail [heɪl] n	Hagel

drizzle ['drɪzl] n	Nieselregen
drizzle v	nieseln
fog n	Nebel
smog n	Smog
mist [mɪst] n	Dunst
haze n	Dunst
visibility [ˌvɪzə'bɪləti] n	Sichtweite
thunderstorm n	Gewitter
lightning n	Blitz
thunder n	Donner
front n	Front *(Luftmassengrenze zwischen unterschiedlich warmen Luftmassen)*
warm front	Warmfront
cold front	Kaltfront
occluded front	Okklusionsfront
inversion [ɪn'vɜːʃn] n	Inversion(-swetterlage)

» It's raining cats and dogs. / It's lashing down. / It's raining hard.
Es schüttet wie aus Eimern.
Temperatures are expected to rise to 25° Centigrade / Celsius.
Die Temperaturen erreichen voraussichtlich 25° Celsius.
During the day it will be cloudy with sunny intervals.
Im Tagesverlauf ist es teils bewölkt, teils heiter.

Climate

climate ['klaɪmət] n	Klima
climate factor	Klimafaktor
climatic variation	Klimaschwankung
climate classification	Klimaklassifikation
climate change / climatic change	Klimaveränderung
climate graph / climograph / climatograph	Klimadiagramm
climatic adj	klimatisch
climatologist n	Klimatologe
climatology n	Klimatologie

» Climate describes the average weather conditions of a region over a longer period of time.
Das Klima beschreibt die Gesamtheit der Wetterabläufe in einer Region über einen längeren Zeitraum.

2 Physical environment › 2.3 Climate

atmosphere ['ætməsfɪə] n	Atmosphäre / Gashülle » Abb. 20
troposphere ['trɒpəʊˌsfɪə] n	Troposphäre
tropopause ['trɒpəʊˌpɔːz] n	Tropopause
stratosphere ['strætəʊˌsfɪə] n	Stratosphäre
stratopause ['strætəʊˌpɔːz] n	Stratopause
mesosphere ['mesəʊˌsfɪə] n	Mesosphäre
thermosphere ['θɜːmɒˌsfɪə] n	Thermosphäre
exosphere ['eksəʊfɪə] n	Exosphäre
ionosphere [aɪ'ɒnəsfɪə] n	Ionosphäre

layer of air n	Luftschicht
gravity ['grævəti] n	Schwerkraft
oxygen ['ɒksɪdʒən] n	Sauerstoff
carbon dioxide [ˌkɑːbəndaɪ'ɒksaɪd] n	Kohlendioxid / CO_2
aerosol ['eərəsɒl] n	Aerosol *(feinste Partikel in der Luft)*
ozone ['əʊzəʊn] n	Ozon
ozone layer n	Ozonschicht
ozone hole n	Ozonloch
ozone concentration n	Ozonkonzentration
greenhouse effect n	Treibhauseffekt
greenhouse gas n	Treibhausgas
filter v	filtern

solar energy n	Sonnenenergie
radiation [ˌreɪdi'eɪʃn] n	Strahlung / Ausstrahlung
short wave radiation	Kurzwelleneinstrahlung *(Wärme)*
long-wave radiation	langwellige Wärmestrahlung
radiation balance / radiation budget	Strahlungshaushalt / Strahlungsbilanz
radiation / radiant energy	Strahlungsenergie
radiation fog	Strahlungsnebel
ultraviolet [ˌʌltrə'vaɪələt] adj	ultraviolett
solar constant n	Solarkonstante
absorption [əb'zɔːpʃn] n	Absorption / Aufnahme
absorb v	absorbieren
insolation n	Einstrahlung / Insolation
convection [kən'vekʃn] n	Konvektion
reflection [rɪ'flekʃn] n	Reflexion / Abstrahlung
reflect v	reflektieren
scattering ['skætərɪŋ] n	Streuung
albedo [al'biːdəʊ] n	Albedo *(Reflexion des Sonnenlichts durch die Erdoberfläche oder Wolken)*

> About 24% of the incoming radiation is absorbed by the atmosphere.
> Etwa 24% der einfallenden Strahlung wird von der Atmosphäre absorbiert.
> A small amount is reflected back into space from the surface of the earth.
> Ein kleiner Betrag wird von der Erdoberfläche zurück in den Weltraum reflektiert.

global energy (heat) budget n	globaler Wärmehaushalt
heat transfer n	Wärmetransport
radiation deficit n	Einstrahlungsdefizit
position of the sun n	Sonnenstand *(Winkel)*
length of day n	Tageslänge
season n	Jahreszeit
equinox ['iːkwɪnɒks] n	Tag-und-Nacht-Gleiche
summer solstice [ˌsʌme'sɒlstɪs] n	Sommersonnenwende
winter solstice n	Wintersonnenwende
Tropic of Cancer [ˌtrɒpɪkəv'kænsə] n	Nördlicher Wendekreis
Tropic of Capricorn [ˌtrɒpɪkəv'kæprɪkɔːn] n	Südlicher Wendekreis
Arctic Circle n	Polarkreis / Nordpolarkreis
Antarctic Circle [ænˌtɑːktɪk'sɜːkl] n	Südpolarkreis
seasonal climate n	Jahreszeitenklima
diurnal climate [ˌdaɪ'ɜːnlˌklaɪmət] n	Tageszeitenklima
growing season / vegetation period n	Wachstumsperiode

air pressure / atmospheric pressure n	Luftdruck
isobar ['aɪsəbɑː] n	Isobare *(Linie gleichen Luftdrucks auf Karten)*
high pressure n	Hochdruck
area of high pressure	Hochdruckgebiet
low pressure n	Tiefdruck
area of low pressure	Tiefdruckgebiet

cyclone ['saɪkləʊn] n	Zyklone / Tiefdruckgebiet
anticyclone [ˌæntɪ'saɪkləʊn] n	Antizyklone / Hochdruckgebiet
pressure balance	Druckausgleich
pressure gradient	Luftdruckgradient *(Abstand zwischen den Isobaren)*
air mass n	Luftmasse

temperature n	Temperatur
isotherm ['aɪsəʊθɜːm] n	Isotherme *(Linie gleicher Lufttemperatur)*

2 Physical environment › 2.3 Climate

»

mean annual temperature	mittlere Jahrestemperatur
temperature range	Temperaturspanne, ~amplitude
dry adiabatic lapse rate	trockenadiabatischer Temperaturgradient (1°Celsius Temperaturabnahme pro 100m Höhe)
saturated adiabatic lapse rate	feuchtadiabatischer Temperaturgradient

evaporation [ˌɪvæpəˈreɪʃn] n — Verdunstung
evaporate [ɪˌvæpəˈreɪt] v — verdunsten
transpiration [ˌtrænspɪˈreɪʃn] n — Transpiration *(Verdunstung durch Pflanzen)*
evapotranspiration [ɪˌvæpətrænspɪˈreɪʃn] n — Evaporation *(Verdunstung und Transpiration)*
condensation [ˌkɒndenˈseɪʃn] n — Kondensation
condense v — kondensieren
condensation nuclei [ˈnjuːkliaɪ] n pl — Kondensationskerne
dewpoint [ˈdjuːˌpɔɪnt] n — Taupunkt
water vapour n — Wasserdampf
precipitation [prɪˌsɪpˈɪteɪʃn] n — Niederschlag
precipitation variation — Niederschlagsvariabilität / Niederschlagsschwankung

rainshadow n — Regenschatten
convectional rain(fall) n — Konvektionsniederschlag
advection rain n — Landregen / Advektionsniederschlag
relief rainfall [rɪˈliːf] / orographic rain [ˌɒrəʊˈgræfɪkˈreɪn] — Steigungsregen
humidity [ˌhjuːˈmɪdəti] n — Feuchtigkeit
humid adj — feucht
aridity [ærˈɪdəti] n — Trockenheit
arid [ˈærɪd] adj — trocken
drought [draʊt] n — Dürre
relative humidity n — relative Luftfeuchte
saturated [ˈsætʃreɪtɪd] adj — gesättigt

»

Moisture on the ground evaporates, rises, and condenses when it meets cooler air masses.
Bodenfeuchtigkeit verdunstet, steigt auf und kondensiert, wenn sie auf kühlere Luftmassen trifft.

Atmospheric circulation

atmospheric circulation n	atmosphärische Zirkulation

» general circulation of the atmosphere | allgemeine Zirkulation der Atmosphäre

planetary circulation	planetarische Zirkulation
[ˌplænɪtri'sɜːkjəˌleɪʃn] n	
air stream n	Luftstrom
air motion n	Luftbewegung
vertical (air) motion	vertikale (Luft-)Bewegung
expand v	sich ausdehnen
cool off v	sich abkühlen
Coriolis force [kə'raɪəlɪsˌfɔːs] n	Corioliskraft
deflection [dɪ'flekʃn] n	Ablenkung
deflect / divert v	ablenken
friction ['frɪkʃn] n	Reibung
equatorial low (pressure belt) /	äquatoriale Tiefdruckrinne
equatorial trough [ekwəˌtɔːriel'trɑːf] n	
intertropical convergence zone (ITCZ) n	innertropische Konvergenzzone (ITC)
trade wind n	Passat
North-east trade wind n	Nordostpassat
South-east trade wind n	Südostpassat
monsoon [mɒn'suːn] n	Monsun
southwest / summer monsoon	Sommermonsun
north-east / winter monsoon	Wintermonsun

» advent of the monsoon | Ankunft des Monsuns

subtropical high pressure belt n	subtropischer Hochdruckgürtel
horse latitudes ['hɔːsˌlætɪtjuːdz] n	Rossbreiten
Hadley cell ['hædli sel] n	Hadleyzelle
doldrums ['dɒldrəm] n pl	Kalmen
polar front n	Polarfront
subpolar low (pressure belt) n	subpolare Tiefdruckrinne
polar high n	polares Hoch
Westerlies ['westliz] / westerly winds	Westwindzone / Westwinddrift
['westeliˌwindz] n	
Easterlies / easterly winds n	Ostwindzone

69

2 Physical environment › 2.3 Climate

» Due to Earth's rotation, wind appears to be deflected to the right in the Northern hemisphere. This effect is the result of the Coriolis force.
Aufgrund der Erdrotation wird der Wind auf der Nordhalbkugel scheinbar nach rechts abgelenkt. Dieser Effekt ist das Resultat der Coriolis-Kraft.

Wind systems

planetary winds n	planetarische Winde
geostrophic wind [ˌdʒiːəʊstrɒfɪk'wɪnd] n	geostrophischer Wind *(parallel zu Isobaren)*
jet stream n	Jetstream / Strahlstrom
meander [mi'ændə] v	mäandrieren

maritime air mass ['mærɪtaɪm] n	maritime Luftmasse
land breeze n	Landwind
sea breeze n	Seewind
offshore wind n	ablandiger Wind / Landwind
onshore wind n	auflandiger Wind / Seewind
windward adj	Wind~ / dem Wind zugekehrt
leeward ['liːwəd] adj	Lee~ / dem Wind abgekehrt

whirlwind n	Wirbelsturm
dust devil n	kleiner Wirbelsturm
tornado [tɔː'neɪdəʊ] n	Tornado *(außertropischer Wirbelsturm)*
twister n	Twister *(amerikanische Bezeichnung für Tornado umgangssprachlich)*
hurricane ['hʌrɪkən] n	Orkan / Hurrikan *(trop. Wirbelsturm über dem Golf von Mexiko)*
calm adj	windstill
calm n	Windstille
typhoon [taɪ'fuːn] n	Taifun *(tropischer Wirbelsturm über dem Indischen und Pazifischen Ozean)*

» eye of the hurricane | Auge des Hurrikans

Norther n	polarer Kaltlufteinbruch in Nordamerika
blizzard ['blɪzəd] n	Schneesturm
Mistral ['mɪstrl] n	Mistral *(kalter Nordwind an der südlichen Rhone)*

Bora ['bɔːrə] n	Bora *(kalter Fallwind an der dalmatinischen Küste)*
mountain wind n	Bergwind
valley wind n	Talwind
foehn / föhn [fɜːn] n	Föhn
ascend [ə'send] v	aufsteigen
gain heat [ˌgeɪn'hiːt] v	sich erwärmen
descend [dɪ'send] v	absteigen
Scirocco [ʃɪ'rɒkəʊ] n	Scirocco *(heißer Wind aus der Sahara)*
Harmattan [ˌhɑːrmə'tæn] n	Harmattan *(heißer Wind in Westafrika aus der Sahara)*
carry dust v	Staub mit sich tragen
Chinook [tʃɪ'nʊk] n	Chinook *(warmer Wind in den Rocky Mountains)*

» A foehn is a warm, dry downslope wind that occurs in the lee (on the downwind side) of a mountain range, particularly in the Alps.
Der Föhn ist ein warmer, trockener Fallwind, der auf der Leeseite (windabgewandten Seite) eines Gebirges entsteht, besonders im Alpenraum.

Climate and vegetation zones

climatic region / climatic zone n	Klimazone
vegetation zone n	Vegetationszonen
natural vegetation n	natürliche Vegetation
biome ['baɪəʊm] n	Landschaftszone / Landschaftsgürtel
ecosystem / biome ['baɪəʊm] n	Ökosystem
biosphere ['baɪəʊsfɪə] n	Biosphäre
habitat n	Lebensraum / Standort
species ['spiːʃiːz] n	Art
fauna ['fɔːnə] n	Tierwelt
flora ['flɔːrə] n	Pflanzenwelt

» Ecosystems or biomes are characterised by typical fauna and flora, dependent on climate and soil.
Ökosysteme sind gekennzeichnet durch eine typische Tier- und Pflanzenwelt, die wiederum von Klima und Boden abhängig sind.

continental climate n	Kontinentalklima
continentality n	Kontinentalität

2 Physical environment › 2.3 Climate

maritime climate ['mærɪtaɪmˌklaɪmət] / oceanic climate n wet-dry climate n equatorial climate [ˌekwə'tɔːrielˌklaɪmət] n	maritimes Klima / ozeanisches Klima wechselfeuchtes Klima Äquatorialklima
rainforest n broadleaved [ˌbrɔːd'liːvd] adj deciduous [dɪ'sɪdjuəs] adj evergreen adj coniferous [kəʊ'nɪfərəs] adj	Regenwald Laub~ / laubtragend laubabwerfend immergrün Nadel~ / nadeltragend

tropics n pl
tropical adj
subtropics n
temperate zone n
temperate adj
polar regions n
  subpolar regions
	Tropen
	tropisch
	Subtropen
	gemäßigte Breiten / gemäßigte Zone
	gemäßigt
	Polarregionen
	  subpolare Gebiete

tropical rainforest / equatorial rainforest n jungle n rapid growth n rot v dead adj	tropischer Regenwald Dschungel schnelles Wachstum verrotten abgestorben
constant heat n high humidity [ˌhaɪ'hjuːmɪdəti] n lush [lʌʃ] adj layer of vegetation n emergent [ɪ'mɜːdʒnt] / emergent tree crown n canopy ['kænəpi] n shrub layer ['ʃrʌbˌleɪə] n buttress root ['bʌtrəsˌruːt] n aerial root n tangled roots ['tæŋgldˌruːts] n leaf n undergrowth n epiphyte ['epɪfaɪt] n liana / liane [li'ɑːnə] n strangler ['stræŋglə] n	gleichbleibende Hitze hohe Luftfeuchtigkeit üppig Stockwerkbau Baumriese Baumkrone Blätterdach / Kronenschicht Strauch- und Krautschicht Brettwurzel Luftwurzel Wurzelgeflecht Blatt Unterholz Epiphyt / Aufsitzerpflanze Liane Würger

fungus ['fʌŋgəs] n	Pilz
micro-organism [ˌmaɪkrəʊ'ɔːgnɪzm] n	Mikroorganismus
mycorrhiza ['maɪkəraɪsə] n	Mykorrhiza
nutrient cycle ['njuːtriənt‚saɪkl] n	Nährstoffkreislauf
shallow adj	flach(-gründig)
mangrove ['mæŋgrəʊv] n	Mangrove(-nwald)
Selva ['sɛlvə] n	Selvas *(tropischer Regenwald im Amazonasgebiet)*
cocoa ['kəʊkəʊ] n	Kakao
coffee n	Kaffee
rubber n	Gummi
hardwood n	Hartholz
precious timber n	Edelholz
mahogany [mə'hɒgəni] n	Mahagoni
rosewood n	Palisander
teak n	Teak(-holz)
orchid ['ɔːkɪd] n	Orchidee

» The tropical rainforest is characterised by rapid growth, lush vegetation and high humidity.
Der tropische Regenwald ist gekennzeichnet durch schnelles Wachstum, üppige Vegetation und hohe Luftfeuchtigkeit.

savanna [sə'vænə] / tropical grassland n	Savanne
wet season n	Regenzeit
dry season n	Trockenzeit
alternate [ɔːl'tɜːnət] v	abwechseln
wet savanna n	Feuchtsavanne
dry savanna n	Trockensavanne
bush savanna / thornbush savanna n	Dornsavanne
Sahel n	Sahel
desertification [dɪˌzɜːtɪfɪ'keɪʃn] n	Desertifikation
caatinga ['kɑːtɪŋgə] n	Caatinga *(Trockensavanne in Südamerika)*
acacia [ə'keɪʃə] n	Schirmakazien
baobab ['beɪəʊbæb] n	Baobab
thick bark n	dicke Rinde
eucalyptus [ˌjuːkəl'ɪptəs] n	Eukalyptus
shrivel ['ʃrɪvl] v	austrocknen / schrumpfen

» scattered tufts of grass | vereinzelte Grasbüschel

drought-resistant ['draʊtrɪˌzɪstənt] adj	trockenheitsresistent
xerophyte ['zɪərəʊfaɪt] n	Xerophyt *(an Trockenheit angepasste Pflanze)*
xerophytic adj	an Trockenheit angepasst / xerophytisch
waxy adj	wächsern
thorny adj	dornig
herbivore ['hɜːbɪvɔː] n	Pflanzenfresser
carnivore ['kɑːnɪvɔː] n	Fleischfresser
predator ['predətə] n	Raubtier
scavenger ['skævɪndʒə] n	Aasfresser
termite ['tɜːmaɪt] n	Termite
desert ['dezət] n	Wüste
arid region ['ærɪd] n	Trockengebiet
semi-desert n	Halbwüste
semi-arid adj	semi-arid / halbtrocken
hammada ['hæmədə] n	Hamada
serir ['sɛrir] n	Serir / Kieswüste / Geröllwüste / Reg
erg ['ɜːg] n	Erg
oasis n	Oase
salt pan n	Salzpfanne
exogenous river [ɪk'sɒdʒənəsˌrɪvə] n	Fremdlingsfluss
river oasis n	Flussoase
wadi ['wɒdi] n	Wadi
succulent ['sʌkjələnt] n	Sukkulente *(Fettpflanze)*
cactus n	Kaktus
halophyte ['heɪləʊfaɪt] n	Halophyten
reptile ['reptaɪl] n	Reptil
nocturnal [nɒk'tɜːnl] adj	nächtlich / Nacht~
mediterranean climate [ˌmedɪtər'eɪniən] n	Mittelmeerklima
western margin climate ['westənˌmɑːdʒɪnˌklaɪmət] n	Westküstenklima
eastern margin climate n	Ostküstenklima
summer drought [draʊt] n	Sommertrockenheit
scrub vegetation ['skrʌbˌvedʒɪ'teɪʃn] n	mediterrane Vegetation
sclerophyllous [ˌsklerəʊ'fɪləs] adj	Hartlaub~
maquis [mæk'i] n	Macchie
garigue [gə'riːg] n	Garigue *(mediterrane Vegetation in Frankreich)*
chaparral [ʃæpərəl] n	Chaparral *(Buschland im Westen der USA)*

Plants in mediterranean climates

cork oak	Korkeiche	thyme	Thymian
olive	Olive	lavender	Lavendel
gorse	Stechginster	rosemary	Rosmarin

steppe [step] / temperate grassland n   Steppe
pampas ['pæmpəs] n   Pampa *(Steppe in Argentinien)*
prairie ['preəri] n   Prärie *(nordamerikanische Steppe)*
buffalo grass n   Büffelgras
feather grass n   Federgras
short grass prairie n   Kurzgrassteppe
bison ['baɪsən] n   Bison

deciduous tree [dɪˌsɪdjuəsˈtriː] n   Laubbaum
deciduous forest n   Laubwald
   deciduous and mixed forest   sommergrüner Mischwald

»

shed leaves	Blätter abwerfen

Trees in mixed forest regions

beech	Buche	lime	Linde
oak	Eiche	ash	Esche

boreal coniferous forest [kəʊˈnɪfərəs] n   borealer Nadelwald
boreal [bɒrɪəl] adj   boreal *(dem nördlichen Klima zugehörend)*
cone-bearing adj   mit Zapfen / zapfentragend
taiga ['taɪgə] n   Taiga
tundra ['tʌndrə] n   Tundra
permafrost ['pɜːməfrɒst] n   Dauerfrost(-boden)
frozen adj   gefroren
drift ice n   Treibeis
thaw, thawed, thawn v   auftauen
tree line / timber line n   Baumgrenze / Waldgrenze
snow line n   Schneegrenze
moor [mɔː] n   Moor

pine n   Kiefer
spruce [spruːs] n   Fichte
fir [fɜː] n   Tanne
larch [laːtʃ] n   Lärche

2 Physical environment › 2.4 Landforms

dwarf willow ['dwɔːfˌwɪləʊ] n	Zwergweide
birch [bɜːtʃ] n	Birke

heather ['heðə] n	Heide
moss n	Moos
lichen ['laɪkən] n	Flechte
cushion plant ['kʊʃnˌplɑːnt] n	Polsterpflanze

reindeer ['reɪndɪə] n	Rentier
caribou ['kærɪbuː] n	Karibu *(nordamerikanisches Rentier)*
moose [muːs] n	Elch
arctic fox n	Polarfuchs / Blaufuchs
arctic hare [ˌɑːktɪk'heə] / blue hare n	Schneehase
polar bear n	Eisbär

altitudinal vegetation zone n	Höhenstufe der Vegetation » Abb. 19
montane tree line n	montane Baumgreneze
montane adj	Gebirgs~
alpine zone n	alpine Stufe
puna [pjuːnə] n	Puna *(Vegetation der alpinen Stufe in tropischen Hochgebirgen)*
cloud forest / fog forest n	Nebelwald

Vegetation zones in tropical mountains » Abb. 19

tierra caliente	Tierra caliente (heiß)
tierra templada	Tierra templada (gemäßigt)
tierra fria	Tierra fria (kalt)
tierra helada	Tierra helada (eisig)
tierra nevada	Tierra nevada ("Schneeland")

2.4 Landforms

geomorphology [ˌdʒiːəʊmɔːˈfɒlədʒi] n	Geomorphologie
landform n	Landform
landscape n	Landschaft
relief [rɪ'liːf] n	Oberflächengestalt / Relief

Mountains, hills and valleys

mountain n	Berg » Abb. 9
mountainous ['maʊntɪnəs] adj	bergig / gebirgig

peak n	Bergspitze
summit / mountain top n	Berggipfel
saddle ['sædl] n	Sattel
col ['kɑːl] n	Pass
ridge [rɪdʒ] n	Kamm
spur [spɜː] n	Sporn
slope [sləʊp] n	Berghang
hill n	Hügel
hilly adj	hügelig
steep adj	steil
gentle adj	flach
rounded adj	gerundet
rocky adj	felsig
crag n	Fels
craggy adj	felsig
rugged adj	zerklüftet
elevation [ˌelɪ'veɪʃn] n	Höhenlage / Höhe
highland n	Hochland
mountains n	Gebirge
low mountain range	Mittelgebirge
high mountains	Hochgebirge
mountain range / range n	Gebirgszug / Gebirgskette
mountain ridge n	Bergrücken

»

A mountain or hill can be ...	steep. gentle. rounded. craggy. rugged.	Ein Berg oder Hügel kann ...	... steil ... ... sanft ... ... gerundet ... ... felsig ... ... zerklüftet ...	sein.

plain n	Ebene
lowland plain	Tiefebene
lowland n	Tiefland
plateau ['plætəʊ] n	Hochebene / Plateau
escarpment [ɪ'skɑːpmənt] / cuesta ['kwestə] / scarp [skɑːp] n	Schichtstufe
dip slope n	Stufenfläche
scarp slope n	Trauf
shield n	Rumpffläche
valley n	Tal
valley floor / floor	Talboden

77

Rivers, streams and swamps

river n	Fluss / Strom »Abb. 7
course n	Flusslauf
upstream adj	stromaufwärts
downstream adj	stromabwärts
shallow ['ʃæləʊ] adj	flach
deep adj	tief
raging / torrential [tə'rentʃl] adj	reißend
channel n	Fluss / Fließgewässer
tributary ['trɪbjətri] n	Nebenfluss
distributary n	Nebenarm
flow v	fließen
mouth n	Mündung
flow into v	münden
rise (from), rose, risen v	entspringen
lower course / middle course / upper course n	Unterlauf / Mittellauf / Oberlauf
flood n	Überschwemmung
flood v	überschwemmen
source / spring n	Quelle
river bank n	Flussufer
riverbed n	Flussbett
course of a river n	Flusslauf
delta ['deltə] n	Delta
estuary ['estjʊəri] n	Trichtermündung
rapid ['ræpɪd] n	Stromschnelle
stream n	Bach
creek n	Bächlein
rivulet ['rɪvjələt] n	Rinnsal
lake n	See
pond n	Teich
swamp n	Sumpf
moor [mɔː] n	Moor / Hochmoor
bog [bɒg] n	Sumpf
peat bog n	Torfmoor
marsh n	Sumpf
marshland	Sumpfland
marshy	sumpfig

» The source of the river Rhine is in Switzerland. In its course downstream, it turns from a stream to a deep river, flows through Lake Constance, passes Austria, France and Germany and finally flows into the North Sea in the Netherlands.
Die Quelle des Rheins ist in der Schweiz. Auf seinem Lauf stromabwärts wandelt er sich von einem Bach zu einem tiefen Fluss, fließt durch den Bodensee, an Österreich, Frankreich und Deutschland vorbei und mündet schließlich in den Niederlanden in die Nordsee.

Oceans and the sea

ocean n	Meer / Ozean
the sea n	die See / das Meer
coast n	Küste » Abb. 11
shore n	Küstenlinie / Strand
tide [taɪd] n	Gezeiten / Tide
low tide	Ebbe
high tide	Flut
wave n	Welle
tidal wave	Flutwelle
surf / surge n	Brandung
breakers n pl	Brandung
beach n	Strand
bay n	Bucht
marine deposit n	Meeresablagerung
landfill n	Aufschüttung *(durch den Menschen)*

Glacial » Abb. 10

Ice Age / glacial ['gleɪsɪəl] n	Eiszeit / Glazial
interglacial	Warmzeit / Interglazial
postglacial	Nacheiszeit / Postglazial
glaciation [ˌgleɪsɪ'eɪʃn]	Vereisung / Vergletscherung
periglacial	periglazial *(Formen und Prozesse am Rand einer Vereisung)*
glacial deposition [ˌgleɪsɪəlˌdepə'zɪʃn]	glaziale Ablagerung
glacial erosion [ˌgleɪsɪəlɪ'rəʊʒn]	glaziale Erosion
glacial series	glaziale Serie
ablation [ə'bleɪʃn] n	Ablation *(Abschmelzen und Verdunsten von Gletschereis)*
nivation [nə'veɪʃn] n	Schnee-Erosion / Nivation
frost shattering / plucking n	Frostsprengung
frost heaving n	Frosthub

2 Physical environment › 2.4 Landforms

freeze-thaw n	Einfrieren und Auftauen
striation / scratch marks [straɪ'eɪʃn] n	Gletscherschliff
solifluction [ˌsɒlɪ'flʌkʃn] n	Bodenfließen / Solifluktion
eustatic change in sea-level ['juːstætɪk] n	eustatische Meeresspiegelschwankung

» At the time of the last glacial, around 18 000 years ago, ice covered most parts of Britain, all of Scandinavia and the northern parts of Germany.
In der letzten Eiszeit vor etwa 18 000 Jahren waren große Teile der Britischen Inseln, ganz Skandinavien und die nördlichen Regionen Deutschlands eisbedeckt.

glacier ['glæsiə] n	Gletscher » Abb. 10
valley glacier	Talgletscher
snowfield n	Schneefeld
snout / glacier snout [ˌgleɪsiə'snaʊt] n	Gletscherzunge
firn / névé ['neveɪ] n	Firn
zone of accumulation [əˌkjuːmjə'leɪʃn] n	Nährgebiet / Akkumulation
zone of ablation n	Zehrgebiet / Ablation
avalanche ['ævlɑːnʃ] n	Lawine
crevasse [krɪ'væs] n	Gletscherspalte
bergschrund [bɜːg'ʃrənd] n	Bergschrund (Spalte zwischen Gletscher und Fels)
mouth / glacier mouth n	Gletschertor
glacial stream n	Gletscherbach

» Glaciers can advance and retreat.
Gletscher können vorrücken und zurückweichen.

ice sheet n	Inlandeis
nunatak ['nʌnəˌtæk] n	Nunatak (über die Oberfläche von Inlandeismasse aufragender Berg oder Fels)

iceberg ['aɪsbɜːg] n	Eisberg
calve [kɑːv] v	kalben
drifting ice n	Eisdrift

moraine [mɒr'eɪn] / till n	Moräne » Abb. 10
terminal moraine	Endmoräne
ground moraine	Grundmoräne
ablation moraine / lateral moraine	Seitenmoräne
medial moraine	Mittelmoräne
older moraine	Altmoräne
young moraine	Jungmoräne

finger lake / ribbon lake n	Zungenbecken
drift n	Geschiebe
till n	Geschiebelehm / Geschiebemergel
scree [skriː] n	Schuttkegel / Schutthalde
kame n	Kame *(Landform über Toteisablagerung)*
mudstream / rock stream n	Mure

» Moraines develop when the debris carried by the glacier is deposited.
Moränen entstehen durch die Ablagerung des durch den Gletscher transportierten Schutt.

cirque [sɜːk] / corrie ['kɒri] / combe [kuːm] n	Kar
arête [ær'et] n	Grat zwischen benachbarten Karen
horn / pyramidal peak n	Pyramide / Karling

valley n	Tal
V-shaped valley	Klamm / Kerbtal
trough / U-shaped valley	Trogtal
hanging valley	Hängetal
fjord [fjɔːd] / fiord n	Fjord

outwash plain / sandur ['sændə] n	Sander
Urstromtal / glacial valley n	Urstromtal
erratic block / erratic [ɪ'rætɪk] n	Findling / erratischer Block

drumlin ['drʌmlɪŋ] n	Drumlin
roche moutonnée [rəʊtʃ mʊtə'ne] n	Rundhöcker
esker ['eskə] n	Os *(Pl. Oser – wallartige Ablagerung unter dem Eis)*
pingo ['pɪŋgə] n	Pingo *(Hügel, der aus einem Eiskern und dem durch Auffrieren darüber gelagerten Erdreich besteht)*
ice wedge n	Eiskeil
patterned ground n	Frostmusterboden

Fluvial

fluvial ['fluːvɪəl] adj	Fluss~ / fluviatil
stream (of water) n	Fließgewässer
flooding n	Überflutung
floodplain n	Überflutungsebene / Talaue

2 Physical environment › 2.4 Landforms

braided stream / braided river n	Fluss mit zahlreichen Seitenarmen / Binnendelta
confluence [ˈkɒnfluəns] n	Zusammenfluss
converge [kənˈvɜːdʒ] v	zusammenfließen

》

The river bursts its banks.	Der Fluss quillt über die Ufer.
Water levels subside.	Die Wasserstände gehen zurück.

erosion [ɪˈrəʊʒn] n	Erosion
vertical erosion	Tiefenerosion
lateral erosion	Seiteneroison
headward erosion / spring sapping	rückschreitende Erosion
erode [ɪˈrəʊd] v	erodieren
base level n	Erosionsbasis
current [ˈkʌrnt] n	Strömung / Stromstrich
riffle [ˈrɪfl] n	seichter Abschnitt
pothole [ˈpɒthəʊl] n	Strudelloch / Kolk
boulder [ˈbəʊldə] n	Felsblock
deposition n	Ablagerung
river deposit	Flussablagerung
levée [ˈlevi] n	natürlicher Damm / natürlicher Deich
embankment [ɪmˈbæŋkmənt] n	Böschung / Uferböschung
river terrace n	Terrasse / Talterrasse
alluvial fan / alluvial cone n	Schwemmfächer
alluvium [əˈluːviəm] n	Flusssediment
silt [sɪlt] n	Schlamm / Schlick
gravel n	Kies
quicksand n	Treibsand
rejuvenation [rɪˌdʒuːvnˈeɪʃn] n	Verjüngung / Flussverjüngung
knick point [ˈnɪkˌpɔɪnt] n	Scheitelpunkt / Knickpunkt

stream n	Fluss
exotic stream / exogenous stream [ɪkˈsɒdʒənəsˌstriːm]	Fremdlingsfluss
perennial stream [prˈeniəlˌstriːm]	perennierender Fluss (*dauerhaft fließender Fluss*)
intermittent stream [ˌɪntəˈmɪtntˌstriːm] / ephemeral stream [ɪˈfemrlˌstriːm]	periodisch fließender Fluss

slope n	Gefälle
aspect n	Exposition / Hangausrichtung
bend n	Krümmung / Flussschlinge

point bank n	Sandbank *(am Gleithang eines Mäanders)*
meander [miˈændə] n	Mäander
meander v	mäandrieren
cut through v	durchstoßen
ox-bow lake / cut-off / horseshoe lake n	Altarm
bluff [blʌf] / river cliff n	Prallhang
slip-off slope / convex bank n	Gleithang
cut-off meander spur / river cliff n	Umlaufberg
rapid n	Stromschnelle
cascade [kæsˈkeɪd] n	Kaskade
cataract [ˈkætrækt] n	Katarakt

» An ox-bow lake comes into being when a meander is finally cut through by the river.
Ein Altarm entsteht, wenn ein Mäanderbogen schließlich vom Fluss durchstoßen wird.

head of the valley n	Talschluss
hollow [ˈhɒləʊ] n	Talkessel
ravine [rəˈviːn] n	Klamm
gorge [gɔːdʒ] n	Schlucht
canyon [ˈkænjən] n	Canyon / Schlucht
V-shaped valley n	Kerbtal
antecedent valley [ˌæntɪˈsiːdntˌvæli] n	Druchbruchstal
butte [bjuːt] / mesa [ˈmeɪsə] n	Zeugenberg / Spitzkuppe
gully [ˈgʌli] n	Rinne / Schlucht / Runse
gullying n	Zerschluchtung
waterfall n	Wasserfall
plunge pool [plʌndʒˈpuːl] n	Fallkolk *(Wasserloch unterhalb eines Wasserfalls)*

karst [ˈkɑːst] n	Karst
karst scenery / karst landscape	Karstlandschaft
karstification	Verkarstung
surface karst	nackter Karst
underground karst	bedeckter Karst
cockpit karst / karst towers	Kegelkarst
corrosion [kəˈrəʊʒn] n	Korrosion / Zersetzung
dissolve v	auflösen

clints and grykes / grikes [ˈgraɪks] n	Karren
dry valley n	Trockental
underground stream / underground aquifer [ˈækwɪfə] n	unterirdischer Fluss

2 Physical environment › 2.4 Landforms

swallow hole / swallow sink n	Schluckloch / Flussschwinde / Versinkung
intermittent spring / karst spring n	Karstquelle
resurgence [rɪˈsɜːdʒəns] n	Wiederauftauchen
doline [ˈdəʊlaɪn] / sinkhole n	Doline
polje n	Polje *(Karsthohlform)*
dripstone cave [ˈdrɪpstəʊnˌkeɪv] n	Tropfsteinhöhle
stalagmite [ˈstæləgmaɪt] n	Stalagmit
stalactite [ˈstæləktaɪt] n	Stalaktit

Wind

air n	Luft
aeolian [iːˈəʊliən] adj	äolisch
deflation [dɪˈfleɪʃn] n	Ausblasung / Winderosion
blow, blew, blown v	blasen / wehen
abrasion [əˈbreɪʒn] n	Windschliff / Abrasion
drifting sand / wind-blown sand n	Flugsand
desert pavement / stone pavement	Hammada / Felswüste
reg n	Steinwüste
serir [səˈriːr] n	Steinwüste *(Ägypten, Libyen)*
desert varnish n	Wüstenlack
dune / sand dune n	Düne / Sanddüne
seif [siːf] n	Längsdüne
barchan [ˈbɑːkən] n	Barchan / Sicheldüne
shifting dune / wandering dune n	Wanderdüne
yardang [ˈjɑːdæŋ] n	Windhöcker / Jardang
mushroom rock / pedestal rock / zeugen n	Pilzfelsen
natural arch [ˌnætʃrlˈɑːtʃ] n	Felsbogen » Abb. 11

» Abrasion leads to desert varnish (the desert surface looks polished), mushroom rocks or natural arches.
Windschliff führt zu Wüstenlack (die Wüstenoberfläche sieht wie poliert aus), Pilzfelsen oder Felsbögen.

Coastal » Abb. 11

coast n	Küste
coastline	Küstenverlauf
coastal plain	Küstenebene

bay / bight n	Bucht
headland n	Landspitze / Landzunge
lagoon [lə'guːn] n	Lagune
barrier reef ['bæriə͵riːf] n	Barriereriff / Wallriff
coral reef ['kɒrəl͵riːf] n	Korallenriff
cliff n	Kliff
beach / shore n	Strand
sandy beach	Sandstrand
swash [swɒʃ] n	auslaufende Welle / Roller
backwash	Brandungsrückstrom
sandbank n	Sandbank
berm [bɜːm] n	Strandwall
mud flats / tidal flats n	Watt
sand flats	Sandwatt
mud flats	Schlickwatt
tidal inlet ['taɪdl͵ɪnlet] / tideway ['taɪdweɪ] n	Priel / Gezeitenstromrinne
lock n	Siel
islet ['aɪlət] / hallig n	Hallig
shoal [ʃəʊl] / shallow / flat n	Untiefe
silting zone n	Verlandungszone
coastal dune n	Küstendüne
shore ice n	Küsteneis

tides n	Gezeiten
low tide	Ebbe / Niedrigwasser
high tide	Flut
tidal range n	Tidenhub
storm tide n	Sturmflut
tidal wave / tsunami n	Flutwelle
longshore current n	Brandungsströmung
surf / surge n	Brandung
breakers n pl	Brandung
break, broke, broken v	brechen *(Welle)*

coast / coastline n	Küste
type of coastline	Küstenform
high coast	Steilküste
rocky coast	Felsenküste
cliff coast	Kliffküste
unconsolidated rock coast [͵ʌnkən'sɒlɪdeɪtɪdrɒk͵kəʊst]	Lockergesteinsküste
fjord coast / sea loch [siːlɒk]	Fjordküste
skerry-coast	Schärenküste

2 Physical environment › 2.4 Landforms

skerry	Schären
haff-coast / lagoon coast / regulated coast	Ausgleichsküste / Haffküste
shallow bay n	Bodden
spit (of land) n	Nehrung
lido coast [ˌliːdəʊˈkəʊst]	Nehrungsküste
coast with mud flats	Wattenküste
drowned coastline / submerged coast	Senkungsküste
raised coast / elevated shoreline	Hebungsküste
raised beach n	gehobener Strand
ria [ˈriːə] n	Ria *(Meeresbucht, die durch Eindringen von Wasser in ein Kerbtal entstanden ist)*
concordant coastline [kənˌkɔːdntˈkəʊstlain]	Längsküste
discordant coastline	Querküste / Diagonalküste

abrasion platform [əˈbreɪʃn] n	Abrasionsplatte
blowhole n	Blowhole *(Loch am Ende einer senkrechten Spalte durch die Wasser nach oben spritzt)*
stack n	Brandungspfeiler
wave-cut platform / shore platform n	Abrasionsplattform / Schorre
wave-cut notch n	Brandungshohlkehle
undercut v	unterhöhlen
undercut adj	unterhöhlt

dike / dyke [daɪk] n	Deich
land in front of the dikes	Deichvorland
main dike	Hauptdeich
coastal protection n	Küstenschutz
groyne [grɔɪn] / breakwater groyne n	Buhne / Lahnung
revetment [rɪˈvetmənt] n	Ufersicherung *(meist Betonmauer)*
beach replenishment [rɪˈplenɪʃmənt] n	Küstenaufschüttung
breakwater n	Wellenbrecher
land reclamation [lændˌrekləˈmeɪʃn] n	Landgewinnung
polder [ˈpɒldə] n	Polder

salt marsh n	Salzmarsch
old coastal marsh / old marshland n	alte Marsch
young marshland / new marshland n	junge Marsch
coastal sandy heathland [ˌkəʊstlsændɪˈhiːθlənd] n	Geest

2.5 Hydrology

Resource water

hydrology [haɪˈdrɒlədʒi] n	Hydrologie
hydrological	hydrologisch
hydrological cycle [haɪˈdrəʊlɒdʒɪklˌsaɪkl] n	Wasserhaushalt / Wasserkreislauf
store n	Wasservorrat
water cycle n	Wasserkreislauf
water table n	Grundwasserspiegel
aquifer [ˈækwɪfə] n	wasserführende Schicht
spring n	Quelle
spring line	Quellhorizont
percolation [pɜːklˈeɪʃn] / infiltration n	Versickerung
percolate [ˈpɜːkleɪt] v	versickern
runoff n	Abfluss
surface runoff	Oberflächenabfluss
delayed runoff	verzögerter Oberflächenabfluss
immediate runoff	direkter Oberflächenabfluss
throughflow [ˈθruːfleʊ] n	Durchfluss
permeable [ˈpɜːmiəbl] adj	durchlässig
pervious [ˈpɜːviəs] adj	durchlässig / durchdringbar
soil moisture n	Bodenfeuchtigkeit

» The hydrological cycle refers to the cycle of water between atmosphere, lithospere and biosphere.
Der Wasserkreislauf bezieht sich auf den Kreislauf des Wassers zwischen Atmosphäre, Gesteinsschicht und Biosphäre.

closed system	geschlossenes System
imbalance of the global water cycle	Ungleichgewicht des globalen Wasserkreislaufs
human impact on the water cycle	menschlicher Einfluss auf den Wasserkreislauf

water supply and distribution n	Wasserwirtschaft
water supply n	Wasserversorgung
water disposal n	Wasserentsorgung
water management n	Wasserbewirtschaftung
water supply management	Wasserbevorratung
water withdrawal / water abstraction n	Wasserentnahme
water rights n	Wasserentnahmerecht
water production n	Wassergewinnung
water exchange n	Wasseraustausch

87

2 Physical environment › 2.5 Hydrology

water pipe(line) n	Wasserleitung
waterworks n	Wasserwerk
water conduit [wɔːtə͵kɒndjuɪt] n	Wasserzuleitung

» Water is used for domestic, industrial, agricultural and recreational purposes.
Wasser wird im Haushalt, zu industriellen, landwirtschaftlichen und Erholungszwecken genutzt.

global water shortage	globale Wasserknappheit
feeding of water into	Wassereinleitung in
(biological) quality of the water	Gewässergüte

fresh water n	Süßwasser
salt water / sea water n	Salzwasser
surface water ['sɜːfɪs͵wɔːtə] n	Oberflächenwasser
meltwater n	Schmelzwasser
ground water n	Grundwasser
ground water resources [rɪ'zɔːsɪz]	Grundwasserreserven
unspiked water n	Rohwasser
drinking water n	Trinkwasser
industrial water [ɪn'dʌstrɪəl͵wɔːtə] / service water ['sɜːvɪs͵wɔːtə] n	Brauchwasser
waste water / sewage ['suːɪdʒ] n	Abwasser
hard water n	hartes Wasser *(hoher Kalkgehalt)*

body of water n	Gewässer
artesian [ɑː'tiːzɪən] adj	artesisch
artesian basin [ɑː'tiːzɪənbeɪsn] n	artesisches Becken
channel n	Fließgewässer
velocity [vɪ'lɒsəti] / stream velocity n	Fließgeschwindigkeit
direction of flow n	Fließrichtung
river regime [rɪvə͵reɪ'ʒiːm] n	Flusshaushalt / Fussregime
perennial stream [pr'enɪəl͵striːm] / perennial river n	permanenter Fluss / perennierender Fluss
intermittent river n	periodischer Fluss / intermittierender Fluss / episodischer Fluss
river profile n	Gefällskurve *(Gefällsverhältnisse eines Flusses in seinem Längsprofil)*
long profile n	Längsprofil
current n	Strömung
eddy ['edi] n	Wirbel / Fließwirbel

load n	Schuttbelastung
suspension n	Schwebstoffe im Fluss / Flusstrübe
drainage ['dreɪnɪdʒ] / draining ['dreɪnɪŋ] n	Entwässerung
drain v	entwässern
drained adj	entwässert
drainage pattern n	Entwässerungssystem
basin / river basin / catchment area n	Flusseinzugsgebiet
watershed / water divide / water parting n	Wasserscheide
discharge ['dɪstʃɑːdʒ] n	Wasserführung
draining ditch n	Entwässerungskanal
peripheral drainage runway [pə'rɪfrl̩ˌdreɪnɪdʒˌrʌnwei]	periphere Entwässerungsrinne
centrifugal drainage runway [ˌsentry'fjuːgl̩ˌdreɪnɪdʒˌrʌnwei]	zentrifugale Entwässerungsrinne
river capture ['rɪvəˌkæptʃə] / river piracy ['rɪvəˌpaɪrəsi] n	Flussanzapfung

» The river regime describes the seasonal variations in the volume of a river.
Der Flusshaushalt beschreibt die jahreszeitlichen Schwankungen des Wasserstandes.

reservoir ['rezəvwɑː] / water storage ['wɔːtəˌstɔːrɪdʒ] n	Wasserspeicher
retaining basin n	Rückhaltebecken
infiltration pool [ˌɪnfɪl'treɪʃn] / percolation pool [ˌpɜːkleɪʃn'puːl] n	Sickerteich
barrage BE ['bærɑːdʒ] / dam [dæm] n	Staudamm/Talsperre/Staustufe » Abb. 8
reservoir / artificial reservoir n	Stausee / Speichersee
percolation plant [ˌpɜːkleɪʃn'plænt] n	Versickerungsanlage
weir [wɪə] n	Wehr
water distribution sluice [wɔːtəˌdɪstrɪ'bjuːʃn̩ˌsluːs] n	Wasserausgleichsschleuse
flooding n	Überschwemmung
flood v	überschwemmen / überfluten
flood protection	Hochwasserschutz

» obligation to feed water into the system | Wasserzuführungsverpflichtung

waterway n	Wasserweg
canal / waterway n	Kanal / Wasserstraße
shipping lane n	Fahrrinne
shipping lane depth n	Fahrwassertiefe

2 Physical environment › 2.5 Hydrology

regulated river course n	begradigter Flusslauf
sluice [sluːs] n	Staustufe
side canal n	Randkanal
cut-off canal n	Stichkanal
connecting canal / junction [ˈdʒʌŋkʃn] n	Verbindungskanal
lowering of the ground water table n	Grundwasserabsenkung
drainage of ground water n	Grundwasserableitung
ground water pump n	Grundwasserpumpe
water pollution n	Gewässerbelastung / Gewässerverschmutzung
overheating of water n	Gewässerüberwärmung
eutrophication [ˈjuːtrɒpɪkeɪʃn] n	Eutrophierung
algal bloom n	Algenblüte
lack of oxygen n	Sauerstoffmangel
die v	umkippen
waste heat n	Abwärme
water reserve n	Wasserschutzgebiet
sewage n	Abwasser
sewage disposal / sewage treatment	Abwasserentsorgung / Abwasseraufbereitung
sewage plant / sewage works n	Kläranlage / Abwasserbehandlungsanlage
sludge [slʌdʒ] n	Klärschlamm

»

restoration of rivers and lakes	(Gewässer)renaturierung
cleaning up of rivers and lakes	Gewässersanierung
unclarified sewage / untreated sewage	ungeklärtes Abwasser

The biological balance in the lake has been upset by water pollution.
Das biologische Gleichgewicht des Sees ist durch Gewässerverschmutzung gestört worden.

The lake died because of the rubbish tip near its bank.
Durch die Mülldeponie in Ufernähe ist der See umgekippt.

Marine ecosystems

marine ecosystem [məˌriːnˈiːkəʊˌsɪstəm] n	marines Ökosystem
marine [məˌriːn] adj	Meeres~
submarine relief n	Meeresboden

surface of the sea n	Meeresoberfläche
ocean current / ocean drift / sea current / marine current	Meeresströmung
ocean depth / depth of the sea n	Meerestiefe
deep (sea) n	Tiefe / Tiefsee
abyssal (sea) [ə'bɪsl] n	Tiefsee
shelf area n	Schelfgebiet
continental shelf n	Kontinentalschelf
bordering sea / border sea n	Randmeer
ocean(ic) circulation n	ozeanische Zirkulation
ocean conveyor ['əʊʃnkən‚veɪə] n	globales Förderband
thermohaline circulation [‚θɜːməʊhəlainsɜːkjeˈleɪʃn] n	Vertikalkonvektion *(thermohaline K.)*
surface circulation n	Oberflächenzirkulation
salt content / salinity n	Salzgehalt
pressure gradient n	Druckunterschied
density n	Dichte(-unterschied)
deep water current n	Tiefenströmung
buoyancy ['bɔɪənsi] n	Auftrieb
thermocline [‚θɜːməʊˈklain] n	thermische Sprungschicht

swell n	Woge / Dünung / Seegang
heavy swell / large swell	hoher Seegang
heavy sea / rough sea	schwerer Seegang / starker Seegang

The tides

tides	Gezeiten	**spring tide**	Springflut
tidal range	Tidenhub	**storm tide**	Sturmflut
ebb tide	Ebbe	**neap tide**	Nipptide
retreating tide / falling tide	auslaufende Flut / Ebbe	**low tide**	Niedrigwasser
incoming tide	auflaufende Flut	**tidal current**	Gezeitenstrom

surge [sɜːdʒ] n	Woge / Brandung
wave n	Welle
wave length n	Wellenlänge
crest n	(Wellen-)Kamm
trough [trɒf] n	(Wellen-)Trog
plunge line n	Brechpunkt der Welle
break, broke, broken v	brechen
tidal wave / tsunami n	Flutwelle / Tsunami
danger of tsunamis	Flutwellengefahr
frictional drag n	Reibungswiderstand
fetch n	Streichlänge *(Einwirkungsdistanz des Windes an der Wasseroberfläche)*

2 Physical environment › 2.5 Hydrology

» Waves are usually created by the transfer of energy from the wind blowing over the surface of the sea.
Wellen entstehen gewöhnlich durch die Übertragung von Energie durch den über die Meeresoberfläche wehenden Wind.
The maximum distance of water over which winds can blow to create waves is called the fetch.
Die größte Wasserfläche, über die Winde zur Erzeugung von Wellen blasen können, nennt man Streichlänge.

salt water n — Salzwasser
primary production n — Primärproduktion
nutrient cycle ['njuːtriənt͵saɪkl] n — Nährstoffhaushalt / Nährstoffkreislauf
protein ['prəʊtiːn] n — Eiweiß
organic matter n — organische Stoffe
anorganic adj — nichtorganisch
plankton n — Plankton
  phytoplankton [͵faɪtə'plæŋktən] — Phytoplankton
  zooplankton [͵zuːə'plæŋktən] — Zooplankton

Marine species

predatory fish	Raubfisch	tuna	Thunfisch
herring	Hering	whale	Wal
cod	Kabeljau / Dorsch	shark	Hai
haddock	Schellfisch	krill	Krill
mackerel	Makrele	alga	Alge
small crustaceans	Kleinkrebse	algal bloom	Algenblüte

sea-water pollution n — Meerwasserverschmutzung
oil pollution n — Ölpest
dumping n — Verklappung

mud flats / tidal flats n pl — Watt
dry out v — austrocknen
brackish water n — Brackwasser
desalinisation BE / desalinization AE — Aussüßung
[diː͵sælɪnaɪ'zeɪʃn] n
shallow water zone n — Flachwasserzone
silting zone n — Verlandungszone

salt water biotope — Salzwasserbiotop
['sɔːlt͵wɔːtə͵baɪəʊtəʊp] n
salty soil n — Salzboden

washing out of salt n		Salzausspülung	
halophyte bush [ˈheɪləʊˌfaɪtˈbʊʃ] n		Salzbusch	
common glasswort [ˌkɒmənˈglɑːwɜːt] /		Queller	
marsh samphire [ˌmɑːʃˈsæmfaɪə] n			
salt meadow n		Salzwiese	

Coastal fauna

mud shrimp	Schlickkrebs	plaice	Scholle
prawn / shrimp	Garnele	periwinkle	Strandschnecke
(blue) mussel	Miesmuschel	green crab / shore crab	Strandkrabbe
cockle	Herzmuschel	arctic tern	Küstenseeschwalbe
barnacle	Seepocke	puffin	Papageientaucher
feather duster worm	Röhrenwurm	sea raven / cormorant	Kormoran

coastal defence n	Küstenschutz
dike [daɪk] / dyke n	Deich
main dike n	Hauptdeich
main retaining dike n	Hauptabschlussdamm
flood barrier [flʌdˈbæriə] n	Sperrwerk
lighthouse / beacon [ˈbiːkn] n	Leuchtturm
Thames Barrier [ˈtɛmzˌbæriə] n	Themse-Barriere
Delta Scheme [ˈdɛltəˌskiːm] n	Deltaplan (Niederlande)

2.6 Endangered environments

Natural hazards

natural hazard [ˌnætʃrəlˈhæzəd]	Naturgefahr
natural disaster n	Naturkatastrophe
occurence n	Vorkommen
earthquake n	Erdbeben
disastrous earthquake n	Katastrophenbeben
early-warning system n	Frühwarnsystem
tremor [ˈtrɛmə] n	Erschütterung
volcanic eruption [vɒlˈkænɪkɪˌrʌpʃn] n	Vulkanausbruch
eruption plume [ɪˌrʌpʃnˈpluːm] n	Ausbruchsschlot
mud flow [ˈmʌdˌfləʊ] / lahar [ˈlɑːhɑː] n	Schlammlawine / Lahar
avalanche [ˈævlɑːnʃ] n	Lawine

2 Physical environment › 2.6 Endangered environments

» Natural hazards can be divided into climatic, geomorphological or geological, and biological hazards.
Man unterteilt die Naturgefahren in klimatische, geomorphologische oder geologische sowie biologische Gefahren.

storm n	Sturm
hurricane [ˈhʌrɪkən] n	Hurrikan
hurricane warning	Hurrikan-Warnung

»
centre of the hurricane	Zentrum des Hurrikans
eye of the hurricane	Auge des Hurrikans

tropical cyclone [ˌtrɒpɪklˈsaɪkləʊn] n	tropischer Wirbelsturm / Taifun
typhoon [taɪˈfuːn] n	Taifun / tropischer Wirbelsturm
tornado [tɔːˈneɪdəʊ] n	Tornado
originate v	entstehen
heat energy v	Wärmeenergie
predict v	vorhersagen
exceed [ɪkˈsiːd] v	überschreiten
uproot v	entwurzeln
disrupt v	unterbrechen
torrential rain [təˈrenʃlˌreɪn] n	sintflutartiger Regenfall
path n	Pfad / Weg / Verlauf

»
spiral upward	in einer Spirale nach oben bewegen
erratic course	unvorhersehbarer Verlauf
reach land / make landfall	auf Land treffen / auf das Festland treffen / Land erreichen

The meteorologists had been unable to predict the landfall of the hurricane.
Die Meteorologen waren nicht in der Lage, vorherzusagen, wann der Hurrikan auf das Festland treffen würde.

The tropical cyclone was accompanied by torrential rains and strong winds that uprooted trees and destroyed overhead power cables.
Der tropische Wirbelsturm wurde von sintflutartigem Regen und starken Winden begleitet, die Bäume entwurzelten und Überlandleitungen zerstörte.

flooding n	Überschwemmung / Überflutung
tsunami n	Tsunami
mudslide n	Schlammlawine

landslide n	Erdrutsch
velocity [vɪˈlɒsəti] n	Geschwindigkeit
storm surge / tidal surge n	Flutwelle
storm wave n	Sturmwelle
flash flood n	flutartige Überschwemmung / Sinflut
spring tide n	Springflut

Man-made hazards

climatic change n	Klimawandel / Klimaänderung
global warming n	globale Erwärmung
rise in sea level n	Meeresspiegelanstieg
coastal flooding n	Küstenüberschwemmung
pack ice / sea ice n	Packeis
melting sea ice	schmelzendes Packeis
adjust to v	sich anpassen an
pollution n	Belastung / Verschmutzung
environmental pollution	Umweltbelastung / -verschmutzung
organic pollution	organische Belastung
thermal pollution	thermische Belastung
pollutant / contaminant n	Schadstoff
pollute v	verschmutzen / verpesten / verseuchen
contamination [kənˌtæmɪˈneɪʃn] n	Verseuchung / Verschmutzung
toxic adj	toxisch / giftig
release v	abgeben / freisetzen

low		geringe	
moderate	level of pollution	mäßige	Belastung
critical		kritische	

environmental		Umweltverschmutzung / Umweltbelastung	
water		Wasserverschmutzung	
air	pollution	Luftverschmutzung	
atmospheric		Luftverschmutzung	
soil		Bodenverschmutzung	

organic	pollution	organische	Belastung
thermal		thermische	

cause			verursachen
fight	pollution	Verschmutzung	bekämpfen
reduce			reduzieren / verringern

pollution	increases	Verschmutzung	nimmt zu
	decreases		nimmt ab

smog n	Smog
acid rain [ˌæsɪdˈreɪn] n	saurer Regen
acidification n	Versäuerung
sulphur dioxide [ˌsʌlfədaɪˈɒksaɪd] n	Schwefeldioxid
dying of the woods n	Waldsterben
greenhouse effect n	Treibhauseffekt
greenhouse gas n	Treibhausgas
ozone hole [ˌəʊzəʊnˈhəʊl] n	Ozonloch
ozone layer n	Ozonschicht
carbon dioxide [ˌkɑːbndaɪˈɒksaɪd] n	Kohlendioxid
emission n	Emission / Ausstoß
emit v	abgeben / emittieren
emission of waste heat n	Abwärme-Emission
build up v	aufbauen
chlorofluorocarbon (CFC) [ˌklɔːrəˌflɔːrəˈkɑːbn] n	Fluorchlorkohlenwasserstoff (FCKW)
aerosol propellant [ˈeərəsɒlprəˌpələnt] n	Treibgas
solvent n	Lösungsmittel
refrigerant n	Kühlmittel
nitrous oxide [ˌnaɪtrəsˈɒksaɪd] n	Stickoxide
methane [ˈmiːθeɪn] n	Methan
vehicle exhausts [ˈvɪəklɪɡˌzɔːst] n	Autoabgase / Kraftfahrzeugabgase
desertification n	Desertifikation
drought [draʊt] n	Dürre
year of drought	Dürrejahr
probability of droughts	Dürrewahrscheinlichkeit
overgrazing n	Überweidung
overcultivation n	Überkultivierung
water pollution n	Gewässerverschmutzung
toxic waste dumping n	Schadstoffeinleitung
acid dumping n	Säureeinleitung / Verklappung
heavy metal n	Schwermetall
eutrophication [ˈjuːtrɒpɪkeɪʃn] n	Eutrophierung
pesticide [ˈpestɪsaɪd] n	Pflanzenschutzmittel / Pestizid
biocide [ˌbaɪəˈsaɪd] n	Biozid
refuse / waste n	Müll / Abfall
(waste) disposal [dɪˈspəʊzl] n	(Abfall-)Entsorgung
toxic waste / hazardous waste [ˈhæzədəs] n	Sonderabfall
rubbish dump n	Müllhalde
household waste / domestic waste n	Haushaltsmüll

incineration [ˌɪnˌsɪnrˈeɪʃn] n	Verbrennung
landfill n	Deponie / Geländeauffüllung

waste dump n	Mülldeponie
waste reduction n	Müllreduzierung
waste management n	Abfallbeseitigung / Abfallentsorgung
composting plant n	Kompostierungsanlage
refuse incineration plant / refuse combustion plant n	Müllverbrennungsanlage

salinisation *BE* / salinization *AE* n	Versalzung
derelict land [ˈderəlɪktˌlænd] n	aufgelassenes Land
contaminated land [kənˈtæmɪneɪtɪdˌlænd] n	verunreinigtes Land / vergiftetes Land
detergent [dɪˈtɜːdʒnt] n	Waschmittel
domestic cleaner n	Haushaltsreiniger
biodegradable [ˌbaɪədɪˈgreɪdəbl] adj	biologisch abbaubar

deforestation [diːˌfɒrɪˈsteɪʃn] n	Abholzung / Deforestation
deforest v	abholzen
forest clearance [ˈklɪərns] n	Rodung / Abholzung
clearance rate n	Abholzungsrate / Abholzungsgeschwindigkeit
overexploitation of forests [ˈəʊvəˌeksplɔɪˈteɪʃn] n	Holzraubbau
clear v	roden
logging n	Holzeinschlag
forest fire n	Waldfeuer
fuelwood [ˈfjuːəlˌwʊd] n	Feuerholz
scorch [skɔːtʃ] v	abbrennen / verbrennen

» The costs of pollution are borne by the consumers.
Die Kosten der Verschmutzung werden von den Verbrauchern getragen.

2 Physical environment › 2.6 Endangered environments

Sustainability

sustainability [səˌsteɪnəˈbɪləti] n	Nachhaltigkeit
sustainable adj	nachhaltig
sutainable development n	nachhaltige Entwicklung
sustainable forestry	nachhaltige Forstwirtschaft
sustainability triangle	Nachhaltigkeitsdreieck
ecology n	Ökologie
ecological adj	ökologisch
ecological footprint n	ökologischer Fußabdruck
environment [ɪnˈvaɪrnmənt] n	Umwelt
environmental protection n	Umweltschutz
environmental movement n	Umweltbewegung
environmental monitoring n	Umweltbeobachtung
environmentalist / conservationist n	Umweltschützer
conserve v	konservieren / bewahren
eco-friendly adj	umweltfreundlich
extinction [ɪkˈstɪŋkʃn] n	Aussterben

»
protect the environment	die Umwelt schützen
fight extinction	das Aussterben bekämpfen
to be in danger of extinction	vom Aussterben bedroht sein

biodegradable [ˌbaɪəʊdɪˈɡreɪdəbl] adj	biologisch abbaubar
recycling n	Recycling / Wiederverwertung
recycle v	recyceln / wiederverwerten
pollution control n	Umweltschutz
low pollution adj	schadstoffarm
pollution-free adj	schadstofffrei

resources n pl	Rohstoffquellen / Ressourcen
finite resources [ˈfaɪnaɪtrɪˈzɔːsɪz]	begrenzte Ressourcen
renewable resources	erneuerbare Rohstoffe
renewable energy	erneuerbare Energie
non-renewable resources	nicht-erneuerbare Rohstoffe
energy-efficient adj	energieeffizient *(sparsam im Umgang mit Energie)*

»
save energy	Energie sparen

insulation / (heat) insulation n	Isolierung / Wärmedämmung
insulate v	isolieren
double-glazing n	Doppelverglasung

» Sustainable development meets the needs of the present without compromising the ability of future generations to meet their own needs. (Brundlandt Report, 1987)
Nachhaltige Entwicklung bedient die Bedürfnisse der Gegenwart, ohne die Fähigkeit zukünftiger Generationen zu schmälern, ihre eigenen Bedürfnisse zu befriedigen.
Sustainable management means to use materials that can either be renewed, recycled or replaced.
Nachhaltiges Wirtschaften bedeutet, Materialien zu benutzen, die entweder erneuert, wiederverwendet oder ersetzt werden können.

conservation	Erhaltung / Schutz
conversation of the countryside n	Landschaftspflege / Landschaftsschutz
landscape reserve / preservation area n	Landschaftsschutzgebiet
nature reserve n	Naturpark
national park n	Nationalpark
area of ecological regeneration n	ökologischer Regenerationsbereich
wildlife sanctuary ['waɪldlaɪfˈsæŋktʃʊəri] n	Wildschutzgebiet

3 Human environment

3.1 Industry

industry, *pl* industries n	Industrie
industrial adj	industriell
industrialisation [ɪnˌdʌstrɪəlaɪˈzeɪʃn] *BE* / industrialization *AE* n	Industrialisierung / Industrieentwicklung
incipient industrialisation [ɪnˈsɪpɪəntɪnˌdʌstrɪəlaɪˌzeɪʃn]	Industrialisierungsansatz
industrial development	industrielle Erschließung
deindustrialisation n	Entindustrialisierung
produce v	produzieren / herstellen
manufacture [ˌmænjəˈfæktʃə] v	produzieren / herstellen

» the Industrial Revolution | die Industrielle Revolution

industrial production n	industrielle Produktion
primary industry [ˈpraɪmrɪˌɪndəstrɪ] n	Primärindustrie
secondary industry n	Sekundärindustrie / Verarbeitungsindustrie
main industry n	Hauptindustrie
key industry n	Schlüsselindustrie
branch of industry / manufacturing branch n	Industriezweig / Branche
basic industry / primary industry n	Grundstoffindustrie
processing industry n	weiterverarbeitende Industrie
heavy industry n	Schwerindustrie / Montanindustrie
capital goods industry n	Investitionsgüterindustrie

manufacturing industry [ˌmænjəˈfæktʃərɪŋˌɪndəstrɪ] n	verarbeitende Industrie / produzierendes Gewerbe
manufacturing process n	Verarbeitungsprozess
processing n	Weiterverarbeitung
semi-processed [semɪprəʊˈsəst]	halbfertig(-gestellt)
finished adj	fertig(-gestellt)
assembly plant n	Montagewerk
light industry n	Leichtindustrie
processing / refinement [rɪˈfaɪnmənt] n	Veredelung
finishing industry n	Veredelungsindustrie / Veredelungsbetrieb
trade n	Handwerk / Gewerbe

business enterprise / industrial undertaking n	Gewerbebetrieb
cottage industry [ˌkɒtɪdʒ'ɪndəstri] n	Heimindustrie / Heimarbeit
home-work / outwork *BE* n	Heimarbeit
support industry n	Zuliefererbetrieb / Zuliefererindustrie
small-scale industry n	Kleinbetrieb
growth industry n	Wachstumsbranche
high technology industry n	High-Tech-Branche
industrial monostructure [ɪnˌdʌstriəlmɒnəʊ'strʌktʃə] n	industrielle Monostruktur
innovation n	Innovation / Erneuerung
research and development (R&D) n	Forschung und Entwicklung
service industry n	Dienstleistungsbranche
industrial location n	Industriestandort
locational triangle [ləˌkeɪʃnl'traɪæŋgl] n	Standortdreieck

Industrialisation: The development of industry

Developing industry – Industrieentwicklung als Prozess, sich entwickelnde Industrie
Weber's model of industrial location introduces the locational triangle.
Webers Modell der Industriestandorte führt das Standortdreieck ein.

industrial region / industrial district n	Industrieregion / Industriegebiet
industrial area n	Industriegebiet
industrial plant n	Industrieanlage
industrial park / industrial estate *BE* n	Gewerbefläche / Gewerbegebiet
trading estate / industrial estate / trade zone n	Industrieanlage / Industriepark
disused industrial site n	Industriebrache
industrial density [ɪnˌdʌstriəl'densiti] n	Industriedichte

industrial concern [ɪnˌdʌstriəlkən'sɜːn] n	Industrieunternehmen
corporation / firm / company n	Firma
factory n	Fabrik
engineer [ˌendʒɪn'nɪə] n	Ingenieur
industrial worker n	Industriebeschäftigter
skilled worker n	Facharbeiter
unskilled adj	ungelernt

assembly line / conveyor belt [kən'veɪəbelt] n	Fließband
conveyor system n	Förderbandanlage
mechanisation [ˌmekənaɪˌzeɪʃn] n	Mechanisierung
automation [ˌɔːtə'meɪʃn] n	Automatisierung

3 Human environment › 3.1 Industry

mass production n	Massenproduktion
overproduction / surplus production n	Überproduktion
lean production n	schlanke Produktion
just-in-time production n	Just-in-time-Produktion *(ohne Lagerung)*

»

advanced manufacturing techniques	verbesserte Herstellungsmethoden / verbesserte Herstellungstechniken

Mass production has led to massive overproduction.
Massenproduktion hat zu enormer Überpoduktion geführt.

With just-in-time production, companies do not need large storekeeping facilities.
Bei Just-in-time-Produktion benötigen Firmen keine großen Lagerungsmöglichkeiten mehr.

location n	Standort
industrial location	Industriestandort
location theory	Standorttheorie
locational triangle [lə‚keɪʃnl'traɪæŋgl]	Standortdreieck
locational advantage	Standortvorteil
least cost location	kostengünstigster Standort
locate v	sich ansiedeln
factor of production n	Produktionsfaktor
means of production n	Produktionsmittel
production costs n	Produktionskosten
location factor n	Standortfaktor
footloose ['fʊtluːs] adj	nicht standortgebunden

raw material oriented adj	rohstofforientiert
workforce / labour force n	Arbeitskräfte
labour supply / labour reserve ['leɪbərɪ‚zɜːv] / labour resource ['leɪbərɪ‚zɔːs] n	Arbeitskräftepotential
labour cost n	Arbeitskosten
labour intensive adj	arbeitsintensiv
capital intensive adj	kapitalintensiv
capital goods n	Investitionsgüter
industrial linkage / clustering of industries n	industrielle Verflechtung
agglomeration economy [ə‚glɒmə‚reɪʃnɪ'kɒnəmi] n	Agglomerationsvorteil
growth pole n	Wachstumspol

industrial inertia [ɪnˌdʌstriəlɪˈnɜːʃə] n	Unbeweglichkeit des Industriestandorts
industrial restructuring n	industrieller Strukturwandel
free choice of location	freie Standortwahl
Manufacturing Belt / Rust Belt	Industriegebiet im Nordosten der USA
Newly Industrialising Country (NIC)	Schwellenland
special economic zone	Wirtschaftssonderzone (China)
Organisation of Petroleum Exporting Countries	Organisation erdölexportierender Staaten (OPEC)
Ruhr area / Ruhr district	Ruhrgebiet
Rhenish Brown Coal Mining Area	Rheinisches Braunkohlerevier

Natural resources

raw material n	Rohstoff / Grundstoff
resource [rɪˈzɔːs] n	Ressource / Rohstoff / Bodenschatz
primary resource	Primärrohstoff
fossil resource	fossiler Rohstoff
deposit n	Vorkommen / Lagerstätte
vein n	Ader / Gang
exploration [ˌekspləˈreɪʃn] n	Suche / Erforschung
prospecting n	Prospektion
exploitation [ˌeksplɔɪˈteɪʃn] n	Abbau / Ausbeutung / Verwertung
exploit v	abbauen
exploitable	abbaubar / abbauwürdig
recoverable adj	förderbar / abbaubar
extraction n	Förderung
extract v	fördern / gewinnen
mine v	abbauen / fördern
exhaustion [ɪgˈzɔːstʃn] n	Erschöpfung
depletion [dɪˈpliːʃn] n	Abbau / Raubbau / Erschöpfung
deplete [dɪˈpliːt] v	aufbrauchen / erschöpfen
reserve n	Reserve
shortage n	Mangel / Knappheit

3 Human environment › 3.1 Industry

»

be endowed with sth | mit etw. ausgestattet sein

These deposits of fossil resources are not being exploited for technical reasons.
Diese Vorkommen fossiler Rohstoffe werden aus technischen Gründen nicht abgebaut.

All reserves that we were endowed with are depleted.
Alle Reserven, mit denen wir ausgestattet waren, sind erschöpft.

mineral		mineralischer	
natural		natürlicher	
renewable	resource	erneuerbarer	Rohstoff
non-renewable		nicht-erneuerbarer	
recyclable		wiederverwertbarer	
non-recyclable		nicht-wiederverwertbarer	
exploited	deposit	erschöpftes	Vorkommen
economically exploitable		wirtschaftlich abbaubares	

energy source / source of energy n — Energieträger
fuel ['fjuːəl] n — Brennstoff / Treibstoff
fossil fuel — fossiler Brennstoff
consume v — verbrauchen / konsumieren
consumption n — Verbrauch / Konsum
energy consumption — Energieverbrauch

»

raw material for the production of energy | Energierohstoff

coal n — Kohle
bituminous coal [bɪ'tʃuːmɪnəs] / hard coal / black coal n — Steinkohle
anthracite ['ænθrəsaɪt] n — Anthrazitkohle
coal-bearing adj — kohleführend
coal field n — Kohlefeld
coal measure / Coal Equivalent (CE) n — Steinkohleeinheit

»

tonne (ton) of coal equivalent (TCE) | Einheit, die aus der Verbrennungsenergie von einer metrischen Tonne Kohle errechnet wird.

Dry Metric Ton Unit (DMTU) | Einheit, die sich aus dem Gewicht einer metrischen Tonne Erz minus dem Wassergehalt mit einem Metallgehalt von 1 % errechnet.

lignite ['lɪgnaɪt] / brown coal n	Braunkohle » Abb. 17
seam [siːm] n	Flöz
lignite seam ['lignait ˌsiːm]	Braunkohlenflöz
gas n	Gas
natural gas	Erdgas
gas fields	Erdgasfelder
liquid gas	Flüssiggas
production area / area of extraction n	Fördergebiet
oil / crude oil n	Erdöl / Rohöl
fuel oil n	Heizöl
oilfield n	Erdölfeld
offshore oilfield	Offshore-Fördergebiet *(vor der Küste gelegen)*
oil platform n	Ölplattform
oil rig / drilling rig n	Bohrplattform / Bohrinsel
drilling device n	Bohrgerät
oil spill / oil pollution n	Ölpest
tanker n	Tanker
uranium [jʊə'reɪniəm] n	Uran

ore [ɔː] n	metallisches Erz
heavy metal n	Schwermetall
non-ferrous metal [ˌnɒn'ferəs] n	Buntmetall
light metal / alloy ['ælɔɪ] n	Leichtmetall
precious metal n	Edelmetall
metal alloy / alloying metal n	Legierungsmetall
iron (ore) ['aɪənˌɔː] n	Eisen(-erz)
lead [led] n	Blei
lead compound	Bleiverbindung
copper ['kɒpə] n	Kupfer
zinc [zɪŋk] n	Zink
tin n	Zinn
manganese ['mæŋgəniːz] n	Mangan
aluminium n	Aluminium
bauxite ['bɔːksaɪt] n	Bauxit / Tonerde
antimony ['æntɪməni] n	Antimon
chrome [krəʊm] n	Chrom
cadmium ['kædmiəm] n	Kadmium
cobalt ['kəʊbɔːlt] n	Kobalt
molybdenum [mə'lɪbdənəm] n	Molybdän
nickel ['nɪkl] n	Nickel
mercury ['mɜːkjri] n	Quecksilber
vanadium [və'neɪdiəm] n	Vanadium
tungsten ['tʌŋstən] n	Wolfram

3 Human environment › 3.1 Industry

titanium [tɪ'teɪniəm] n	Titan
steel stabiliser n	Stahlveredler
gold n	Gold
silver n	Silber
platinum n	Platin

asbestos [æs'bestɒs] n	Asbest
graphite ['græfaɪt] n	Graphit
salt n	Salz
rock salt	Steinsalz
salt dome	Salzstock
potash n	Kali / Pottasche
potash salt ['pɒtæʃ] n	Kalisalz
potash mine	Kalisalzgewinnung
phosphate ['fɒsfeɪt] n	Phosphat
saltpetre BE / salpeter AE ['sælpiːtə] n	Salpeter
sulfur ['sʌlfə] n	Schwefel
clay n	Ton
kaolin ['keɪəlɪn] / China clay n	Kaolin
marble ['mɑːbl] n	Marmor
diamond n	Diamant
precious stone / gemstone ['dʒemstəʊn] n	Edelstein
cement [sɪ'ment] n	Zement
cellulose ['seljələʊs] n	Zellulose
India rubber [ˌɪndiə'rʌbə] n	Kautschuk

energy / power n	Energie
primary energy	Primärenergie
secondary energy	Sekundärenergie
useful energy	Nutzenergie
energy production / power generation	Energieerzeugung / Stromerzeugung
energy / power supply	Energieversorgung / Stromversorgung
energy consumption ['enədʒɪkən,sʌmʃn]	Energieverbrauch
energy transfer	Energietransport
energy crisis	Energiekrise
electricity n	Elektrizität
electric power n	Strom
base load power n	Grundlast
power line n	Hochspannungsleitung / Starkstromleitung
power cut n	Stromausfall

| feed in, fed, fed v | einspeisen |
| district heating / long-distance heat supply n | Fernwärme |

»

international power generation and distribution agreement	Stromverbund
integrated system	Verbundnetz
generation of electrical energy	Verstromung

power station n	Kraftwerk
coal power station	Kohlekraftwerk
lignite power station	Braunkohlenkraftwerk
mixed fuelling [ˌmɪkst'fjuːəlɪŋ] n	Mischfeuerung
nuclear power station	Kernkraftwerk
thermal power station	Wärmekraftwerk
storage power station	Speicherkraftwerk
hydroelectric power station [ˌhaɪdrəʊɪ'lektrɪk]	Wasserkraftwerk
emission n	Emission / Ausstoß
emission of waste heat	Abwärme-Emission
combustion efficiency [kəm'bʌstʃnɪˌfɪʃnsi] / efficiency n	Wirkungsgrad

nuclear energy n	Kernenergie
nuclear fission [ˌnjuːkliə'fɪʃn] n	Kernspaltung
pressurised water reactor (PWR) n	Druckwasserreaktor (DWR)
fast breeder reactor n	Schneller Brüter
reprocessing plant n	Wiederaufbereitungsanlage
reactor core n	Reaktorkern
fuel rods n	Brennstäbe
coolant ['kuːlənt] n	Kühlflüssigkeit
control rods ['kɒntrəʊlˌrɒds] n	Steuerstab
generator n	Generator
protective containment vessel [prəˌtektɪvkən'teɪnməntˌvəsl] n	Reaktorsicherheitsbehälter / Sicherheitsbehälter
cooling tower n	Kühlturm
radioactive waste / nuclear waste n	radioaktiver Abfall
high-level nuclear waste	stark verseuchter radioaktiver Abfall
uncontrolled chain reaction n	unkontrollierte Kettenreaktion
total melt-down / ultimate MCA (maximum credible accident) n	Super-Gau (größter anzunehmender Unfall)
core melt-down [kɔː'meltdaʊn] n	Kernschmelze / Super-Gau

107

radioactive contamination n	radioaktive Verseuchung
nuclear accident n	Reaktorunfall

renewable energy / alternative energy n	erneuerbare Energie / alternative Energie
solar power / solar energy n	Solarenergie / Sonnenenergie
solar furnace ['səʊləˌfɜːnɪs] n	Solar(schmelz)ofen
solar panel n	Sonnenkollektor
solar cell n	Solarzelle
photovoltaic [ˌfəʊtevɒl'teɪk] n	Photovoltaik
wind power / wind energy n	Windenergie
wind farm n	Windfarm / Windpark
windmill / wind turbine n	Windgenerator / Windrad / Windkraftturbine
hydro-electricity n	durch Wasserkraft gewonnene Energie
dam n	Damm
reservoir ['rezəvwɑː] n	Stausee / Speichersee
barrage BE ['bærɑːdʒ] / dam [dæm] n	Staudamm / Talsperre / Staustufe
geothermal heat n	Erdwärme
geothermal energy n	geothermale Energie
tidal power ['taɪdlˌpaʊə] n	Gezeitenkraft
wave energy n	Wellenenergie
bioenergy n	Bioenergie
biogas n	Biogas
biomass [ˌbaɪəʊ'mæs] n	Biomasse
biofuel n	Biokraftstoff
energy crop n	Energiepflanze (z. B. Raps)
oilseed rape n	Raps
ethanol ['eθənɒl] n	Äthanol / Ethanol
firewood / fuel wood n	Brennholz
chips n	Späne (meist Plural)
pellets ['pelɪts] n	Holzpellets (meist Plural)

Industries

mining (industry) n	Bergbau
mine / pit / colliery ['kɒljəri] n	Bergwerk / Zeche
mine / hard coal mine n	Zeche / Steinkohlenzeche
pit closure ['pɪtˌkləʊʒə]	Zechenschließung
disused mine pit	stillgelegte Zeche
mine building	Zechengebäude
mining community	Bergarbeitersiedlung

coal (mining) district n	Revier / Montan-Revier
underground / below ground n	unter Tage
underground mining / deep shaft mining n	Tiefbau
open-pit mining / opencast mining n	Tagebau
exploited opencast mine	ausgekohlter Tagebau

coal n	Kohle
hard coal / bituminous coal / black coal n	Steinkohle
coal heap	Kohlenhalde
shaft [ʃɑːft] n	Schacht
adit ['ædɪt] n	Stollen
gallery n	Sohle / Stollen
recultivation [riːˌkʌltɪ'veɪʃn] n	Rekultivierung

» | area which has subsided due to mining operations | Bergsenkungsfläche |

lignite ['lɪgnaɪt] / brown coal n	Braunkohle » Abb. 17
lignite mining / lignite pit / lignite mine	Braunkohlebergbau
open cast lignite mining / mining	Braunkohlentagebau
bucket wheel excavator n	Schaufelradbagger
spreader n	Absetzer *(zur Ablagerung des abgebaggerten Obermaterials)*
relocation [ˌriːlə'keɪʃn] / resettlement [ˌriː'setlmənt] n	Umsiedlung
resettle v	umsiedeln
briquette factory [brɪ'ket] n	Brikettfabrik
coke n	Koks
coke v	verkoken
coking coal	Kokskohle
coke works	Kokerei
coal milling plant n	Kohlenstaubanlage
coal conversion n	Kohleveredelung
coal gasification n	Kohlevergasung

mine v	abbauen
mining area n	Abbaufläche
direction of mining n	Abbaurichtung
overburden [ˌəʊvə'bɜːdn] / spoil / mining waste n	Abraum
mine dump / spoil heap / colliery waste tip n	Abraumhalde / Halde

3 Human environment › 3.1 Industry

rubbish railway n	Abraumbahn
iron and steel industry [ˌaɪənænd'stiːlˌɪndəstri] n	Eisen- und Stahlindustrie
iron and steel production n	Eisen- und Stahlproduktion
iron and steel manufacturing industry	Eisen- und Stahl verarbeitende Industrie
pig iron n	Roheisen
smelting (of iron) n	Verhüttung / Eisenverhüttung
smelt [smelt] v	verhütten
iron and steel works n	Hüttenwerk
integrated steelworks	integriertes Hüttenwerk
blast furnace ['blɑːstˌfɜːnɪs] n	Hochofen
slag [slæg] n	Schlacke
forge ['fɔːdʒ] n	Hammerwerk
steel production n	Stahlerzeugung
steel plant / mill / steelworks n	Stahlwerk
tube mill [tjuːb] / tubeworks n	Röhrenwerk
oxygen steel converter [ˌɒksɪdʒən'stiːlkənˌvɜːtə] n	Oxygenstahlkonverter
foundry ['faʊndri] n	Gießerei
rolling mill n	Walzwerk
metal production n	Metallerzeugung
metal industry n	Metallindustrie
metal goods n	Metallwaren
ore [ɔː] n	Erz
ore dressing plant	Erzaufbereitungsanlage
smelting of non-ferrous metals n	Buntmetallverhüttung
smelting of aluminium n	Aluminiumverhüttung
alloy smelting works ['ælɔɪ] n	Legierungsmetallhütte
cable factory n	Kabelwerk
energy production / power generation n	Energieerzeugung
conversion into electricity n	Verstromung
nuclear industry n	Atomindustrie
chemical industry n	chemische Industrie / Chemieindustrie
chemical products / chemicals n	Chemieprodukte / Chemikalien
plastics n	Kunststoff
fibre n	Faser
synthetic fibre [sɪn'θetɪk] / artificial fibre [ˌɑːtɪ'fɪʃl] / man-made fibre	Kunstfaser

petrochemical industry petrochemische Industrie
[ˌpetrə'kemɪklˌɪndəstri] n
oil industry n Erdölverarbeitung
petroleum [pə'trəʊliəm] / petrol ['petrl] n Benzin
diesel ['diːzl] n Diesel
refine [rɪ'faɪn] v raffinieren
oil refinery n Erdölraffinerie
oil company n Erdölgesellschaft
gasworks n Gaswerk
gas-liquefying plant Gasverflüssigungsanlage
['gæsˌlɪkwɪfaɪɪŋ'plɑnt] n
pipeline n Pipeline / Rohrleitung
  pipeline network   Pipeline-Verbundnetz
gas pipeline n Erdgasleitung
  long-distance gas pipeline   Erdgas(fern)leitung
gasometer [gæs'ɒmɪtə] n Erdgasspeicher

chlorine plant ['klɔːriːn] n Chlorwerk
fertiliser factory ['fɜːtɪlaɪzə] n Düngemittelfabrik
cellulose factory / wood pulp works n Zellulosefabrik
paper production n Papiererzeugung
paper mill n Papierfabrik
paper processing / paper industry n Papierverarbeitung
pharmaceutical industry Pharmaindustrie /
[ˌfɑːmə'sjuːtɪkl] n   Arzneimittelindustrie
cement manufacturing n Zementherstellung
building industry / construction Bauindustrie
  industry n

mechanical engineering / machine Maschinenbau
  production n
engine manufacturing n Motorenbau
machine and instrument producing Gerätebau
  industry n

»

car		
automobile	production	(Kraft)Fahrzeugbau, Automobilindustrie
vehicle	manufacturing	

car assembly plant n Automobilmontagewerk
car manufacturer n Autohersteller
car supply industry n Zubehörindustrie (Auto)
rail vehicle production n Schienenfahrzeugbau

3 Human environment › 3.1 Industry

shipbuilding industry n	Schiffbau
shipyard n	Werft

electronics n	Elektronik
electronic adj	elektronisch
electrical adj	elektrisch / Elektro~
electrical engineering	Elektrotechnik
semiconductor [ˌsemɪkənˈdʌktə] n	Halbleiter
micro-electronics [ˌmaɪkrəʊˌɪlekˈtrɒnɪks] n	Mikroelektronik
micro-electronics firm	mikroelektronischer Betrieb
microchip n	Mikrochip
microchip plant	Mikrochip-Hersteller
silicon chip [ˈsɪlɪkəntʃɪps] / silicon wafer [ˈsɪlɪkənweɪfə] n	Siliziumchip
nanotechnology [ˌnænəʊtekˈnɒlədʒi] n	Nanotechnologie
biotechnology n	Biotechnologie
information technology (IT) n	Informationstechnologie
technology park / technology estate n	Technologiepark
communications engineering / telecommunications n	Nachrichtentechnik
precision mechanics n	Feinmechanik
precision engineering n	Präzisionstechnik
optics [ˈɒptɪks] n	Optik
optical industry n	Optik

aeronautical industry [ˌeərəˈnɔːtɪklˌɪndəstri] n	Flugzeugindustrie
aerospace [ˌeərəspeɪs] n	Luft- und Raumfahrttechnik
space technology n	Raumfahrttechnik

consumer n	Verbraucher(in) / Konsument(in)
consumer good / consumer product	Konsumgut
consumer (goods) industry	Verbrauchsgüterindustrie / Konsumindustrie
textile industry n	Textilindustrie
clothing n	Bekleidung
leather goods n pl	Lederwaren
footwear industry / shoe industry n	Fußbekleidungsindustrie / Schuhindustrie
printing industry n	Druckgewerbe
wood industry / lumber industry [ˈlʌmbəˌɪndəstri] n	Holzindustrie
plywood factory [ˌplaɪwʊdˈfæktri] n	Sperrholzfabrik
furniture [ˈfɜːnɪtʃə] n	Möbel

household goods n	Haushaltswaren
ceramics industry / pottery industry n	Keramikindustrie
porcelain / china n	Porzellan
porcelain industry ['pɔːslɪn‚ɪndəstri] n	Porzellanindustrie
glass industry n	Glasindustrie
jewellery ['dʒuːəlri] n	Schmuckwaren
food industry and semi-luxury industry n	Nahrungs- und Genussmittelindustrie
dairy industry n	Milchverarbeitungsindustrie
brewery ['bruːri] n	Brauerei
fish processing industry n	Fischverarbeitung
canning factory [kænɪŋ] n	Konservenfabrik
tobacco products n	Tabakwaren

»

processing of agricultural products	Verarbeitung landwirtschaftlicher Produkte

3.2 Agriculture

agriculture ['æɡrɪkʌltʃə] / farming n	Landwirtschaft
agricultural adj	landwirtschaftlich
agricultural landscape	landwirtschaftliche Nutzfläche
arable ['ærəbl] adj	landwirtschaftlich nutzbar
arable farming	Ackerbau
arable land / farmland / cultivated area	Ackerland

»

unsuitable for agriculture	landwirtschaftlich nicht nutzbar
used for agricultural purposes	landwirtschaftliche Nutzung

cultivation ['kʌltɪ'veɪʃn] n	Anbau / Kultivierung
cultivation area	Anbaugebiet
cultivation boundary	Anbaugrenze
cultivation / breeding	Zucht
area under cultivation	Agrarlandschaft
cultivate v	anbauen / kultivieren
farm v	bewirtschaften
livestock breeding / animal husbandry n	Viehzucht
crop n	Feldfrucht / Ernte

3 Human environment › 3.2 Agriculture

produce ['prɒdju:s] n	Erzeugnisse / Produkte
produce *AE* n	Obst und Gemüse

»
cultivation of crops or produce	Anbau von Getreide oder Gemüse
cultivation of land	Bebauung (Bestellung) des Lands
bring land under cultivation	Land bebauen

crop rotation n	Anbaufolge / Fruchtwechsel
grafting [grɑ:ftɪŋ] n	Veredelung *(bei Pflanzen)*
high yield variety [ˌhaɪjiːldˈvəraɪəti] n	Hochleistungssorte
green revolution n	Grüne Revolution
food production n	Nahrungsmittelproduktion
food shortage n	Lebensmittelknappheit / Nahrungsknappheit
food surplus ['fu:dˌsɜ:pləs] n	Nahrungsmittelüberschuss
food supply n	Lebensmittelversorgung / Nahrungsversorgung
diet [daɪət] n	Ernährung
feed, fed, fed v	ernähren
food security n	Ernährungssicherheit
staple (food) ['steɪpl] n	Grundnahrungsmittel

farmer n	Bauer / Farmer
smallholder / peasant (farmer) n	Kleinbauer
landowner / landlord n	Landbesitzer
landless adj	ohne Landbesitz
farm hand / agricultural labourer n	Landarbeiter
seasonal worker n	Saisonarbeiter

field n	Feld
plot / lot *AE* / parcel of land n	Parzelle
open fields / farmlands / corridor n	Flur
open-field system	Flurform
block field pattern n	Blockflur
fragmented land / mixed location n	Gemengelage
wide strip field pattern n	Breitstreifenflur
hide n	Hufe
common land n	Allmende

land use n	Landnutzung / Bodennutzung / Flächennutzung
cultivated land n	Kulturland

meadow ['medəʊ] n	Wiese
wet meadows	Feuchtgrünland
pasture ['pɑːstʃə] n	Weide
natural pasture	Naturweide
grazing [ɡreɪzɪŋ] n	Beweidung
improved grassland n	Kunstweide
mountain pasture n	Gebirgsweide
permanent grassland / grassland n	Dauergrünland / Grünland
grain cultivation n	Getreideanbau
permanent agriculture n	Dauerfeldbau
dry farming n	Trockenfeldbau
rainfed agriculture / farming n	Regenfeldbau
irrigation farming n	Bewässerungsfeldbau
terrace agriculture ['terɪsˌæɡrɪkʌltʃə] / terracing n	Terrassenfeldbau
hoe culture ['həʊˌkʌltʃə] / hoe cultivation n	Hackbau
shifting cultivation n	Wanderfeldbau
intensification [ɪnˌtensɪfɪ'keɪʃn] n	Intensivierung
cultura mista n	Stockwerkkultur / Etagenbau
fallow ['fæləʊ] n	Brache
fallow adj	brachliegend
yield [jiːld] n	Ertrag / Gewinn
yield v	Ertrag abwerfen

»

alternating cultivation and fallow periods		Anbau-Brache-Rotation	
heavy light acid	soil	schwerer leichter saurer	Boden
rich poor	harvest	reiche schlechte	Ernte
low-yield	ertragsarm		
high-yield	ertragsstark / ergiebig		

farm n	Bauernhof
relocation n	Aussiedlung
relocated farm	Aussiedlerhof
country estate n	Landgut / Gut
work the land v	Land bearbeiten
size of farm area n	Betriebsfläche
farm size n	Betriebsgröße
farm building n	Wirtschaftsgebäude

3 Human environment › 3.2 Agriculture

» building for agricultural use | landwirtschaftlich genutztes Gebäude

barn [bɑːn] n	Scheune
stables ['steɪblz] n	Stallung
granary ['grænri] n	Getreidespeicher
silo ['saɪləʊ] n	Silo
cow shed ['kaʊʃed] n	Kuhstall
sheep shed n	Schafstall
pigsty ['pɪgstaɪ] n	Schweinestall
milking parlour / milking parlor *AE* n	Melkkammer
milk v	melken
glasshouse / greenhouse / hothouse n	Treibhaus / Gewächshaus
polytunnel / polythene greenhouse structure n	Folienhaus / Folientunnel
cold storage n	Kühlhaus

mechanisation n	Mechanisierung
appropriate technology n	angepasste Technologie
plough [plaʊ] n	Pflug
plough v	pflügen
tractor n	Traktor / Schlepper
harvester ['hɑːvɪstə] n	Erntemaschine
combine harvester	Mähdrescher
farming activity n	landwirtschaftliche Aktivität
sow [səʊ] v	säen
plant v	pflanzen / anbauen
harvest v	ernten
agricultural machinery store n	Landmaschinenhandel

» clear land for cultivation | roden

livestock n	Vieh / Viehbesatz
livestock production	Viehwirtschaft
keeping of livestock n	Viehhaltung
cattle farmer / herder [hɜːdə] n	Viehhalter
keeping of cattle	Viehhaltung
herd [hɜːd] n	Herde
fattening n	Mast
fattening bay	Mastbucht
fattening of cows	Rindermast
rear [rɪə] v	aufziehen

breed, bred, bred v	züchten
racehorse breeding	Rennpferdzucht
cross-breeding	Kreuzung
artificial insemination [ˌɑːtɪfɪʃlɪnsemɪ'neɪʃn] n	künstliche Befruchtung
cattle pen n	Viehpferch
watering place n	Viehtränke
cattle trough ['kætlˌtrɒf] / feeding trough n	Futtertrog
fence n	Zaun
electrified wire fence	elektrischer Zaun
graze v	weiden (lassen) / grasen
feed / fodder n	Futtermittel
feed, fed, fed	füttern
feedlots	Feedlot / Mastparzelle
silage ['saɪlɪdʒ] n	Silage
shear [ʃɪə], shore, shorn v	scheren

seed n	Saat / Saatgut
seedling	Setzling
hybridisation BE [ˌhaɪbrɪdaɪ'zeɪʃn] / hybridization AE n	Kreuzung
manure [mə'njʊə] / fertiliser n	Dünger / Düngemittel
dung [dʌŋ] / manure n	Dung / Mist
liquid manure	Gülle
mineral fertiliser	Mineraldünger
manuring / fertilising	Düngung
fertilise	düngen
use of fertiliser	Düngerausbringung
guano ['gwɑːnəʊ] n	Guano
nitrogen ['naɪtrədʒən] n	Stickstoff
potash n	Pottasche / Kali
phosphate n	Phosphat
nutrient-demanding plant n	Starkzehrer
less demanding plant n	Schwachzehrer
plant disease n	Pflanzenkrankheit
pest n	Schädling
plant protection n	Pflanzenschutz
pesticide ['pestɪsaɪd] / biocide n	Schädlingsvernichtungsmittel / Biozid
insecticide [ɪn'sektɪsaɪd] n	Insektenvernichtungsmittel / Insektizid
herbicide ['hɜːbɪsaɪd] n	Unkrautvernichtungsmittel / Herbizide
fungicide ['fʌŋgɪsaɪd] n	Pilzvernichtungsmittel / Fungizid

3 Human environment › 3.2 Agriculture

irrigation n	Bewässerung / Beregnung
irrigated land	Bewässerungsland
irrigate	bewässern
irrigation channel / irrigation ditch	Bewässerungskanal / Bewässerungsgraben
irrigation by means of wells	Brunnenbewässerung
boom irrigation	(fahrbare) Bewässerungsanlage
centre pivot irrigation	Kreisberegnung(-sanlage)
trickle irrigation / drip irrigation	Tröpfchenbewässerung
wells in a row n	Brunnengalerie
sprinkler ['sprinklə] n	Berieselungsanlage / Rasensprenger
salination [sælɪ'neɪʃn] n	Versalzung
schistosomiasis [ˌʃɪstəʊʃəʊmaɪəsɪs] / bilharzia [bɪl'hɑːzɪə] n	Schistosomiasis / Bilharziose
tank n	Wasserbecken *(in Indien)*
Archimedes' screw [ˌɑːkɪ'miːdiːz'skruː] n	archimedische Schraube
shaduf [ʃə'dʌf] n	Shaduf

viticulture ['vɪtɪˌkʌltʃə] n	Weinbau
vineyard ['vɪnjəd] n	Weinberg / Rebfläche
vintage ['vɪntɪdʒ] n	Weinernte
wine grower n	Winzer
press v	keltern
winepress n	Kelter

soil degradation ['sɔɪlˌdegre'deɪʃn] n	Bodenzerstörung

»

exhaust		Boden erschöpfen
damage to	the soil	Bodenschädigung
exhaustion of		Bodenverarmung

Agricultural products

agricultural product n	landwirtschaftliches Erzeugnis
crop n	Anbauprodukt / Feldfrucht
food crop	Nahrungspflanze
cash crop	Marktfrucht
fodder crop ['fɒdə]	Futterpflanze
crop failure	Missernte
energy crop	Energiepflanze

grow (sth), grew, grown v	(etw.) anbauen
grow for sale	zum Verkauf anbauen
easy to grow	anspruchslos
resistant / hardy adj	widerstandsfähig / resistent
cultivated plant n	Nutzpflanze / Kulturpflanze
plant employed in industry	Industriepflanze
main crop of cultivation n	Hauptanbauart
permanent crop n	Dauerkultur
specialised crop n	Sonderkultur
catch crop / cover crop n	Zwischenfrucht
grain / corn / cereal ['sɪərɪəl] AE n	Getreide / Korn
wheat [wiːt] n	Weizen
spring wheat	Sommerweizen
winter wheat	Winterweizen
rye [raɪ] n	Roggen
barley ['bɑːli] n	Gerste
oats [əʊts] n pl	Hafer
rice n	Reis
high yield rice variety	Hochertragsreis
flooded field / paddy field n	Nassfeld (Reis)
maize / (sweet) corn AE n	Mais
corn n	Körnermais
millet ['mɪlɪt]	Hirse
sorghum ['sɔːgəm]	Sorghumhirse

》

bread basket		Kornkammer
cotton	belt	Baumwollgürtel (USA)
dairy		Milchwirtschaftsgürtel (USA)

root crops / row crops n	Hackfrüchte / Blattfrüchte
potato, pl potatoes n	Kartoffel
early potato	Frühkartoffel
sweet potato	Süßkartoffel
Colorado beetle n	Kartoffelkäfer
manioc ['mænɪɒk] n	Maniok / Kassava
yam [jæm] n	Jams(-wurzel)
taro ['tærəʊ] n	Taro / Wasserbrotwurzel
sugar beet n	Zuckerrübe
sugar cane n	Zuckerrohr

3 Human environment › 3.2 Agriculture

oil-bearing crops n pl	Ölsaaten
oil palm n	Ölpalme
oilseed rape n	Raps
sunflower n	Sonnenblume
olive n	Olive
grove [grəʊv] n	Hain

soybean n	Sojabohne
peanut n	Erdnuss

vegetables ['vedʒtəblz] n pl	Gemüse
field vegetables	Feldgemüse
early vegetables	Frühgemüse
legume ['legjuːm] / pulse n	Hülsenfrucht
bean n	Bohne
pea n	Erbse
lentil ['lentl] n	Linse
onion ['ʌnjən] n	Zwiebel
leek [liːk] n	Lauch
cabbage ['kæbɪdʒ] n	Kohl
asparagus [ə'spærəgəs] n	Spargel
cut asparagus	Spargel stechen
tomato, pl tomatoes n	Tomate
zucchini [zʊ'kiːni] / courgette [kɔː'ʒet] n	Zucchini
eggplant n	Aubergine
lettuce ['letɪs] n	Salat
paprika n	Paprika
chili n	Pepperoni
pepper n	Pfeffer
cooking banana n	Kochbanane

fruit n	Obst
fruit plantation / orchard ['ɔːtʃəd] n	Obstkultur
apple n	Apfel
pear [peə] n	Birne
plum n	Pflaume
cherry n	Kirsche
peach n	Pfirsich
quince [kwɪns] n	Quitte
apricot n	Aprikose
melon n	Melone
grapes n	Weintrauben / Trauben (meist Pl.)
raisin ['reɪzn] n	Rosine
citrus fruit ['sɪtrəsˌfruːt] n	Zitrusfrucht

orange n	Apfelsine / Orange
lemon n	Zitrone
tangerine [ˌtændʒrˈiːn] n	Mandarine
tropical fruit n	Südfrucht
pineapple [ˈpaɪnæpl] n	Ananas
banana n	Banane
papaya n	Papaya
mango n	Mango
walnut n	Walnuss
almond [ˈɑːmənd] n	Mandel
coconut palm [ˌkəʊkənʌtˈpɑːm] n	Kokospalme
date palm n	Dattelpalme

» plant cultivated for the production of semi-luxuries (i.e. tabacco) — Genusspflanze (z. B. Tabak)

coffee n	Kaffee
coffee bean	Kaffeebohne
roast [rəʊst] v	rösten
grind [graʊnd], ground, ground v	mahlen
cocoa (beans) [ˈkəʊkəʊ] n	Kakao(-bohnen)
cocoa tree	Kakaostrauch
cocoa butter	Kakaofett / Kakaobutter
tea n	Tee
tea shrub [ˈtiːʃrʌb]	Teestrauch
tea leaf, *pl* leaves	Teeblatt
pick tea	Tee pflücken
vine n	Weinrebe
wine n	Wein
hop n	Hopfen
beer n	Bier
tobacco n	Tabak
poppy [ˈpɒpi] n	Mohn

flower plantation / cultivation of flowers n	Blumenanbau
cut flower n	Schnittblume
bulb [bʌlb] n	Blumenzwiebel
tree nursery n	Baumschule

legume [ˈleɡjuːm] n	Leguminose / Hülsenfrüchte
clover [ˈkləʊvə] n	Klee
alfalfa grass [ˌælˈfælfəɡrɑːs] n	Luzerne / Alfalfa

3 Human environment › 3.2 Agriculture

fibre plant ['faɪbəˌplɑːnt] n	Faserpflanze
cotton n	Baumwolle
flax [flæks] n	Flachs
hemp [hemp] n	Hanf
sisal ['saɪsl] n	Sisal
jute [dʒuːt] n	Jute
mulberry tree ['mʌlbri] n	Maulbeerbaum
silkworm breeding ['sɪlkwɜːmˌbriːdɪŋ] / sericulture [ˌserɪ'kʌltʃə] n	Seidenraupenzucht

rubber / India rubber n	Kautschuk
rubber / latex ['leɪteks] n	Gummi
tap [tæp] v	anzapfen

livestock n	Vieh
young stock	Jungvieh
cattle n pl	Vieh / Rinder
dairy cattle ['deəriˌkætl]	Milchvieh
large farm animals n pl	Großvieh
meat n	Fleisch
beef n	Rindfleisch
mad cow disease / BSE *BE* n	Rinderwahnsinn
pig / hog [hɒg] n	Schwein
hog cholera [ˌhɒg'kɒlrə] / swine fever n	Schweinepest
pork n	Schweinefleisch
swine flu n	Schweinegrippe
sheep, *pl* sheep n	Schaf
ewe [juː] n	Mutterschaf
lamb n	Lamm
goat [gəʊt] n	Ziege
water buffalo n	Wasserbüffel
camel n	Kamel

small farm animals n pl	Kleinvieh
chicken, *pl* chicken n	Huhn
free-range adj	in Freilandhaltung
goose [guːs] *pl* , geese [giːs] n	Gans
turkey n	Pute / Truthahn
avian flu n	Vogelgrippe

wood / timber n	Holz
timber ['tɪmbə] n	Nutzholz
precious wood / high grade wood n	Edelholz
teak n	Teakholz

cork oak n	Korkeiche

Agricultural systems

farming system n	Ackerbausystem
agrarian structure [ə'greəriən] / agricultural structure n	Agrarstruktur
type of farm n	Betriebssystem
regional distribution of farm size n	Betriebsgrößenstruktur
system of land use n	Bodennutzungssystem
shifting cultivation n	Wanderfeldbau
slash-and-burn farming n	Brandrodungsfeldbau
three-field (crop) rotation n	Dreifelderwirtschaft
transhumance [træns'hju:məns] n	Wanderweidewirtschaft
livestock farming n	Viehhaltung / Tierproduktion
cattle grazing / ranching n	Rinderweidewirtschaft
pastoral farming ['pɑ:strl] n	Grünlandlandwirtschaft
rotation with grass period n	Feldgraswirtschaft
mixed farming n	Mischbetrieb *(Anbau verschiedener Anbaufrüchte)*
» farm with mixed agriculture (cattle and cultivation)	landwirtschaftlicher Gemischtbetrieb (Viehhaltung und Feldanbau)
monoculture / one-crop agriculture n	Monokultur
feed crop farm n	Futterbaubetrieb
plantation farming n	Plantagenwirtschaft
oasis agriculture [əʊ'eɪsɪs ˌægrɪkʌltʃə] n	Oasenwirtschaft
market gardening/vegetable growing n	Marktgemüseanbau / Gemüseanbau
contract cultivation n	Vertragsanbau
agroforestry [ˌægrəʊ'fɒrɪstri] n	Agroforstwirtschaft *(Kombination von Land- und Forstwirtschaft)*
cultivation of cash crops n	marktorientierter Anbau
operate commercially v	kommerziell bewirtschaften
commercial farming n	gewerbliche Landwirtschaft
cash crop farm n	Marktfruchtbetrieb
extensive farming n	extensive Bewirtschaftung
full-time farming n	Vollerwerbsbetrieb
full-time farmer n	Vollerwerbslandwirt
part-time farming n	Nebenerwerbsbetrieb / Zuerwerbsbetrieb

3 Human environment › 3.2 Agriculture

family farm n	landwirtschaftlicher Familienbetrieb
agricultural service supply agency n	Lohnunternehmen
self-sufficiency [ˌselfsə'fɪʃnsi] n	Selbstversorgung
subsistence (farming) [səb'sɪstns] n	Selbstversorgung *(durch Landwirtschaft)*
horticulture ['hɔːtɪkʌltʃə] n	Gartenbau
market gardening firm n	Gartenbaubetrieb / Gärtnerei
cultivation in hot houses n	Glashauskultur
tree nursery n	Baumschule
land reform n	Landreform
ownership n	Besitzverhältnis
latifundium, *pl* latifundia n	Großgrundbesitz / Latifundium
big farmer / big land owner n	Großbauer
splitting up of possessions n	Besitzzersplitterung
fragmentation [ˌfrægmən'teɪʃn] n	Zersplitterung
fragmentation of land n	Flurzersplitterung
land consolidation [ˌlændkənˌsɒlɪ'deɪʃn] n	Flurbereinigung
lot n	Besitzparzelle
tenure ['tenjə] n	Pacht
consolidate v	zusammenlegen / konsolidieren
redistribute [ˌriːdɪ'strɪbjuːt] v	umverteilen / neu verteilen
land tenure n	Landbesitz
tenant ['tenənt] n	Pächter
cash tenancy ['kæʃˌtenənsi]	Pachtverhältnis *(Pachtzahlungen)*
rent v	pachten / mieten
absentee landowner [ˌæbsntiː'lænlɔːd] n	Landbesitzer, der nicht auf seinem Land lebt

» boundary of a field or cluster of fields which has the same crop rotation | Schlaggrenze

The fragmentation of land in some areas of Germany is the result of inheritance laws.
Die Flurzersplitterung in einigen Gegenden Deutschlands ist das Ergebnis des Vererbungsrechts.
They ordered inheritance by equal division, known as "Realteilung".
Dies regelte die Erbschaft durch eine Aufteilung zu gleichen Teilen, die „Realteilung".
In other areas, the inheritance system led to "Anerbenrecht" – one relative, usually the eldest son, inheriting the complete property.
In anderen Gebieten führte das Vererbungsrecht zu Anerbenrecht – ein Verwandter, meist der älteste Sohn, erbte den gesamten Besitz.

co-operative n	Genossenschaft / Kooperative
collective farming n	Kollektivierung
agricultural cooperative n	Landwirtschaftliche Produktionsgenossenschaft (LPG)
nationalisation *BE* / nationalization *AE* n	Verstaatlichung
state-owned farm n	Staatsfarm
kibbutz [kɪ'bʊts] n	Kibbuz *(Israel)*
sovkhozy n	Sowchose *(ehemalige Sowjetunion)*
kolkhoz [ˌkɒl'kɒz], *pl* kolkhozy, kolhozes n	Kolchose *(ehemalige Sowjetunion)*
people's commune [ˌpiːplz'kɒmjuːn] n	Volkskommune *(China)*
ranch n	Ranch
fattening of bulls n	Bullenmast
fattening of calves n	Kälbermast
alpine meadow / alpine pasture [ˌælpaɪn'pɑːstʃə] n	Alm
alpine herdsmen's hut [ˌælpaɪn'hɜːdzmənsˌhʌt] n	Almhütte
nomad ['nəʊmæd] n	Nomade
semi-nomad n	Halbnomade
dairy farming n	Milchproduktion / Milchwirtschaft / Milchviehhaltung
milk processing plant n	milchverarbeitender Betrieb
factory farming n	Massentierhaltung
poultry farming [ˌpəʊltri'fɑːmin] n	Geflügelhaltung
battery farming n	Geflügelhaltung in Legebatterien
battery-caged adj	im Käfig gehalten
subsidy ['sʌbsɪdi] n	Subvention / Fördermittel
subsidise ['sʌbsɪdaɪz] *BE* / subsidize *AE* v	subventionieren / fördern
grant [grɑːnt] v	gewähren
quota ['kwəʊtə] n	Quote
farm-gate price n	Erzeugerpreis

》

Common Agricultural Policy (CAP)
(Europäische) Gemeinsame Agrarpolitik (GAP)
European Agricultural Fund for Rural Development (EAFRD)
Europäischer Landwirtschaftsfonds für die Entwicklung des ländlichen Raum (ELER)
European Agricultural Guidance and Guarantee Fund (EAGGF)
Europäischer Ausrichtungs- und Garantiefonds für die Landwirtschaft
ACP producers (African, Caribbean, Pacific)
AKP-Produzenten (Afrika, Karibik, Pazifik)

Food industry

food industry n	Lebensmittelindustrie
food processing n	Lebensmittelherstellung
process (sth) v	(etw.) verarbeiten

commercial farming n	kommerzielle Landwirtschaft
agribusiness / factory farming n	Agribusiness
agro-industrial farm n	agroindustrieller Betrieb *(Betrieb der agrarische Rohstoffe für die Industrie anbaut)*
genetically modified food / GM-food n	gentechnologisch veränderte Lebensmittel
genetically modified adj	gentechnisch verändert

»
processing of agricultural products	Verarbeitung landwirtschaftlicher Produkte
intensive commercial farming	intensive kommerzielle Landwirtschaft
grow commercially	kommerziell anbauen

dairy industry n	Milchverarbeitungsindustrie
dairy / creamery ['kriːmri] n	Molkerei
cheese factory n	Käserei
cheese spread plant n	Schmelzkäsewerk

meat products n	Fleischwaren
meat packing / meat processing	Fleischverarbeitung
slaughterhouse ['slɔːtəhaʊs] / abattoir ['æbətwɑː] n	Schlachthof
cattle market n	Viehmarkt

beverages / soft drinks n pl	Getränke *(nichtalkoholisch)*
beverage plant ['bevrɪdʒˌplɑːnt]	Getränkeherstellung
brewery ['bruːri] n	Brauerei
beer n	Bier
brandy n	Branntwein / Spirituose
spirits n pl	Spirituosen
sparkling wine n	Schaumwein / Sekt

fishing industry n	Fischereiwirtschaft
fishing capacity n	Fischfangkapazität
fish processing industry n	Fischverarbeitung
catch size / commercial catch n	Fangmenge

whaling ['weɪlɪŋ] n	Walfang
fish meal n	Fischmehl

overfishing n	Überfischung
overfish v	überfischen
fish population / fish stock n	Fischbestand
fishing grounds / fishing bank n	Fischgrund / Fischfangregion
spawning ground [spɔːnɪŋ] n	Laichplatz
quantity of fish caught n	Fangmenge
trawl [trɔːl] v	mit Schleppnetz fischen
trawler fleet n	Trawler-Flotte
mesh opening / mesh size n	Maschenweite
aquaculture ['ækwə,kʌltʃə] n	Aquakultur
fish meal production / fish flour production n	Fischmehlproduktion

can v	einmachen / in (Konserven-)Dosen füllen
canning factory n	Konservenfabrik
food canning industry n	Konservenindustrie

» canned (food) / tinned (food) | (Lebensmittel) in Dosen

ready-made meal n	Fertiggericht
frozen food n	Tiefkühlkost
sugar mill / sugar factory / sugar refinery n	Zuckerfabrik

Ecological agriculture

agriculture ['ægrɪkʌltʃə] / farming n	Landwirtschaft
ecological agriculture	ökologische Landwirtschaft
environmentally friendly farming	umweltverträgliche Landwirtschaft
organically adj	biologisch / biodynamisch
organically grown	biologisch angebaut
biocapacity n	Biokapazität
biodiversity [,baɪəʊdaɪ'vɜːsəti] n	Biodiversität / Artenvielfalt
carrying capacity / sustainable stock n	Tragfähigkeit
habitat (of plants) ['hæbɪtæt] n	Standort
habitat-adapted	standortangepasst
sustainable [sə'steɪnəbl] adj	nachhaltig

3 Human environment › 3.2 Agriculture

set-aside system n Verbot einer landwirtschaftlichen Nutzung *(zur Schonung der Bestände des Bodens)*
animal husbandry [ˈænɪmlˌhʌzbəndri] n Viehhaltung
species-appropriate husbandry artgerechte Haltung

»

alternative	farming / agriculture	alternative	Landwirtschaft
organic		biologische	
conventional		konventionelle	

soil n Boden
soil conservation (measure) Bodenschutz / Bodenerhaltungs(-maßnahme)
soil compaction Bodenverdichtung
soil degradation Bodenzerstörung
contour ploughing [ˈkɒntʊəˌplaʊɪŋ] n Konturpflügen
strip-farming / strip-cultivation n Streifenkultur
protective plantation [prəˌtektɪvplænˈteɪʃn] n Schutzpflanzung
strip of protective vegetation n Schutzstreifen
protective forest strip n Waldschutzstreifen
windbreak [ˈwɪnbreɪk] n Windschutzhecke

»

protection from	erosion	Erosionsschutz
protection against		

manure [məˈnjʊə] / fertiliser n Dünger / Düngemittel
organic fertiliser organischer Dünger
dung [dʌŋ] / manure n Dung / Mist
manure (sth) v (etw.) düngen
green manure Gründüngung
compost [ˈkɒmpɒst] n Kompost
composting plant Kompostierungsanlage
mulch [mʌlʃ] v mulchen

»

preservation of soil fertility	Erhaltung der Bodenfruchtbarkeit
keeping animals in a near-natural environment	artgerechte Tierhaltung
organically produced food	ökologisch produziertes Lebensmittel
eco-seal of approval	Biosiegel

3.3 Population Characteristics

population [ˌpɒpjə'leɪʃn] n	Bevölkerung
world population	Weltbevölkerung
local population	ortsansässige Bevölkerung
population structure	Bevölkerungsstruktur
population composition	Bevölkerungszusammensetzung
population distribution	Bevölkerungsverteilung
population density	Bevölkerungsdichte
optimum population	optimale Bevölkerungsdichte
populated adj	bevölkert / bewohnt
populate v	bevölkern
demography [dɪ'mɒgrəfi] n	Demografie / Bevölkerungsforschung
demographic adj	Bevölkerungs~
demographic data [ˌdɪ'mɒgræfɪkˌdeɪtə]	Bevölkerungszahlen
census ['sensəs] n	Zensus / Volkszählung
micro-census [maɪkrəʊ'sensəs]	Mikrozensus

inhabitant [ɪn'hæbɪtnt] n	Einwohner
inhabit v	bewohnen
citizen ['sɪtɪzn] n	Bürger *(Bewohner einer Stadt)*
settlement n	Besiedlung
settle v	besiedeln
recent settler / colonist / pioneer	Neusiedler
colony n	Kolonie
colonist n	Kolonist / Siedler
colonise *BE* / colonize *AE* v	kolonialisieren / besiedeln / siedeln
colonial [kə'ləʊniəl] adj	kolonial
dweller ['dwelə] n	Bewohner

overpopulation n	Überbevölkerung
underpopulation n	Unterbevölkerung
depopulation n	Entvölkerung
populous ['pɒpjələs] adj	dicht besiedelt / dicht bevölkert
overcrowded adj	überfüllt

》

densely populated	dicht besiedelt / dicht bevölkert
sparsely populated	dünn besiedelt

ethnic ['eθnɪk] adj	ethnisch
ethnic structure	ethnische Struktur
ethnic group	Bevölkerungsgruppe
ethnic minority	ethnische Minderheit
descent [dɪ'sent] n	Herkunft / Abstammung
foreigner ['fɒrɪnə] / alien ['eɪliən] n	Ausländer
foreign / alien adj	ausländisch
foreign employee	ausländischer Arbeitnehmer
guest-worker n	Gastarbeiter / ausländischer Arbeitnehmer
xenophobic [ˌzenə'fəʊbɪk] adj	ausländerfeindlich

» hostile to foreigners | ausländerfeindlich

race n	Rasse
multiracial [ˌmʌlti'reɪʃl] adj	multirassisch / vielrassig
multiracial state	Vielvölkerstaat
multicultural [ˌmʌlti'kʌltʃrl] adj	multikulturell
tribe [traɪb] / clan n	Sippe
indigenous [ɪn'dɪdʒɪnəs] / native adj	indigen / einheimisch
indigenous people / native n	Ureinwohner / ursprüngliche Bevölkerung
aborigine [ˌæbə'rɪdʒni] (Australia) n	Ureinwohner (Australien)
melting pot n	Schmelztiegel

» proportion of foreigners / percentage of foreigners | Ausländeranteil

integration n	Integration / Eingliederung
integrate v	integrieren / eingliedern
integrated adj	integriert / fester Bestandteil
tension ['tenʃn] n	Spannung
tolerance ['tɒlrns] n	Toleranz / Duldung
tolerant adj	tolerant
discrimination n	Diskriminierung / Ausgrenzung
segregation [ˌsegrɪ'geɪʃn] n	Segregation / Trennung
segregate v	trennen
apartheid [ə'pɑːtaɪt] n	Apartheid (frühere Rassentrennung in Südafrika)
ghetto ['getəʊ] n	Ghetto
reservation n	Reservat

Native American n	Amerikanische Ureinwohner *(Indianer)*
coloured person n	Farbiger
person of mixed parentage n	Mischling
mulatto n	Mulatte
mestizo n	Mestize *(europäisch-indianisch)*
pygmy n	Pygmäen

sex / gender ['dʒendə] n	Geschlecht
gender ratio ['dʒendəˌreɪʃiəʊ]	Geschlechterverhältnis
sex ratio	Sexualproportion
gender equity ['dʒendəˌekwɪti]	Gleichberechtigung *(von Mann und Frau)*
female adj	weiblich
male adj	männlich
married adj	verheiratet
single adj	alleinstehend
divorced [dɪ'vɔːst] adj	geschieden
separated adj	getrennt
family n	Familie

» (be a) single parent | alleinerziehend

life expectancy n	Lebenserwartung
adult ['ædʌlt] n	Erwachsener
retirement age [rɪ'taɪəmənt‿eɪdʒ] n	Rentenalter
elderly people / the elderly n	ältere Menschen
household n	Haushalt
single household / one-person household	Einpersonenhaushalt

living conditions n pl	Lebensbedingungen
quality of life / quality of living n	Lebensqualität
prosperity [prɒs'perəti] n	Wohlstand
income n	Einkommen
dink [dɪŋk] n *(dual income, no kids)*	Dink *(kinderlose (Ehe-)Paare mit zwei Einkommen)*
yuppie ['jʌpi] n *(young urban professionals)*	Yuppie *(junge, in der Stadt lebende Beschäftigte mit Hochschulabschluss)*
poverty ['pɒvəti] n	Armut
poor adj	arm

» below the poverty line | unterhalb der Armutsgrenze

3 Human environment › 3.3 Population

subsistence level n	Existenzminimum
marginalised *BE* / marginalized *AE* ['mɑːdʒɪnlaɪzd] adj	an den Rand gedrängt
need n	Bedürfnis
in need	bedürftig
supply n	Versorgung
daily supply	tägliche Versorgung
degree of supply	Versorgungsgrad
health n	Gesundheit
sanitation [ˌsænɪ'teɪʃn] n	Gesundheitspflege / Hygiene
staple food n	Grundnahrungsmittel
malnutrition [ˌmælnjuː'trɪʃn] n	Fehlernährung
undernutrition n	Unterernährung
living space / housing n	Wohnraum / Wohnfläche
subsidised housing ['sʌbsɪdaɪzdˌhaʊsɪŋ] / council housing	Sozialwohnungen
council flat ['kaʊnslˌflæt] n	Sozialwohnung
education n	Bildung
school education	Schulbildung
educated adj	gebildet
illiteracy [ɪ'lɪtrəsi] n	Analphabetismus
illiterate [ɪ'lɪtrət] n	Analphabet
literacy rate ['lɪtrəsiˌreɪt]	Alphabetisierungsrate
nursery school n	Kindergarten
primary school n	Grundschule
secondary school n	weiterführende Schule
college / university n	Hochschule
graduate n	Hochschulabsolvent(in) / Absolvent(in)
graduate v	einen akademischen Grad erwerben / einen Abschluss machen

» graduate from college / university | einen Hochschulabschluss machen

social structure n	Sozialstruktur
social status n	sozialer Status
deprived [dɪ'praɪvd] adj	sozial benachteiligt
social benefit / social security n	Sozialhilfe
social facility [ˌsəʊʃlə'sɪləti] n	Sozialstation / Sozialeinrichtung
social class n	Gesellschaftsklasse

upper		Oberschicht
middle	class	Mittelschicht
lower		Unterschicht

caste [kɑːst] n Kaste / soziale Gruppe *(in Indien)*
untouchable / dalit n Unberührbarer / Dalit *(in Indien)*

European Social Fund (ESF) | Europäischer Sozialfond (ESF)

religion / denomination [dɪˌnɒmɪˈneɪʃn] n Religionszugehörigkeit / Konfessionszugehörigkeit
world religion n Weltreligion
Christianity n Christentum
Christian n Christ
Catholic n Katholik
Catholic adj katholisch
Protestant [ˈprɒtɪstnt] n Protestant
Protestant adj protestantisch
Islam [ˈɪzlæm] n *(ohne Artikel)* Islam
Muslim [ˈmʊzlɪm] n Muslim
Muslim adj muslimisch
Jewry [ˈdʒʊərɪ] n Judentum
Jew [dʒuː] n Jude
Jewish [ˈdʒuːɪʃ] adj jüdisch
Hinduism n Hinduismus
Hindu n Hindu
Hindu adj hinduistisch
Buddhism n Buddhismus
Buddhist n Buddhist
Buddhist adj buddhistisch
natural religion n Naturreligion

Development

population development n Bevölkerungsentwicklung
population growth n Bevölkerungswachstum
  natural growth rate   natürliche Bevölkerungswachstumsrate
fertility [fəˈtɪləti] n Fruchtbarkeit / Fertilität
  fertility rate   Fruchtbarkeitsrate / Fruchtbarkeitsziffer

3 Human environment › 3.3 Population

population explosion n	Bevölkerungsexplosion
population change n	Bevölkerungsveränderung
population structure n	Bevölkerungsstruktur
carrying capacity n	Tragfähigkeit
surplus of women ['sɜːpləsəv‚wɪmɪn] / excess of women n	Frauenüberschuss
age structure / age distribution n	Altersstruktur / Altersaufbau
population pyramid n	Bevölkerungspyramide
age-sex pyramid n	Alterspyramide
age group n	Altersgruppe
cohort ['kəʊhɔːt] n	Geburtsjahrgang
economically active population / working population n	wirtschaftlich aktive Bevölkerung
non-economically active population	nicht wirtschaftlich aktive Bevölkerung
old-age dependency ratio n	Altenquotient
superannuation [‚suːprˌænjuˈeɪʃn] (of the population) n	Überalterung (der Bevölkerung)
old age / senescence [sɪˈnesns] n	Vergreisung
demographic transition [‚dɪˈmɒɡræfɪktrænˌzɪʃn] n	demographischer Übergang
fertility behaviour [fəˈtɪlətɪbɪˌheɪvjə] n	generatives Verhalten
birth rate n	Geburtenrate
birth surplus / excess of births over deaths n	Geburtenüberschuss
death rate n	Sterberate
mortality [mɔːˈtæləti] n	Sterblichkeit
infant mortality	Säuglingssterblichkeit
child mortality	Kindersterblichkeit
infant mortality rate	Kindersterbeziffer
life expectancy n	Lebenserwartung
double v	sich verdoppeln
increase n	Anstieg / Zunahme
fluctuate [ˈflʌktʃueɪt] v	schwanken / fluktuieren
family planning n	Familienplanung
birth control n	Geburtenkontrolle
contraception [‚kɒntrəˈsepʃn] n	Verhütung
contraceptive n	Verhütungsmittel / Empfängnisverhütungsmittel
use a contraceptive	verhüten
sterilisation [‚sterlaɪˈzeɪʃn] n	Sterilisation
abortion [əˈbɔːʃn] n	Abtreibung
one-child policy n	Ein-Kind-Politik (China)

»

There can be a population	decline. decrease. increase.	Es kann eine Bevölkerungs~ ...	~abnahme ... ~verminderung ... ~zunahme ...,	geben.
The population	declines. decreases. increases.	Die Bevölkerung	nimmt ab. verringert sich. wächst an / nimmt zu.	
The population structure can be	expansive stationary contractive / shrinking	Die Bevölke- rungsstruktur kann ...	... sich ausdehnen. ... stationär ... ... schrumpfende ...	sein.
	rapidly falling death rate steadily rising birth rate		rasant fallende Sterberate stätig steigende Geburtenrate	
	low high	life expectancy	geringe hohe	Lebenserwartung

The demographic transition model describes a sequence of change over a period of time in the relationship between birth and death rates and overall population change. (Waugh)
Das Modell des demographischen Übergangs beschreibt eine Folge von Veränderungen der Relation von Geburten- und Sterberaten und allgemeiner Bevölkerungsveränderung in einem bestimmten Zeitraum. (Waugh)

Migration

migration [maɪˈgreɪʃn] n   Wanderung
migration movement   Wanderungsbewegung
migration balance   Wanderungsbilanz / Wanderungssaldo
migration gain   Wanderungsgewinn
migration loss   Wanderungsverlust
migration flow   Wanderungsstrom
out-migration   Abwanderung
in-migration   Zuwanderung (regional)
rural-urban migration   Landflucht
[ˈrʊərlˌɜːbnmaɪˌgreɪʃn]
internal migration   Binnenwanderung
migrate v   wandern / abwandern
mobility [məˈbɪləti] n   Mobilität
emigration [ˌemɪˈgreɪʃn] n   Auswanderung
emigration rate   Auswanderungsquote

3 Human environment › 3.3 Population

emigrate (to) v	auswandern (nach)
emigrant ['emɪgrənt] n	Auswanderer
immigration [ˌɪmɪ'greɪʃn] n	Einwanderung
immigrate (into) v	einwandern (in)
immigrant ['ɪmɪgrənt] n	Einwanderer / Zuwanderer
illegal immigrant	illegaler Einwanderer
return migration / remigration n	Rückwanderung
country of origin [ˌkʌntrɪɒv'ɒrɪdʒɪn] n	Herkunftsland
home country / native land n	Heimatland
push and pull factor n	Push-und-Pull-Faktor
abroad [ə'brɔːd] adv	im Ausland

»

Migration movements can be	permanent. semi-permanent. temporary. seasonal. daily.	Wanderungs- bewegungen können	dauerhaft für einige Jahre zeitlich begrenzt jahreszeitlich bedingt täglich	erfolgen.
external international voluntary forced internal regional		migration	grenzüberschreitende internationale freiwillige erzwungene interne regionale	Migration

commuter [kə'mjuːtə] n	Pendler
daily commuter	Tagespendler
cross-border commuter	Grenzpendler
commute	pendeln
migrant worker n	Wanderarbeiter
guest worker n	Gastarbeiter
economic migrant n	Wirtschaftsflüchtling / Arbeitsmigrant
recruit [rɪ'kruːt] v	anwerben

»

relatives following the 'gastarbeiters'	nachziehende Familienangehörige der Gastarbeiter

asylum [ə'saɪləm] n	Asyl
asylum seeker [ə'saɪləmˌsiːkə]	Asylbewerber
right of asylum	Anrecht auf Asyl / Asylrecht
seek asylum, sought asylum	um Asyl bitten
grant sb asylum	jdm. Asyl gewähren

» ask for political asylum | um politisches Asyl bitten

applicant ['æplɪkənt] n	Bewerber
apply for [ə'plaɪ]	beantragen
assert [ə'sɜːt] v	geltend machen
attain [ə'teɪn] v	erreichen / erlangen
registration [ˌredʒɪ'streɪʃn] n	Anmeldung
acceptance [ək'septəns] n	Akzeptanz
border ['bɔːdə] / boundary ['baʊndri] / frontier [frʌn'tɪə] n	Grenze
border crossing point / point of entry	Grenzübergang
border patrol (officer) [ˌbɔːdəpə'trəʊl]	Grenzschutz(beamter)
state boundary / national boundary	Staatsgrenze
federal state boundary	Ländergrenze
boundary of territory	Territorialgrenze
transnational [træns'næʃnl] adj	grenzüberschreitend
passport n	Pass / Ausweis
territory n	Hoheitsgebiet
host country ['həʊstˌkʌntri] / receiving country [rɪ'siːvɪŋˌkʌntri] n	Aufnahmeland
country of destination n	Zielland
flight [flaɪt] n	Flucht
flee [fliː], fled, fled v	flüchten
refuge ['refjuːdʒ] / shelter ['ʃeltə] / asylum n	Zuflucht
refugee [ˌrefjʊ'dʒiː] n	Flüchtling
refugee from poverty	Armutsflüchtling
environmental refugee [ɪnˌvaɪərn'mentl]	Umweltflüchtling
refugee camp	Flüchtlingslager
migration of refugees	Flüchtlingsbewegung
aid to refugees	Flüchtlingshilfe
forced migration [fɔːstmaɪ'greɪʃn] n	erzwungene Migration
expulsion [ɪk'spʌlʃn] / (forced) displacement [ˌfɔːstdɪ'spleɪsmənt] n	Vertreibung
displaced person n	Vertriebene/r / Heimatvertriebene(r) / Flüchtling
resettlement n	Umsiedlung
political resettling	politisch begründete Umsiedlung
persecution [ˌpɜːsɪ'kjuːʃn] n	Verfolgung
persecute v	verfolgen

3 Human environment › 3.4 Trade, services and consumer

conflict n	Konflikt
tribalism ['traɪblɪzm] n	Tribalismus *(Bevorzugung von Stammesangehörigen)*
emergency shelter [ɪ'mɜːdʒnsiˌʃeltə] n	Notquartier
tent camp / tent city [tent] n	Zeltstadt
squatter settlement ['skwɒtəˌsetlment] n	illegale Siedlung
shanty town ['ʃæntiˌtaʊn] n	Barackensiedlung / Elendsviertel

»

United Nations High Commissioner for Refugees (UNHCR)	Hoher Flüchtlingskommissar der Vereinten Nationen (UNHCR)
Commissioner for Migration, Refugees, and Integration	Beauftrage/r für Migrantion, Flüchtlinge und Integration
Geneva Refugee Convention	Genfer Flüchtlingskonvention
Maastricht Treaty	Vertrag von Maastricht
Schengen Zone	Schengen-Gebiet (umfasst nahezu alle EU-Staaten, erlaubt Verkehr innerhalb des Gebiets ohne Grenzkontrollen)
Schengen Agreement	Schengener Abkommen

3.4 Trade, services and consumer

Trade

trade n	Handel
trade activities	Handelsaktivitäten
economy [ɪ'kɒnəmi] n	Wirtschaft
economic activities	wirtschaftliche Unternehmungen
world trade / global trade n	Welthandel
home trade / domestic trade [dəˌmestɪk'treɪd] n	Binnenhandel
foreign trade [ˌfɒrɪn'treɪd] n	Auslandshandel
overseas trade n	Überseehandel
trading links n pl	Handelsverbindungen
production n	Produktion / Herstellung / Erzeugung
consumption [kən'sʌmpʃn] n	Verbrauch / Konsum
consume v	konsumieren
demand n	Nachfrage
supply n	Angebot
regions of supply	Angebotsregionen
regions of demand	Nachfrageregionen

138

trade balance / balance of trade n	Handelsbilanz
trade deficit ['treɪd͵defɪsɪt] n	Handelsdefizit
trade surplus ['treɪd͵sɜːpləs] n	Handelsüberschuss
domestic market n	Binnenmarkt
export n	Ausfuhr / Export
import n	Einfuhr / Import
goods n pl	Güter / Waren
services n pl	Dienstleistung

»
gain access to a market	Zugang zu einem Markt erlangen

Trade develops out of regional economic differences. It serves to balance production and consumption by moving raw materials, goods and services from regions of supply to regions of demand.
Handel entsteht aus regionalen wirtschaftlichen Unterschieden. Er dient dazu, Produktion und Verbrauch durch das Verschieben von Rohstoffen, Waren und Dienstleistungen von Angebotsregionen zu Nachfrageregionen auszugleichen.

US companies complain that they cannot gain access to Japanese markets.
Amerikanische Unternehmen beklagen sich darüber, dass sie keinen Zugang zu den japanischen Märkten bekommen können.

promotion n	Förderung
guideline n	Richtlinie
barrier ['bæriə] n	Schranke / Barriere
market barrier	Marktbarriere

visibles ['vɪzəblz] n pl	Waren / Güter *(sichtbar; die ein- und ausgeführt werden)*
visible trade	Güterverkehr / Warenverkehr
visible imports	Wareneinfuhren
visible exports	Warenausfuhren

»
EU export of visibles in the machine, electronic, building and automobile sector in 1991 amounted to nearly 585 million dollars.
Die europäischen Ausfuhren im Warenverkehr in den Bereichen Maschinenbau, Elektronik, Bauwesen und Automobilbau beliefen sich 1991 auf fast 585 Millionen Dollar.

invisibles [ɪn'vɪzəblz] n pl	Dienstleistungen *(unsichtbar; die ein- und ausgeführt werden)* / Dienstleistungsverkehr
invisible trade	Dienstleistungsverkehr im Außenhandel

invisible imports	Einfuhr von Dienstleistungen
invisible exports	Ausfuhr von Dienstleistungen
finances n	Finanzen
tourism n	Tourismus

》

	... visible trade	Warenbilanz
	... invisible trade	Dienstleistungsbilanz
	... current accounts	Leistungsbilanz
balance of	... capital movements	Kapital(verkehrs)bilanz
	... payments	Zahlungsbilanz
	... trade surplus	Handelsbilanzüberschuss
	... trade deficit	Handelsbilanzdefizit

barter trade [ˌbɑːtəˈtreɪd‚] n	Tauschhandel / Warentauschgeschäft / Kompensationsgeschäft
bartering [ˈbɑːtrɪŋ] n	Tauschhandel / Tauschverkehr
receipts [rɪˈsiːts] n pl	Einnahmen / Eingänge
outgoings *BE* / expenditures *AE* [ɪkˈspendɪtʃəz] n pl	Ausgaben / Ausgänge
outflow n	Abfluss
currency outflow [ˈkʌrensiˌaʊtfləʊ]	Devisenabfluss

》

A country's receipts and outgoings are reflected in its balance of trade.
Die Außenhandelseingänge und -ausgänge eines Landes spiegeln sich in seiner Zahlungsbilanz wider.

trade war n	Handelskrieg
free trade n	Freihandel
trade barrier [ˈtreɪdˌbæriə] n	Handelsschranke / Handelshemmnis
tariff [ˈtærɪf] n	Zolltarif / Zoll
impose [ɪmˈpəʊz] v	auferlegen / errichten
abolish [əˈbɒlɪʃ] v	entfernen / beseitigen
entrepôt trade [ˌɑ̃ːntrəpəʊˈtreɪd] n	internationaler Handel
free-port trade n	Wiederausfuhrhandel *(via Freihafen)*
free-port [ˈfriːpɔːt] n	Freihafen *(unterliegt keiner Zollgrenze)*
re-export n	Reexport / Wiederausfuhr
re-export v	reexportieren / wieder ausführen
re-import n	Reimport / Wiedereinfuhr
re-import v	reimportieren / wiedereinführen

single market policy | Binnenmarktpolitik

The main purpose of EU Single Market policy is to remove trade barriers.
Der Hauptzweck der europäischen Binnenmarktpolitik besteht darin, Barrieren abzubauen.

Hamburg and Rotterdam are two of Europe's largest ports for entrepôt trade.
Hamburg and Rotterdam sind zwei der größten Wiederausfuhrhäfen Europas.

product n	Produkt
produce [prəˈdjuːs] v	produzieren / herstellen
produce [ˈprɒdjuːs] n	Erzeugnis / Obst und Gemüse
growth rate [ˈgrəʊθˌreɪt] n	Zuwachsrate
boom [buːm] n	Boom / Aufschwung / Hochkonjunktur
boom v	boomen / florieren
economic bloc n	Wirtschaftsblock
terms of trade n	Handelsbedingungen / Terms of Trade / Austauschverhältnis
price n	Preis
value [ˈvæljuː] n	Wert
amount (to) [əˈmaʊnt] v	sich belaufen auf / betragen
equivalent [ɪˈkwɪvlənt] n	Gegenwert / Äquivalent

The terms of trade for a lorry/truck (6–10 tonnes) amounted to the equivalent of 6 tonnes of coffee in 1985, today to 32 tonnes of coffee.
Das Austauschverhältnis für einen LKW (6–10 t) belief sich 1985 auf den Gegenwert von 6 t Kaffee, heute 32 t Kaffee.

arrangement n	Vereinbarung / Abmachung / Absprache
agreement n	Übereinkunft / Vereinbarung / Einverständnis
mutual agreement [ˌmjuːtʃuələˈgriːmənt]	gegenseitiges Einverständnis

General Agreement on Tariffs and Trade (Gatt) | das Gatt-Abkommen

transport n	Transport / Beförderung
transport system	Verkehrswesen
transport network	Verkehrsnetz
access [ˈækses] n	Zugang
competition n	Wettbewerb

3 Human environment › 3.4 Trade, services and consumer

competitiveness [kəm'petɪtɪvnəs] n	Wettbewerbsfähigkeit
improve v	verbessern

rigid ['rɪdʒɪd] adj	starr / fest
quota ['kwəʊtə] n	Quote / Kontingent
preferential [ˌprefr'enʃl] adj	Vorzugs~ / bevorzugt / Präferenz~
deny [dɪ'naɪ] v	verweigern
prohibit [prə'hɪbɪt] v	verbieten / untersagen
protectionism [prə'tekʃnɪzm] n	Protektionismus
protectionist adj	protektionistisch
voluntary export restraint (VER) ['vɒləntriekspɔːtrɪˌstreɪnt] n	freiwillige Exportbeschränkung
non-tariff trade barrier [ˌnɒn'tærɪf 'treɪdˌbæriə] n	nichttarifäres Handelshemmnis
red tape n	(übermäßige) Bürokratie
restrain [rɪ'streɪn] v	beschränken
sanction ['sæŋʃn] n	Sanktion
embargo [ɪm'bɔːgəʊ] n	Embargo

distribution [ˌdɪstrɪ'bjuːʃn] n	Vertrieb
distributor n	Vertriebsagent (in)
distribution management	Vertriebsmanagement
distribution centre *BE* / distribution center *AE*	Auslieferungszentrum
distribution channel	Vertriebskanal

»   take measures | Maßnahmen ergreifen

In a distribution centre goods are processed and moved on to wholesalers, retailers and distributors.
In einem Auslieferungszentrum werden Güter abgewickelt und an Groß- und Einzelhändler oder Vertriebsagenten weitergeleitet.

manufacturer n	Hersteller
manufactured goods n pl	Industriewaren / Industriegüter
wholesale trade [ˌhəʊlseɪl'treɪd] n	Großhandel
wholesale adj	Großhandels~
intermediary [ˌɪntə'miːdiəri] n	Zwischenhändler / Mittelsperson

» A distribution channel is the route by which a product is moved from producer to consumer.
Ein Vertriebskanal ist der Weg eines Produktes vom Hersteller zum Kunden.
It usually consists of a chain of intermediaries, including wholesalers, retailers and salesmen or sales agents.
Er besteht gewöhnlich aus einer Kette von Mittelspersonen, die Großhändler, Einzelhändler und Vertriebsagenten umfasst.

direct distribution n	Direktvertrieb
mail order n	Postversand
mail order catalogue *BE* / mail order catalog *AE* n	Versandhauskatalog
mail order company / mail order house n	Versandhaus
middleman n	Zwischenhändler(in)
principal ['prɪnsəpl] n	Auftraggeber (in)
agent n	Auftragnehmer(in) / Vermittler(in) / Vertreter(in)

» An agent is empowered to act on behalf of the manufacturer in dealing with a third party.
Ein Vermittler ist ermächtigt, im Auftrag des Herstellers zu handeln, wenn er mit Dritten verhandelt.

commission [kə'mɪʃn] n	Provision
part-time agent n	Teilzeitvertreter(in)
doorstep selling *BE* / door to door selling *AE* n	Haustürverkauf

» on one's own account | auf eigene Rechnung

The agent buys and sells on his own account.
Der Vertreter kauft und verkauft auf eigene Rechnung und im eigenen Namen.

merchant ['mɜːtʃnt] n	Händler
mail shot *BE* / direct mailing *AE* n	Briefwerbung / Postwurfsendung
home shopping n	Homeshopping / Teleshopping
wholesaler ['həʊlˌseɪlə] n	Großhändler(in) / Großhandelsunternehmen
in bulk [ɪn'bʌlk] adv	in (großen) Mengen / en gros

3 Human environment › 3.4 Trade, services and consumer

commodity [kəˈmɒdəti] n Wirtschaftsgut / an der Warenbörse
 gehandeltes Gut
primary product n Primärprodukt

» Commodities such as wheat, corn or other primary products are mostly traded in bulk.
Wirtschaftsgüter wie Weizen, Mais oder andere Primärprodukte werden zumeist en gros gehandelt.

warehouse n Lager
price ex warehouse [ˌpraɪseksˈweəhaʊs] Preis ab Lager
warehousing Warenlagerung
warehouse v lagern

» Goods are often warehoused strategically, in order to ensure punctual delivery.
Güter werden oft strategisch gelagert, um pünktliche Lieferung zu gewährleisten.

just-in-time (JIT) adj just-in-time / gerade (noch) rechtzeitig
just-in-time delivery bedarfsorientierte Lieferung
just-in-time production bedarfsorientierte Produktion

» Today many manufactured goods are delivered just-in-time in order to save costs for warehousing.
Heute werden viele Industriegüter just-in-time geliefert um Lagerungskosten zu sparen.

retailer [ˈriːteɪlə] n Einzelhändler(in)
retailer n Einzelhandelsunternehmen
 sole retailer [ˈsəʊlˌri teɪlə] BE / selbständige(r) Einzelhändler(in)
 independent retailer AE
retail trade n Einzelhandel
retail adj Einzelhandels~
supermarket n Supermarkt
opening hours n pl Öffnungszeiten
late-night shopping n spätabendliches Einkaufen
24/7 adv ununterbrochen / ständig
 (24 Stunden am Tag / sieben Tage die Woche)

department store n Kaufhaus
showroom n Ausstellungsraum
multiple store BE / chain store AE n Kette / Filialgeschäft

speciality shop ['speʃlti] n	Spezialgeschäft
specialist shop / specialist trade n	Fachhandel
stockist ['stɒkist] / specialist shop n	Fachgeschäft
merchandise ['mɜːtʃndaɪs] n	Handelsware
stock n	Bestand / Vorrat
in stock adj	vorrätig / auf Lager
stock up v	wieder (auf)füllen / Vorräte anlegen
assortment [əˈsɔːtmənt] / range (of goods) n	(Waren-) Sortiment

» Retailers will generally increase their stocks of merchandise before the Christmas season.
Kurz vor der Weihnachtszeit erhöhen Einzelhändler normalerweise ihre Warenvorräte.

dealer n	Händler
sole retailer BE / independent retailer AE n	selbständige(r) Einzelhändler(in)
own brand BE / generic brand AE n	Hausmarke / Eigenmarke
super store BE / outlet store AE n	Verbrauchermarkt *(Markt mit mindestens 2.700 qm Verkaufsfläche und Parkplätzen in Stadtrandlage)*
hypermarket ['haɪpəˌmɑːkɪt] n	Verbrauchermarkt / Selbstbedienungswarenhaus *(Markt ab ca. 5.000 qm Verkaufsfläche)*
hard discount store n	Discountgeschäft

» The range of goods in hard discount stores consists of own brands to a great extent.
Das Sortiment in Discountgeschäften besteht zu einem großen Teil aus Eigenmarken.

shopping precinct [ˈʃɒpɪŋˌpriːsɪŋt] n	Einkaufszone / Ladenstraße
shopping mall n	Einkaufspassage *(überdacht)*
franchising [ˈfrænʃaɪzɪŋ] n	Franchising *(vertraglich straff geführtes Filialsystem mit Alleinverkaufsrecht)*
franchise [ˈfrænʃaɪz] n	Franchise / Alleinverkaufsrecht
franchisee n	Franchisenehmer(in)
franchisor BE / franchiser AE n	Franchisegeber(in) / Konzessionserteiler(in)
convenience store [kənˈviːnɪənsˌstɔː] n	Laden an der Ecke
corner shop n	Tante-Emma-Laden
grocery store [ˈgrəʊsrɪˌstɔː] n	Lebensmittelgeschäft

3 Human environment › 3.4 Trade, services and consumer

price n	Preis
cost n	Kosten
sales n pl	Absatz
turnover ['tɜːn,əʊvə] n	Umsatz
annual turnover [ˌænjuəl'tɜːn,əʊvə]	Jahresumsatz
price n	Preis
price v	den Preis festsetzen
price tag	Preisschild
price list	Preisliste
running expenses n pl	laufende Kosten
cover (costs) v	(Kosten-)decken
unit price n	Stückpreis / Preis je Einheit
VAT [ˌviːeɪ'tiː] (value added tax) n	Mehrwertsteuer
sales tax n	Umsatzsteuer / Verkaufssteuer
purchase price ['pɜːtʃəsˌpraɪs] n	Kaufpreis
delivery costs n pl	Versandkosten
overheads ['əʊvəhedz] n pl	Gemeinkosten

» recommended retail price | unverbindliche Preisempfehlung

Overheads are figured into the retail purchase price.
Gemeinkosten werden bei der Ermittlung des Verkaufspreises einbezogen.

cost of sales n	Absatzkosten
net price n	Nettopreis
gross selling price [ˌgrəʊsselɪŋ'praɪs] n	Bruttoverkaufspreis
resale price maintenance (RPM) [riːseɪl'praɪsˌmeɪntnəns] n	Preisbindung

Services

service n	Dienstleistung
tertiary ['tɜːʃri] adj	tertiär
tertiarisation [ˌtɜːʃrɪ'zeɪʃn] n	Tertiärisierung
tertiary sector n	Tertiärer Sektor
commerce ['kɒmɜːs] n	Handel / Handelsverkehr
trade n	Handel / Gewerbe / Handelsverkehr
trade v	handeln
sector ['sektə] n	Sektor / Bereich
producer services n pl	unternehmensbezogene Dienstleistungen

consumer services n pl — Basisdienstleistungen / Grundversorgung

»
| state or non-market services | staatliche, nicht marktbezogene Dienstleistungen |
| personal or private services | personenbezogene, private Dienstleistungen |

The tertiary sector of the economy provides services to industry and consumers.
Der tertiäre Sektor der Wirtschaft offeriert der Industrie und den Verbrauchern Dienstleistungen.

Doctors, teachers and policemen offer personal services rather than goods to consumers.
Ärzte, Lehrer und Polizisten bieten dem Verbraucher keine Waren sondern persönliche Dienstleistungen an.

import adj — Import~
export adj — Export~
external adj — extern
domestic / home adj — Binnen~ / Inlands~
foreign adj — Auslands~
distributive [dɪˈstrɪbjətɪv] adj — Vertriebs~
measure v — messen
quantify [ˈkwɒntɪfaɪ] v — mengenmäßig messen / quantifizieren

» The value of services is very hard to measure and quantify.
Der Wert von Dienstleistungen lässt sich nur schwierig messen und in Zahlen ausdrücken.

Growth of services

growth of services n — Wachstum im Dienstleistungsbereich
deindustrialisation BE / deindustrialization AE [ˌdiːɪnˌdʌstrɪlaɪˈzeɪʃn] n — Deindustrialisierung
sub-contracting [ˌsʌbkənˈtræktɪŋ] n — Untervergabe / Weitervergabe
subcontractor n — Subunternehmer(in)
rationalisation BE / rationalization AE [ˌræʃnlaɪˈzeɪʃn] n — Rationalisierung
outsourcing [ˈaʊtsɔːsɪŋ] n — Ausgliederung / Fremdbeschaffung
externalisation of services [ɪkˌstɜːnlaɪˈzeɪʃnəvˌsɜːvɪsɪz] n — Auslagerung von Dienstleistungen

3 Human environment › 3.4 Trade, services and consumer

»

rise in efficiency and productivity	Anstieg der Effektivität und der Produktivität
rise in disposable income	Anstieg des verfügbaren Einkommens
decline of the traditional nuclear family	Rückgang der traditionellen Kernfamilie
emergence of more single adult households	vermehrtes Aufkommen von Ein-Personen-Haushalten

product quality n Produktqualität
labour *BE* / labor *AE* ['leɪbə] n Arbeit
  manual labour körperliche Arbeit
capital intensity n Kapitalintensität
define [dɪ'faɪn] v definieren / bestimmen

»

The quality of the product depends on the quality of the labour.
Die Produktqualität hängt von der Qualität der Arbeit ab.

Most service employment is non-manual.
Die Beschäftigung im Dienstleistungsbereich ist meist nicht mit körperlicher Arbeit verbunden.

Service sectors

service sector n Dienstleistungsbereich / Dienstleistungssektor
form of employment n Beschäftigungsart

»

The service sector is increasingly the main form of employment in a developed country.
Die Dienstleistungsindustrie ist zunehmend die wichtigste Form der Beschäftigung in einem entwickelten Land.

finance n Finanzwesen
retailing ['riːteɪlɪŋ] / retail trade n Einzelhandel
administration [əd₁mɪnɪ'streɪʃn] n Verwaltung
Research and Development (R&D) n Forschung und Entwicklung (F&E)
production planning n Produktionsplanung
marketing n Vermarktung
advertising n Werbung
distribution n Vertrieb
sales n Vertrieb

warehousing n	Lagerhaltung
consultant [kən'sʌltnt] n	Berater(in)
consultancy n	Beratung
market research n	Marktforschung
education n	Erziehung / Bildung
health care n	Gesundheitswesen

» The cost of health care is a growing concern for hospitals.
Die Kosten des Gesundheitswesens stellen ein wachsendes Problem für die Krankenhäuser dar.

legal services n pl	Rechtsleistungen
legal adviser n	Rechtsbeistand
law firm ['lɔːˌfɜːm] / lawyer's office n	Anwaltskanzlei
lawyer ['lɔɪə] n	Rechtsanwalt
partnership of lawyers	Sozietät
social welfare n	Sozialwesen / öffentliche Wohlfahrt
local government n	lokale Regierung
national government n	nationale Regierung
emergency services n pl	Notfalldienste
tourism n	Tourismus
travel agent n	Reiseveranstalter(in)
travel agency n	Reisebüro
cleaning n	Reinigung
domestic work n	Hausarbeit
insurance [ɪnˈʃʊərns] n	Versicherung
banking n	Bankgeschäft / Bankgewerbe
transport BE / transportation AE n	Transport
communications n pl	Kommunikation
restaurant sector n	Gastronomiebereich
hotel business n	Hotelgewerbe
hotel and restaurant sector n	Gastgewerbe
entertainment industry n	Unterhaltungsindustrie
film industry n	Filmindustrie
publishing n	Verlagswesen
leisure industry [ˌleʒəˈɪndəstri] n	Freizeitindustrie

Distribution of services

factor n	Faktor / Umstand
location n	Ort / Standort
decision n	Entscheidung

149

3   Human environment › 3.4 Trade, services and consumer

decision-making | Entscheidungsfindung

» There are a number of factors which influence the locational decisions of service businesses.
Es gibt eine Anzahl von Faktoren, die die Entscheidungsfindung bei der Standortwahl von Dienstleistungsfirmen beeinflussen.

customer proximity ['kʌstəməprɒkˌsɪmeti] n	Kundennähe
telecommunications n pl	Telekommunikation / Fernmeldewesen
traffic infrastructure ['træfɪkɪnfrəˌstrʌktʃə] n	Verkehrsinfrastruktur
personnel [ˌpɜːsn'el] n	Personal
qualified personnel	qualifiziertes Personal
access ['ækses] n	Zugang
accessibility [əkˌsesə'bɪləti] n	Zugänglichkeit / Erreichbarkeit
access v	zugreifen / öffnen

» information access is vital to … | Zugang zu Information ist unerlässlich für …
access information | auf Informationen zugreifen

image n	Image / Ruf
prestige [pres'tiːʒ] n	Prestige / Ansehen
environment [ɪn'vaɪrnmənt] n	Umwelt
distribution of customers n	Kundenverteilung
affluence ['æfluəns] n	Wohlstand / Überfluss
affluent ['æfluənt] adj	wohlhabend / reich
development n	Entwicklung
decentralise BE / decentralize AE [diː'sentrəlaɪz] v	dezentralisieren
decentralisation n	Dezentralisierung
function n	Aufgabe / Pflicht / Funktion
routine task n	Routinetätigkeit
office work / clerical work n	Büroarbeit

» Decentralisation of services can be found in certain functions, especially routine tasks such as clerical work.
Dezentralisierung von Dienstleistungen gibt es in manchen Aufgabenbereichen, besonders in Routinetätigkeiten wie Büroarbeit.

sophisticated [sə'fɪstɪkeɪtɪd] adj	hochentwickelt / hochrangig
back-office n	Abwicklungsstelle *(der innere Arbeitsbereich eines Unternehmens)*
back-office services	Dienstleistungen im Back Office-Bereich
office space n	Bürofläche
suburbanisation *BE* / suburbanization *AE* [sə‚bɜːbnaɪ'zeɪʃn] n	Suburbanisierung
counterurbanisation ['kaʊntə‚ɜːbnaɪ'zeɪʃn] n	Gegenurbanisierung

»

face-to-face meeting	Begegnung von Angesicht zu Angesicht

Suburbanisation is a term used to describe the movement of urban population from within towns and cities to the rural-urban fringe.
Unter Suburbanisierung versteht man die Abwanderung städtischer Bevölkerung aus der Stadt in das städtische Umland.

Counterurbanisation is a demographic and social process.
Gegenurbanisierung ist ein demographischer und sozialer Prozess.

Consumer and market

consumer n	Konsument(in) / Verbraucher(in)
consumerism [kən'sjuːmərɪzm] n	Konsum
consumer acceptance	Akzeptanz beim Verbraucher
consumer behaviour [kən'sjuːmebɪ‚heɪvjə]	Verbraucherverhalten
consumer spending	Verbraucherausgaben
potential consumer	potentielle(r) Konsument(in)
customer / client [klaɪənt] n	Kunde
purchaser ['pɜːtʃəsə] / buyer n	Käufer
prospective buyer [prə‚spektɪv'baɪə]	potentieller Käufer

»

A sudden shift in consumer behavio(u)r is always a threat.
Eine plötzliche Veränderung des Verbraucherverhaltens stellt immer eine Gefahr dar.

demand n	Nachfrage
supply n	Angebot
want n	Bedürfnis
desire [dɪ'zaɪə] n	Wunsch / Verlangen / Begehren

cost of living n	Lebenshaltungskosten
afford sth v	sich etw. leisten
lifestyle n	Lebensstil
standard of living n	Lebensstandard
disposable income n	frei verfügbares Einkommen
savings ratio [ˈseɪvɪŋzˌreɪʃiəʊ] n	Sparquote

》

The savings ratio is the ratio of savings by individuals and households to disposable income.
Die Sparquote ist das Verhältnis von Spareinlagen von Einzelpersonen und Haushalten zu ihren verfügbaren Einkommen.

thrift [θrɪft] n	Sparen / Wirtschaftlichkeit
thrift shop	Secondhandladen *(nicht kommerziell)*
impulse buy(ing) n	Spontankauf
impulse buyer n	Spontankäufer
compulsive buying n	Kaufzwang
hoard [hɔːd] v	horten / hamstern
hoarding n	Hamstern / Anhäufen / Horten
shopping spree [ˈʃɒpɪŋˌspriː] n	Einkaufstour
extravagance [ɪkˈstrævəɡəns] n	Luxus / Verschwendung
browse v	sich umsehen / stöbern
green consumerism n	umweltbewusstes Konsumverhalten
purchasing power [ˈpɜːtʃəsɪŋˌpaʊə] n	Kaufkraft

》

Persons with greater purchasing power are often able to afford a more luxurious lifestyle and a better standard of living.
Personen mit höherer Kaufkraft können sich häufig einen luxuriöseren Lebensstil und einen besseren Lebensstandard leisten.

survey [ˈsɜːveɪ] n	Untersuchung / Studie
survey [səˈveɪ] v	untersuchen
assess [əˈses] v	einschätzen / beurteilen
carry out v	durchführen / betreiben
distinct [dɪˈstɪŋt] adj	verschieden
niche [niːʃ] n	Nische

》

Demographic surveys examine distinct niches in various market segments.
Demographische Studien untersuchen verschiedene Nischen in unterschiedlichen Marksegmenten.

market research n	Marktforschung
consumer research n	Verbraucherforschung
marketing n	Marketing
marketable ['mɑːkɪtəbl] adj	marktfähig
competition n	Wettbewerb
competitor n	Konkurrent(in)
competitive adj	konkurrenzfähig
potential market n	potentieller Markt
consumption [kən'sʌmʃn] n	Konsum / Verbrauch
interview n	Interview
interviewer n	Interviewer(in)
market research interviewer	Marktforscherin
bias ['baɪəs] n	Befangenheit / vorgefasste Meinung
biased ['baɪəst] adj	voreingenommen
unbiased adj	unvoreingenommen
target group n	Zielgruppe
field research / primary market research n	Primärerhebung *(Studie mit eigenen Befragungen und Messungen in der Marktforschung)*
desk research n	Sekundärerhebung *(Marktstudie auf Basis bereits bestehender Daten)*
sales forecast n	Absatzprognose
subset ['sʌbset] n	Teilmenge
market segment [ˌmɑːkɪt'segmənt] n	Marksegment
market segmentation	Marktsegmentbildung

» The interviewers were trained to get unbiased information from the consumers.
Die Befrager waren ausgebildet, unvoreingenommene Informationen von Verbrauchern zu bekommen.

Market segmentation is done in order to focus on subsets of consumers with similar needs.
Marktsegmente werden gebildet, um sich auf Kundengruppen mit ähnlichen Bedürfnissen konzentrieren zu können.

social status / social class n	soziale Position / sozialer Status
stratified ['strætɪfaɪd] adj	geschichtet
systematic [ˌsɪstə'mætɪk] adj	systematisch
category n	Kategorie / Gruppe / Merkmalsklasse
maximise *BE* / maximize *AE* ['mæksɪmaɪz] v	maximieren
optimise *BE* / optimize *AE* v	optimieren
up-market adj	exklusiv / anspruchsvoll

3 Human environment › 3.4 Trade, services and consumer

down-market adj	Massen~ / Billig~
census ['sensəs] n	Volkszählung
pilot survey ['paɪlət‚sɜːveɪ] n	Pilotstudie / Vorlaufsstudie
consumer profile n	Verbraucherprofil
sample ['sɑːmpl] n	Probe
sample v	probieren / testen
sample of people	Querschnitt
quota sample	Quotenauswahlverfahren
free sample	kostenlose Warenprobe / Gratisprobe
marketing mix n	Marketing-Mix / Marketinginstrumentarium
promotion n	Werbung / Verkaufsförderung

»
    a random sample of consumers | stichprobenartig ausgewählte Konsumenten

The marketing mix is made up of the "four Ps": product, price, promotion and place.
Das Marketinginstrumentarium beinhaltet die „4 P" Produkt, Preis, Produktwerbung und Platzierung (Ort).

promotion scheme n	Verkaufsaktion
branding n	Markenkennzeichnung / Kennzeichnung
price-cutting n	Preissenkung
free gift n	Werbegeschenk / Geschenk
discount n	Rabatt
loss leader pricing n	Lockangebot

»
    Buy One Get One Free (BOGOF) | zwei Artikel zum Preis von einem

    point of sale advertising | Werbung am Verkaufsort

Loss leader pricing is the selling of popular products at a loss, in the hopes of attracting customers who will also buy other products.
Lockangebote sind beliebte Produkte, die mit Verlust verkauft werden, in der Erwartung Kunden anzulocken, die auch andere Produkte kaufen werden.

There are six main methods of sales promotion: BOGOF, discounts, competitions, free gifts, product trials and point of sale advertising.
Es gibt sechs wichtige Verkaufsförderungsmaßnahmen: BOGOF, Rabatte, Gewinnspiele, Werbegeschenke, Produktproben und Werbung am Verkaufsort.

after-sales service n	Kundendienst
price war n	Preiskrieg
price leadership n	Preisführerschaft

price discrimination n	Preisdiskriminierung
price plateau ['praɪsˌplætəʊ] n	Preisniveau
common pricing n	Preisabsprache
predatory pricing ['predətriˌpraɪsɪŋ] n	aggressive Preisgestaltung (Dumpingpreise ansetzen)

» hike up prices | Preise stark erhöhen

market-orientated adj	marktorientiert
brand loyalty n	Markentreue
sales gimmick ['seɪlzˌɡɪmɪk] n	Verkaufstrick
product placement n	Produktplatzierung (im Verkauf und in der Werbung)

» The company reduced costs in order to achieve a market-oriented price plateau.
Das Unternehmen senkte seine Kosten um zu einem marktorientierten Preisniveau zu gelangen.

consumer protection n	Verbraucherschutz
monopolies commission BE / antitrust agency AE [ˌæntɪˈtrʌstˌeɪdʒnsi] n	Kartellamt
price agreement / price fixing n	Preisabsprache

3.5 Ecology and economy

The social question

social ['səʊʃl] adj	Gesellschaft~ / gesellschaftlich / sozial
social evils ['səʊʃlˌiːvlz]	soziale Missstände
society n	Gesellschaft
agrarian society [əˈɡreəriənsəˌsaɪəti] / agricultural society	Agrargesellschaft
industrial society	Industriegesellschaft
misery ['mɪzri] n	Elend
destitute ['destɪtjuːt] adj	verarmt / mittellos / notleidend
population explosion n	Bevölkerungsexplosion
factory n	Fabrik
pauperism ['pɔːprɪzm] n	Pauperismus / Armut / Massenarmut
poverty ['pɒvəti] n	Armut
early industrialisation n	Frühindustrialisierung
livelihood ['laɪvlihʊd] n	Auskommen

epidemic [ˌepɪˈdemɪk] n	Epidemie
neglect [nɪˈglekt] n	Verwahrlosung
paid work force n	Lohnarbeiterschaft
working poor n	Erwerbsarme / Geringverdiener / „Working Poor"
support n	Unterstützung / Hilfe
public expense n	Staatskosten
poorhouse n	Armenhaus

》

the social question	die Soziale Frage
to live in poverty	in Armut leben
to fall into poverty	ins Elend geraten

Ireland was once referred to as Europe's "poorhouse".
Irland wurde einmal als das Armenhaus Europas bezeichnet.

Economic background

economy [ɪˈkɒnəmi] n	Wirtschaft
economic adj	wirtschaftlich
economist n	Wirtschaftsexperte
production n	Produktion
producer n	Produzent
capital [ˈkæpɪtl] n	Kapital
machinery [məˈʃiːnri] n	Maschinen
human labour n	menschliche Arbeitskraft
consumer n	Konsument(in) / Verbraucher(in)
goods n pl	Waren
service n	Dienstleistung
need n	Bedarf
basic need	Grundbedürfnis
landed property n	Grundbesitz

division of labour n	Arbeitsteilung
specialisation BE / specialization AE [ˌspeʃlaɪˈzeɪʃn] n	Spezialisierung
optimisation BE / optimization AE [ˌɒptɪmaɪˈzeɪʃn] n	Optimierung
simplification [ˌsɪmplɪfɪˈkeɪʃn] n	Vereinfachung
standardisation BE / standardization AE n	Standardisierung / Vereinheitlichung

mass production n	Massenproduktion
alienation [ˌeɪliə'neɪʃn] n	Entfremdung
alienation from work	Entfremdung von der Arbeit

market economy n	Marktwirtschaft
free-market economy	freie Marktwirtschaft
social market economy	soziale Marktwirtschaft
centrally planned economy	zentrale Planwirtschaft
command economy	Planwirtschaft
price mechanism n	Preismechanismus
pricing process n	Preisfindung
profit n	Gewinn
profit motive n	Gewinnmotiv
distribution [ˌdɪstrɪ'bjuːʃn] n	Verteilung

demand n	Nachfrage
supply n	Angebot
scarcity ['skeəsəti] n	Mangel / Knappheit
surplus ['sɜːpləs] n	Überangebot
oversupply n	Angebotsüberhang
oversupply v	ein Überangebot erzeugen
price drop n	Preisverfall
injustice [ɪn'dʒʌstɪs] n	Ungerechtigkeit
inequality [ˌɪnɪ'kwɒləti] n	Ungleichheit

» A surplus of goods leads to a price drop, whereas a scarcity leads to a rise in prices.
Ein Überangebot an Waren führt zu einem Preisverfall, wohingegen ein Mangel zu einem Preisanstieg führt.

Energy demand

energy n	Energie
energy demand	Energiebedarf
energy supply	Energieversorgung
energy scarcity ['enədʒɪˌskeəsəti]	Energieknappheit / Energiemangel
energy crisis ['enədʒɪˌkraɪsɪs]	Energiekrise
electricity n	Elektrizität
power supply n	Energieversorgung / Stromversorgung
power station / power plant AE n	Kraftwerk

3 Human environment › 3.5 Ecology and economy

generate v	erzeugen
generate electricity	Strom erzeugen

energy source n	Energieträger
primary (source of) energy n	Primärenergie
fossil fuel ['fɒsl͵fjuːel] n	fossiler Brennstoff
hard coal n	Steinkohle
brown coal n	Braunkohle
oil n	Erdöl
natural gas n	Erdgas
wind energy n	Windkraft
hydropower ['haɪdrəʊpaʊə] n	Wasserkraft
solar power [ˌsəʊlə'paʊə] / solar energy n	Sonnenenergie
nuclear power [ˌnjuːklɪə'paʊə] n	Kernenergie
geothermal energy ['ʤiːəʊˌθɜːml'enəʤi] n	geothermische Energie
wave power n	Wellenkraft
ocean current ['əʊʃn͵kʌrənt] n	Meeresströmung
tidal power [ˌtaɪdl'paʊə] n	Gezeitenkraft
tidal power station / tidal power plant	Gezeitenkraftwerk

secondary energy n	Sekundärenergie
transformation n	Umwandlung
effective energy / net energy n	Nutzenergie
electric potential energy n	elektrische Energie

fuel oil n	Heizöl
petrol ['petrl] n	Benzin
diesel ['diːzl] n	Diesel
briquette [brɪ'ket] n	Brikett
liquid gas [ˌlɪkwɪd'gæs] n	Flüssiggas
natural gas n	Erdgas
district heating n	Fernwärme

renewable adj	erneuerbar
non-renewable adj	nicht erneuerbar

alternative energies n	alternative Energiequellen
biomass [ˌbaɪəʊ'mæs] n	Biomasse
biodiesel n	Biodiesel
geothermal energy ['ʤiːəʊˌθɜːml'enəʤi] n	Erdwärme / geothermische Energie
wood pellet [wʊd'pelɪt] n	Holzpellet

» Older heating systems in houses are usually powered by fossil fuels, such as coal, gas, or oil.
Ältere Heizsysteme in Häusern werden oft mit fossilen Brennstoffen betrieben, wie beispielsweise Kohle, Gas oder Öl.
Newer technologies such as solar energy or geothermal systems may help reduce energy costs and prevent global warming.
Neuere Technologien wie Solarenergie oder Erdwärmesysteme können helfen, Energiekosten zu senken und die Erderwärmung zu stoppen.

Ecology and the environment

social adj	Sozial
social justice	soziale Gerechtigkeit
socially responsible	sozial verantwortlich
ecology [iː'kɒləʤi] n	Ökologie
ecological [ˌiːkə'lɒʤɪkl] adj	ökologisch
ecologically forward-looking	ökologisch zukunftsweisend
ground-breaking adj	zukunftsweisend
sustainable [sə'steɪnəbl] adj	zukunftsfähig / nachhaltig
unsustainable adj	unhaltbar / nicht aufrechtzuerhalten
sustainable development	nachhaltige Entwicklung

globalisation BE / globalization AE [ˌgləʊblaɪ'zeɪʃn] n	Globalisierung
consumption [kən'sʌmpʃn] n	Verbrauch / Konsum
economical adj	wirtschaftlich / ökonomisch / sparsam (im Verbrauch sein)
neo-liberalism [ˌniːəʊ'lɪbrlɪzm] n	Neoliberalismus
liberalisation BE / liberalization AE [ˌlɪbrlaɪzeɪʃn] n	Liberalisierung
deregulation n	Deregulierung
privatisation BE / privatization AE [ˌpraɪvɪtaɪ'eɪʃn] n	Privatisierung
exploitation [ˌeksplɔɪteɪʃn] n	Ausbeutung

environmental [ɪnˌvaɪərnmentl] adj	Umwelt~
environmental issues [ɪnˌvaɪərnmentl'ɪʃuːz]	Umweltprobleme
pollution [pə'luːʃn] n	Verschmutzung
pollute [pə'luːt] v	verschmutzen
fumes [fjuːmz] n pl	Abgase

3 Human environment › 3.5 Ecology and economy

emission [ɪ'mɪʃn] n	Emission / Ausstoß
exhaust fumes [ɪg'zɔːstˌfjuːmz] n	Abgase *(von Fahrzeugen)*
smog [smɒg] n	Smog
dumping n	Abladen von Müll
sewage ['suːɪdʒ] n	Abwasser
waste n	Müll / Abfall
household waste	Hausmüll
toxic waste ['tɒksɪkˌweɪst]	Giftmüll
nuclear waste [njuːkliəˌweɪst]	radioaktiver Müll
refuse ['refjuːs] / garbage *AE* n	Abfall / Müll
hazardous materials [ˌhæzədəsˌmə'tɪəriəls] n pl	gesundheitsschädliche Materialien / Gefahrgut
harmful n	schädlich

contamination [kənˌtæmɪ'neɪʃn] n	Verseuchung / Vergiftung / Verschmutzung
pollutant / contaminant n	Schadstoff
effluent ['efluənt] n	Abwasser
purify ['pjʊərɪfaɪ] v	reinigen
filter v	filtern
discharge ['dɪstʃɑːdʒ] v	einleiten
degradable [dɪ'greɪdəbl] adj	abbaubar / zersetzbar
non-degradable	unzersetzbar
biodegradable [ˌbaɪəʊdɪ'greɪdəbl] v	biologisch abbaubar
biodegradable waste	biologisch abbaubarer Müll

greenhouse effect n	Treibhauseffekt
greenhouse gas n	Treibhausgas
global warming n	globale Erwärmung *(der Erdatmosphäre)*
ozone ['əʊzəʊn] n	Ozon
ozone hole	Ozonloch
ozone layer	Ozonschicht
ozone depletion	Schädigung der Ozonschicht
chlorofluorocarbon (CFC) [ˌklɔːrəʊˌflɔːrəʊ'kɑːbn] [ˌsiːef'siː] n	Fluorchlorkohlenwasserstoff (FCKW)
methane ['miːθeɪn] n	Methan
carbon dioxide ['kɑːbndaɪ'ɒksaɪd] n	Kohlendioxid / CO_2

» CFC is a gas harmful to the ozone layer; it contributes to the decline of ozone in the Earth's stratosphere.
FCKW ist ein die Ozonschicht schädigendes Gas und es führt zur Verringerung des Ozongehalts in der Stratosphäre.

Environmental protection

protection n	Schutz
environmental protection n	Umweltschutz
conservation n	Umweltschutz
conservation law	Umweltschutzgesetz
environmental policy n	Umweltpolitik
environment minister / secretary of the environment *AE* n	Umweltminister
ministry for the environment / EPA (United States Environmental Protection Agency) *AE* n	Umweltministerium
environmentalist n	Umweltschützer

» In Great Britain the 'Department for Environment, Food and Rural Affairs' is responsible for the British environmental policy. In the US this department is known as 'Environment Protection Agency'.
In Großbritannien ist das ‚Department for Environment, Food and Rural Affairs' für die britische Umweltpolitik verantwortlich. In den USA wird dieses Ministerium ‚Environment Protection Agency' genannt.

environmentally friendly / environmentally sound adj	umweltschonend / umweltverträglich
organic product n	Bioprodukt / aus biologischem Anbau
energy-saving adj	energiesparend
treatment n	Behandlung
clean adj	sauber
unleaded [ʌn'lədɪd] adj	bleifrei
non-polluting adj	umweltfreundlich
ecosystem [iːkəʊˌsɪstəm] n	Ökosystem
ecological restriction n	ökologische Restriktion
environmental crisis n	Umweltkrise
green issues n pl	Umweltfragen

» So called "green products" (environmentally sound products) are identified by eco-labels.
Sogenannte "Grüne" Produkte (umweltverträgliche Produkte) werden mit Öko-Siegeln gekennzeichnet.

environmental damage n	Umweltzerstörung
time horizon [ˌtaɪmhə'raɪzn] n	Zeithorizont

3 Human environment › 3.6 Urban areas and urbanisation

efficient [ɪ'fɪʃnt] adj
  efficient technology
well-being / prosperity [prɒs'perəti] n
  economic well-being / economic prosperity
ecological viability [ˌiːkə'lɒdʒɪklˌvaɪə'bɪləti] n
generation n
  future generation
ecological barrier n
consumption [kən'sʌmʃn] n
  consumption of resources
  model of consumption
opulent society ['ɒpjələntsə'saɪəti] n
affluence model ['æfluəntsˌmɒdl] n
productivity n
global financial market n
demand for space n
drain of land resources n
restrict / limit v

effizient
  effiziente Technologie
Wohlstand
  materieller Wohlstand

ökologische Tragfähigkeit

Generation
  zukünftige Generation
ökologische Schranke
Verbrauch / Konsum
  Ressourcenverbrauch
  Konsummodell
opulente Gesellschaft
Wohlstandsmodell
Produktivität
globaler Finanzmarkt
Raumanspruch
Flächenverbrauch
einschränken

» Germany's environmental policy provides tax incentives to boost the sales of energy-saving cars and to secure a clean environment for future generations. Deutschlands Umweltpolitik setzt Steueranreize, um den Verkauf von energiesparenden Autos zu fördern und zukünftigen Generationen eine saubere Umwelt zu sichern.

3.6 Urban areas and urbanisation
Urban areas – rural areas

urban ['ɜːbn] adj
rural ['rʊəl] adj
country n
countryside n

städtisch / urban
ländlich
Land
Land

» to live in the countryside | auf dem Land leben

settlement n
residential district / residential area n
area of settlement / settled region n
suburb ['sʌbɜːb] n

Siedlung
Wohngebiet
Siedlungsgebiet
Vorort / Vorstadt

industrial area n	Industriegebiet
commercial zone [kəˈmɜːʃˌzəʊn] n	Gewerbegebiet
business district n	Geschäftsviertel
central business district (CBD) n	Hauptgeschäftszentrum (CBD)
city centre n	Innenstadt / Stadtzentrum

»
to live in the suburbs	in der Vorstadt leben
to commute to work	zur Arbeit pendeln

airport n	Flughafen
port n	Hafen
goods depot / freight yard [ˈfreitˌjɑːd] n	Güterbahnhof
container terminal n	Containerterminal
quay [kiː] n	Kaianlage
railway station / train station n	Bahnhof
sports complex n	Sportanlagen
stadium [ˈsteɪdiəm] n	Stadion
golf course [ˈgɒlfˌkɔːs] n	Golfplatz
exhibition centre n	Messezentrum
shopping centre n	Einkaufszentrum

factory n	Fabrik
warehouse [ˈweəhaʊs] n	Lagerhaus
parking area n	Parkplatz
refinery [rɪˈfaɪnri] n	Raffinerie
landfill n	Mülldeponie

rural settlement [ˌrʊəlˈsetlmənt] n	ländliche Siedlung
country life n	Landleben
agriculture [ˈægrɪkʌltʃə] n	Landwirtschaft
agricultural production	landwirtschaftliche Produktion
natural landscape n	Naturlandschaft
cultural landscape n	Kulturlandschaft *(durch menschliche Aktivität überformt)*
farm n	Bauernhof
ruralise [ˈrʊəlaɪz] v	sich auf Landleben umstellen

town hall n	Rathaus
convention centre [kənˈvenʃnˌsentə] n	Kongresszentrum
courthouse n	Gerichtsgebäude
office building n	Bürogebäude
post office n	Postamt

3 Human environment › 3.6 Urban areas and urbanisation

police station n	Polizeirevier
hospital n	Krankenhaus
fire station n	Feuerwache
museum n	Museum
theatre n	Theater
opera n	Oper
cinema n	Kino
educational institution n	Bildungseinrichtung
university n	Universität
library n	Bibliothek
school n	Schule
church n	Kirche
cathedral n	Dom / Kathedrale
cemetery ['semətri] n	Friedhof
pattern n	Muster
form n	Form
shape n	Form
site n	Ort / Stelle
situation n	Lage / Situation
function n	Funktion
facility n	Möglichkeit / Funktion / Einrichtung
hierarchy ['haɪərɑːki] n	Hierarchie
change n	Wechsel

» The facilities of the CBD include shopping, offices, such as banks or administration, cultural facilities, and many more.
Die Einrichtungen des CBD beinhalten Einkaufsmöglichkeiten, Büros, wie Banken oder Verwaltung, kulturelle Einrichtungen und vieles mehr.

settlement hierarchy n	Siedlungshierarchie
hamlet ['hæmlət] n	Weiler
village n	Dorf
small town n	Kleinstadt
large town n	Großstadt
city n	Stadt
primate city ['praɪmeɪtˌsɪti] n	Primatstadt
capital city n	Hauptstadt / Kapitale
shanty town ['ʃæntiˌtaʊn] n	Elendssiedlung / Barackensiedlung
slum n	Slum / Elendsviertel / Marginalsiedlung
corrugated-iron hut [ˌkɒrəɡeɪtɪd'aɪənˌhʌt] n	Wellblechhütte

workers' housing estate n	Arbeitersiedlung
nucleated village ['njuːklɪeɪtɪdˌvɪlɪʤ] n	Haufendorf *(planlos entwickeltes Dorf)*
linear village n	Reihendorf / Zeilendorf
street village n	Straßendorf
round village n	Rundling / Runddorf
village built around a green n	Angerdorf
industrial village n	Industriedorf
scattered settlement n	Streusiedlung
working-class town n	Arbeiterstadt
strip city n	Bandstadt
mining town n	Bergbaustadt
cathedral town n	Domstadt
fortress town n	Festungsstadt
garden city n	Gartenstadt *(nach E. Howard)*
gold mining town / gold boom town n	Goldgräberstadt
harbour city ['hɑːbəˌsɪti] n	Hafenstadt
trading city n	Handelsstadt
Hanseatic town [ˌhænsi'ætɪkˌtaʊn] n	Hansestadt
spa town [ˌspɑː'taʊn] n	Kurstadt
"sun city" n	Rentnerstadt *(im Süden der USA)*
capital (city) n	Hauptstadt
small town n	Kleinstadt
medium-sized town n	Mittelstadt
upper town n	Oberstadt
large town n	Großstadt
metropolis [mə'trɒpəlɪs] n	Metropole
metropolitan area [ˌmɛtrə'pɒlɪtnˌeərɪə] n	Metropolraum
satellite town [ˌsætlaɪt'taʊn] / spill over town *BE* n	Satellitenstadt
dormitory town [ˌdɔːmɪtri'taʊn] n	Schlafstadt
cosmopolitan city [ˌkɒzmə'pɒlɪtnˌsɪti] / world city / global city n	Weltstadt

» Hamburg, Bremen, and Rostock are old German Hanseatic towns.
Hamburg, Bremen und Rostock sind alte deutsche Hansestädte.
Millions of Japanese employees commute daily from dormitory towns in the metropolitan suburbs to their work place in the city centre.
Millionen japanischer Angestellter pendeln täglich aus Schlafstädten in den Vororten der Metropolen zu ihrem Arbeitsplatz im Zentrum.

3 Human environment › 3.6 Urban areas and urbanisation

Indicators for cities

size [saɪz] n	Größe / Ausmaß
population size	Bevölkerungszahl
inhabitant [ɪn'hæbitnt] n	Einwohner
area n	Gebiet / Fläche
density n	Dichte
population density	Bevölkerungsdichte
housing density	Bebauungsdichte
function n	Funktion
political function	politische Funktion
economic function	wirtschaftliche Funktion
religious function	religiöse Funktion
supply n	Versorgung
distribution n	Distribution / Verteilung
surplus of importance n	Bedeutungsüberschuss
operational area n	Funktionsraum
classification n	Gliederung
utilisation BE / utilization AE [ˌjuːtlaɪ'zeɪʃn] n	Nutzung

» pattern of utilisation | Struktur der Nutzung

use n	Nutzung
civil use	zivile Nutzung
residential district n	Wohngebiet
industrial estate n	Gewerbegebiet / Industriegebiet
central business district (CBD) n	Hauptgeschäftszentrum
settlement system n	Siedlungsstruktur
land use pattern n	Flächennutzung
residential [ˌrezɪ'denʃl] adj	Wohn~
residential building n	Wohngebäude
factory n	Fabrik
shop n	Laden
store / department store n	Kaufhaus / Warenhaus
Social-spatial adj	sozialräumlich
upper-class residential area n	Oberschichtwohngebiet
slum [slʌm] n	Marginalsiedlung

» structure of urban development | Raum- und Siedlungsstruktur
social and geographic differentiation | sozialräumliche Gliederung (räumliche Gliederung nach baulichen und sozialen Merkmalen)

economic structure [ˌiːkəˈnɒmɪk ˈstrʌktʃə] n | Wirtschaftsstruktur
sector [ˈsektə] n | Sektor
  primary sector | primärer Sektor
  secondary sector | sekundärer Sektor
  tertiary sector | tertiärer Sektor
  quaternary sector | quartärer Sektor
  informal sector | informeller Sektor

population structure n | Bevölkerungsstruktur
single-person household n | Einpersonenhaushalt
multi-person-household n | Mehrpersonenhaushalt
ethnic minority [ˈeθnɪkˌmaɪˈnɒrəti] n | ethnische Minderheit

social structure n | Sozialstruktur
worker n | Arbeiter
employee n | Angestellte(r)
lifestyle group n | Lebensstilgruppe

interdependency [ˌɪntədɪˈpendənsi] n | gegenseitige Abhängigkeit
waste disposal n | Entsorgung
recreation [ˌrekriˈeɪʃn] n | Naherholung
(human) labour BE / labor AE [ˈleɪbə] n | Arbeitskräfte
  labour resource | verfügbare Arbeitskräfte
  labour force potential | Arbeitskräftepotenzial
spatial interaction [speɪʃlˌɪntəˈæktʃn] n | räumliche Verflechtung
crossroads n pl | Knotenpunkt
hub [hʌb] n | Drehscheibe

» dependence on other regions | Abhängigkeit von anderen Regionen

3 Human environment › 3.6 Urban areas and urbanisation

Dwellings

flat *BE* / apartment *AE* n	Wohnung / Apartment
freehold apartment / condominium *AE* n	Eigentumswohnung
multiple-family dwelling n	Mehrfamilienhaus
block of flats *BE* / apartment building *AE* n	Wohnblock
single family house / single family home *AE* n	Einfamilienhaus
detached house [dɪˈtætʃtˌhaʊs] n	freistehendes Einfamilienhaus
semi-detached house [ˌsemɪdɪˈtætʃtˌhaʊs] / duplex [ˈduːpleks] *AE* n	Doppelhaushälfte
two-family house n	Zweifamilienhaus
terraced house [ˈterɪstˌhaʊs] / row house *AE* n	Reiheneinfamilienhaus
end terrace n	Reiheneinfamilienendhaus

Traffic

motorway / highway *AE* n	Autobahn
motorway intersection / interchange n	Autobahnkreuz
kerb [kɜːb] *BE* / curb [kɜːb] *AE* n	Bordstein
pavement *BE* / sidewalk *AE* [ˈpeɪvmənt] n	Bürgersteig
thoroughfare [ˈtʌrəfeə] n	Durchgangsstraße
one-way street n	Einbahnstraße
bridge n	Brücke
crash barrier [ˈkræʃˌbæriə] n	Leitplanke
ring road *BE* / beltway *AE* n	Ringstraße
taxi stand / taxi rank n	Taxistand
tunnel [ˈtʌnl] n	Tunnel
pedestrian precinct [pɪˈdestriənˌpriːsɪŋkt] n	Fußgängerzone
speed hump [spiːdˌhʌmp] n	Straßenschwelle / Bodenschwelle
elevated railway n	Hochbahn
railway bridge n	Eisenbahnbrücke
maglev [ˈmæglev] / magnetic levitation [mægˈnetɪkˌlevɪˈteɪʃn] n	Magnetschwebebahn
harbour *BE* / habor *AE* [ˈhɑːbə] / port [ˈpɔːt] n	Hafen

ferry ['feri] n	Fähre
ferry terminal	Fährterminal
marina [məˈriːnə] n	Yachthafen
airport n	Flughafen
airplane n	Flugzeug
hangar [ˈhæŋgə] n	Hangar
dirigible [ˈdɪrɪdʒəbl] / airship n	Luftschiff / Zeppelin
dirigible hangar	Luftschiffhangar
runway n	Rollbahn

Infrastructure

infrastructure [ˈɪnfrəˌstrʌktʃə] n	Infrastruktur
services n pl	Dienstleistung
facilities [fəˈsɪlətiz] n pl	Einrichtung / Anlage
function v	funktionieren
economy [ɪˈkɒnəmi] n	Wirtschaft
society n	Gesellschaft

transport infrastructure n	Verkehrsinfrastruktur
public transport n	öffentlicher Transport (ÖPNV)
pedestrian crossing [pɪˈdestriənˌkrɒsɪŋ] n	Fußgängerüberweg
traffic lights n pl	Verkehrsampel
roadway n	Fahrbahn
central reservation n	Mittelstreifen
street light n	Straßenlaterne
pavement [ˈpeɪvmənt] n	Bürgersteig

energy infrastructure n	Energieinfrastruktur
power supply n	Stromversorgung
electricity cable n	Stromversorgungskabel
gas supply n	Gasversorgung
gas pipe n	Gasrohr

water infrastructure n	Wasserversorgungsinfrastruktur
water main n	Trinkwasserleitung
water supply n	Wasserversorgung
fire hydrant [ˈfaɪəˌhaɪdrənt] n	Hydrant
surface water drain n	Regenwasserabfluss

waste management infrastructure n	Abfallentsorgungsinfrastruktur
sewage disposal [ˈsuːɪdʒˌdɪˈspəʊzl] n	Abwasserentsorgung
recycling n	Recycling / Wiederverwertung

sewer ['səʊə] n	Abwasserkanal
main sewer	Mischwasserkanal
communications infrastructure n	Kommunikationsinfrastruktur
telephone cable n	Telefonkabel

Cities in different historical and cultural environments

cultural environment n	Kulturkreis
region n	Region
world region n	Weltregion

ancient world [ˌeɪnʃnt'wɜːld] n	Antike
polity n	Polis
Roman Empire n	Römisches Reich
planned city n	geplante Stadt
Middle Ages n	Mittelalter
medieval [ˌmədi'iːvl] adj	mittelalterlich

townspeople n	Stadtbewohner / Bürger
town wall n	Stadtmauer
status symbol n	Statussymbol
independence n	Unabhängigkeit
wealth [welθ] n	Wohlstand
stone wall n	Steinmauer
walkway n	Fußgängerweg
tower n	Turm
gate n	Tor
gatehouse	Torhaus

toll n	Wegegeld / Zoll
street n	Straße
main street	Hauptstraße
side street	Seitenstraße
market place n	Marktplatz
market stall	Marktstand
haymarket ['heɪˌmɑːkɪt]	Heumarkt
coal market	Kohlenmarkt
weighbeam ['weɪbiːm] / weighbridge n	Wiegebalken / Waage

pillory ['pɪləri] n	Pranger
announcement [ə'naʊnsmənt] n	Bekanntmachung
public announcement	öffentliche Bekanntmachung
punishment n	Bestrafung

execution [ˌeksɪ'kjuːʃn] n	Hinrichtung

timber frame n	Fachwerk
timber-framed / half-timbered adj	Fachwerk~
wattle ['wɒtl] n	Flechtwerk
daub [dɔːb] n	Lehmbewurf / Lehmverstrich
wattle and daub wall	Flechtwerkwand mit Lehmbewurf
gable ['geɪbl] n	Giebel
gables facing the street	giebelständig
eave ['iːv] n	Traufrinne / Dachrinne
eaves facing the street	traufständig
roof n	Dach
thatched roof [θætʃt'ruːf]	Reetdach / Strohdach
tiled roof [taɪld'ruːf]	Ziegeldach

» In medieval towns the gables usually faced the street.
In mittelalterlichen Städten waren die Häuser normalerweise giebelständig gebaut.

shed [ʃed] n	Schuppen
well n	Brunnen
garden n	Garten
shop n	Geschäft / Laden
goods n pl	Waren
church n	Kirche
parish church	Pfarrkirche
monastery n	Kloster

merchant [mɜːtʃnt] n	Kaufmann
craftsman n	Handwerker
labourer *BE* / laborer *AE* n	Arbeiter
armourer *BE* / armorer *AE* ['ɑːmərə] n	Waffenschmied
carpenter ['kɑːpəntə] n	Zimmermann
cooper ['kuːpə] n	Küfer *(stellt Fässer her)*
draper ['dreɪpə] n	Tuchhändler
embroider [ɪm'brɔɪdə] n	Sticker(in)
glover ['glʌvə] n	Handschuhmacher
hosier ['həʊzɪə] n	Wirkwarenhändler / Strumpfwarenhändler
furrier ['fʌrɪə] n	Kürschner
potter n	Töpfer
shoemaker n	Schuhmacher
smith n	Schmied
locksmith n	Schlosser

3 Human environment › 3.6 Urban areas and urbanisation

tanner n	Gerber
blacksmith n	Hufschmied
tailor n	Schneider
weaver n	Weber
baker n	Bäcker
butcher n	Metzger
fishmonger n	Fischhändler
grocer n	Lebensmittelgeschäft
poulterer ['pəʊltrə] n	Geflügelhändler
vintner n	Weinhändler

castle n	Burg
medieval castle	mittelalterliche Burg
Norman castle	normannische Burg
Carolingian castle	karolingische Burg
Ghibelline castle ['gɪbɪlaɪnˌkɑːsl]	staufische Burg / Stauferburg
castle siege ['kɑːslˌsiːdʒ] n	Burgbelagerung
moat [məʊt] n	Burggraben
castle gate n	Burgtor
castle tower n	Burgturm
drawbridge n	Zugbrücke
keep n	Bergfried
dungeon ['dʌndʒn] n	Kerker

Latin American city n	lateinamerikanische Stadt
gridiron street pattern ['grɪdaɪənˌstriːtˌpætn] n	Rechtecksmuster *(von Straßen)*
grid plan n	schachbrettartiger (Stadt-)Plan
chequered pattern [ˌtʃekəd'pætn] n	Schachbrettmuster
central plaza n	Plaza
government ['gʌvnmənt] n	Regierung
administration n	Verwaltung

African city n	afrikanische Stadt
apartheid [ə'pɑːtaɪt] n	Apartheid / Rassentrennung
core [kɔː] n	Kern
commerce ['kɒmɜːs] n	Handel
residential zone n	Wohngebiet
government sector n	Verwaltungssektor
indigenous [ɪn'dɪdʒɪnəs] adj	einheimisch
mixed adj	gemischt
elite [ɪ'liːt] n	Elite
shanty ['ʃænti] n	Shanty / Wellblechhütte
shanty town	Elendsviertel / Slum

township n	Township *(während Apartheid angelegte abseits gelegene Siedlungen für nicht-weiße Bevölkerung)* / Gemeinde

Islamic city n	orientalisch-islamische Stadt
citadel ['sɪtədel] n	Zitadelle
mosque [mɒsk] n	Moschee
Fridays mosque	Freitagsmoschee
central mosque	Zentralmoschee
local mosque	lokale Moschee *(in Subzentren)*
madrasah [mə'dræʃə] n	Medrese *(Koranschule einer Moschee)*
food market n	Lebensmittelmarkt
local market n	ländlicher Markt
bazaar [bə'zɑː] n	Basar
city wall n	Stadtmauer
burial ground n	Friedhof
public bath / hammam ['hæmæm] n	öffentliche Badeanstalt

Asian city n	asiatische Stadt
port ['pɔːt] n	Hafen
fort [fɔːt] n	Festung / Fort
wholesale market n	Großhandelsmarkt
religious enclave n	Viertel einer bestimmten Religion
linguistic cluster n	Viertel einer bestimmten Sprachgruppe
caste / caste group n	Kaste
caste system	Kastenwesen / Kastensystem
kampong [kam'pɒŋ] n	Kampung / Kampong *(malaiisches Dorf)*

North American city n	US-Amerikanische Stadt
suburbanisation [sə‚bɜːbənaɪ'zeɪʃn] n	Suburbanisierung
Central Business District (CBD) n	Hauptgeschäftszentrum / Kerngebiet
transition zone n	Übergangsbereich
hinterland ['hɪntəlænd] n	Umland
downtown n	Innenstadt
uptown n	Vorort / Villenviertel
skyscraper n	Wolkenkratzer
high-rise n	Hochhaus
apartment building n	Wohnblock
gated community n	bewachtes Wohnviertel *(mit Schranken an den Zugängen)*
edge city n	Edge City *(multifunktionales Außenstadtzentrum)*
chequered pattern [‚tʃekəd'pætn] n	Schachbrettmuster

173

» The Manhattan city plan is one of the most famous grid plans ever. The Streets run at right angles to each other, forming a grid that looks like a chessboard.
Der Stadtplan von Manhattan ist einer der berühmtesten aller schachbrettförmigen Stadtpläne. Die Straßen laufen rechtwinklig zueinander und bilden dabei ein Gitternetz, das einem Schachbrett gleicht.

Central-place theory

central-place theory n	Theorie der Zentralen Orte
economic determinism n	ökonomischer Determinismus

settlement n	Siedlung
settlement hierarchy [ˌˈsetlmənt ˌhaɪəraːki]	Siedlungshierarchie
first-order settlement n	Ort unterer Ordnung
hamlet n	Marktort / Weiler
second-order settlement n	Ort mittlerer Ordnung
village n	Dorf
third-order settlement n	Ort höherer Ordnung
town n	Stadt
city n	Stadt
centre *BE* / center *AE* n	Zentrum
lowest-order centre	Unterzentrum / ländliches Unterzentrum
low-order centre	Grundzentrum
middle-order centre	Mittelzentrum
higher-order centre	Oberzentrum
township centre	Amtsort

isotropic surface [ˌaɪsəˈtrɒpikˌsɜːfɪs] n	unbegrenzte und ebene Fläche
distance n	Abstand / Distanz
regular distance	gleichmäßiger Abstand
transport costs n pl	Transportkosten
rural region n	ländliche Region
catchment area n	Einzugsbereich / Einzugsgebiet
circular catchment area n	(kreis-)runder Einzugsbereich

hexagon [ˈheksəgən] n	Hexagon / Achteck
market area n	Absatzgebiet / Marktgebiet
marketing principle n	Marktprinzip

» The catchment area of a school is rather small, as it mainly consists of the surrounding neighbourhoods, while the catchment area of an airport is usually rather large.
Das Einzugsgebiet einer Schule ist normalerweise eher klein, da es hauptsächlich aus den angrenzenden (Wohn-)Vierteln besteht, während das Einzugsgebiet eines Flughafens normalerweise eher groß ist.

Burgess' concentric model n	Burgess Modell der konzentrischen Ringe
loop [luːp] n	Stadtzentrum
migrant ['maɪgrnt] n	Migrant / Zuwanderer

»
second generation immigrant	zweite Generation der Zuwanderer

residential zone n	Mittelschicht-Wohnzone
zone of working people's homes n	Arbeiterwohnzone
manufacturing zone n	Industriezone
commuting zone [kə'mjuːtɪŋˌzəʊn] n	Pendlerzone
commute n	Pendelstrecke
commute v	pendeln
transition zone / transitional zone n	Übergangszone
social class n	soziale Schicht
landlord / landlady n	Vermieter(in)
tenant ['tenənt] n	Mieter
low-density housing n	Gebiet mit geringer Wohndichte
light manufacturing n	Leichtindustrie
low-class residential n	Wohngebiete der Unterschicht
medium-class residential n	Wohngebiete der Mittel- und Oberschicht

Hoyt's sector model n	Hoyt'sches Sektorenmodell
transport route n	Transportweg
routeway n	Verkehrsweg

Harris and Ullman's multiple nuclei model n	Mehrkernemodell nach Harris und Ullman
nucleus ['njuːklɪəs] pl, nuclei n	Kern
suburb ['sʌbɜːb] n	Vorort

3 Human environment › 3.6 Urban areas and urbanisation

Stages in urbanisation

rapid urbanisation [ˌræpidˌɜːbnaɪˈzeɪʃn] n	schnelles Wachstum
population concentration n	Bevölkerungskonzentration / Bevölkerungsverdichtung
rural area [ˌrʊəlˈeəriə] n	ländlicher Raum
urban area [ˌɜːbnˈeəriə] n	städtischer Raum
suburbanisation [seˌbɜːbənaɪˈzeɪʃn] n	Suburbanisierung
decline [dɪˈklaɪn] n	Niedergang / Verfall
counter urbanisation [ˌkaʊntəˈɜːbənaɪˈzeɪʃn] n	Desurbanisierung
reurbanisation n	Reurbanisierung
stabilise v	stabilisieren
stimulate v	stimulieren

»

outwards growth	nach außen gerichtetes Wachstum
adjacent rural area	angrenzender ländlicher Raum

Effects of urbanisation

poverty [ˈpɒvəti] n	Armut
poverty line	Armutsgrenze
subsidy [ˈsʌbsɪdi] n	Subvention / Hilfsgelder
overcrowded adj	überbevölkert / überfüllt
urban sprawl [ˌɜːbnˈsprɔːl] n	Zersiedelung

»

live below the poverty line		unterhalb der Armutsgrenze leben
receive / grant	a subsidy / eine Subvention	erhalten / gewähren

Garden City Movement n	Gartenstadtbewegung
New Towns n	New Towns *(in GB geplante Städte zur Entlastung der Kernstädte)*
green belt n	Grüngürtel
derelict land [ˈderelɪktˌlænd] n	Brache / Brachland
out-migration n	Abwanderung von Industrie aus den Zentren
convert v	umwandeln
negative spiral n	Negativspirale

proximity [prɒk'sɪməti] n		Nähe
fabric of a building n		Bausubstanz
historic building stock		historische Bausubstanz
restore n		renovieren
improve n		verbessern
gentrification [ˌdʒentrɪfɪ'keɪʃn] n		Gentrifizierung

Regional planning and spatial development

regional development planning n		Raumordnung
Regional Planning Act		Raumordnungsgesetz
regional development plan		Raumordnungsplan
regional planning guideline		Raumordnungsrichtlinie
spatial development n		Raumentwicklung
sustainable spatial development		nachhaltige Raumentwicklung
spatial planning at regional level		regionale Raumordnung
European Spatial Development Perspective (ESDP) n		Europäisches Raumentwicklungskonzept (EUREK)
spatial relevance n		Raumwirksamkeit
spatial research n		Raumforschung
land use n		Landnutzung
spatial fragmentation n		Raumfragmentierung
spatial structure n		Raumgefüge
spatial pattern n		Raummuster
spatial compatibility n		Raumverträglichkeit
waste of space n		Raumverschwendung

---

space-oriented adj		raumbezogen
activity n		Aktivität
behaviour BE / behavior AE [bɪ'heɪvjə] n		Verhaltensweise
intervention [ˌɪntə'venʃn] n		Eingriff
public authorities n pl		öffentliche Hand
changing the spatial structure adj		raumverändernd
regional planning n		Raumplanung
measure ['meʒə] / action n		Maßnahme
examine / check v		prüfen
fathom sth (out) ['fæðm] v		(etw.) ergründen

» A regional planning act provides the framework for spatial development in a certain area.
Ein Raumordnungsgesetz gibt die Rahmenbedingungen der Raumentwicklungen eines bestimmten Gebietes vor.

Spatial analysis: indicators

spatial analysis n	Raumanalyse
soil fertility [sɔɪl,fə'tɪləti] n	Bodenfruchtbarkeit
abundance of species [ə'bʌndənsəv'spiːʃiːz] n	Artenvielfalt
stretch of water n	Gewässer
slope [sləʊp] n	Hangneigung
employee [ɪm'plɔɪiː] / employed persons n	Beschäftigte(r) / Angestelle(r)
employment structure n	Beschäftigtenstruktur
per capita income n	Pro-Kopf-Einkommen
headquarters n	Firmenhauptsitz
industry structure n	Branchenstruktur
age structure / age distribution n	Altersstruktur
commuter stream [kə'mjuːtəstriːm] n	Pendlerstrom
habitat density n	Siedlungsdichte

3.7 World development: stages and indicators

Stages

development [dɪ'veləpmənt] n	Entwicklung
world development	Weltentwicklung
developing country n	Entwicklungsland
underdeveloped country	unterentwickeltes Land
industrial(ised) country [ɪn'dʌstriəlaɪzd‚kʌntri] n	Industrieland

north-south divide [‚nɔːθ'saʊθdɪ'vaɪd] n	Nord-Süd-Gefälle
rich adj	reich
poor adj	arm

decline [dɪ'klaɪn] v	zurückgehen
decrease [dɪ'kriːs] v	zurückgehen / abnehmen
crash v	abstürzen
collapse [kə'læps] v	zusammenbrechen
drop v	fallen
plummet ['plʌmɪt] v	stürzen
fall, fell, fallen v	fallen
plunge [plʌndʒ] v	stürzen / fallen
slide v	abrutschen / abfallen
weaken ['wiːkn] v	schwächen

»

	to be in decline to be on the decline	nachlassen / zurückgehen	
plunge ... lose ground ... decline ...	dramatically spectacularly considerably	dramatisch außergewöhnlich beträchtlich	... stürzen ... an Boden verlieren ... zurückgehen
Prices are on the decrease.		Die Preise lassen nach.	

The Price of sth is on the increase / decrease.
Der Preis von etw. lässt nach / steigt an.

increase [ɪnˈkriːs] v — ansteigen / wachsen / zunehmen
rise v — ansteigen
climb v — ansteigen
soar [sɔː] v — sprunghaft ansteigen
gain v — dazu gewinnen
surge [sɜːdʒ] v — plötzlich ansteigen
jump v — springen
rally [ˈræli] v — sich erholen
strengthen [ˈstreŋθn] v — stärken

»

rocket upwards	in die Höhe schießen

flatten out [ˌflætnˈaʊt] v — (sich) verflachen
hold steady [ˌhəʊldˈstedi] v — (sich) stabil halten
recover [rɪˈkʌvə] v — sich erholen
level off v — (sich) einpendeln
stabilise BE / stabilize AE [ˈsteɪblaɪz] v — (sich) stabilisieren

slow adj — langsam
disastrous [dɪˈzɑːstrəs] adj — katastrophal / verheerend
steady adj — gleichmäßig
massive adj — massiv / enorm
slight adj — leicht
alarming adj — besorgniserregend
perilous [ˈperɪləs] adj — gefährlich
sharp adj — scharf
rapid adj — schnell
gradual adj — graduell / stufenweise
heavy adj — schwer / stark

3 Human environment › 3.7 World development: stages and indicators

» Gold prices hold steady, while other metals surge.
Die Goldpreise halten sich stabil, während andere Metalle stark ansteigen.

economy [ɪˈkɒnəmi] n	Wirtschaft
industrial market economy	Industrieland mit Marktwirtschaft
centrally planned economy	Planwirtschaft

»

high income oil exporter	ölexportierendes Land mit hohen Gewinnen
middle income developing country	Entwicklungsland mit mittlerem Einkommen
low income developing country	Entwicklungsland mit niedrigem Einkommen

Stages in development

MEDC – more economically developed country	wirtschaftlich stark entwickeltes Land
LEDC – less economically developed country	wirtschaftlich weniger entwickeltes Land
NIC – newly industrialising country	Schwellenland (NIC)
LDC – less developed country	wenig entwickeltes Land
LDC – least developed country	am wenigsten entwickeltes Land
low income country	Länder mit niedrigem Einkommen
middle income country	Länder mit mittlerem Einkommen
high income country	Länder mit hohem Einkommen

»

Asian Tigers	Tigerstaaten

Indices

HDI – human development index n	HDI – Index der menschlichen Entwicklung
HDR – human development report n	HDR – Bericht zur menschlichen Entwicklung
average [ˈævrɪdʒ] adj	durchschnittlich
average n	Durchschnitt
life expectancy n	Lebenserwartung
level of education n	Bildungsgrad / Wissensstand
adult literacy [ˌædʌltˈlɪtrəsi] n	Erwachsenenalphabetisierungsrate
standard of living n	Lebensstandard
purchasing power [ˌpɜːtʃəsɪŋˈpaʊə] n	Kaufkraft
purchasing power parity (ppp)	Kaufkraftparität (KKP)

cost of living n	Lebenshaltungskosten

gross adj	brutto
GNP – gross national product n	BSP – Bruttosozialprodukt
GDP – gross domestic product n	BIP – Bruttoinlandsprodukt
GNI – gross national income n	BNE – Bruttonationaleinkommen

consumption n	Verbrauch / Konsum
investment n	Investition
gross investment [ˌgrəʊsɪn'vesmənt] n	Bruttoinvestition
government spending n	Staatsausgaben
net foreign investment n	Gesamtwert ausländischer Investitionen
value n	Wert
output value	Produktionswert
total value	Gesamtwert
per capita income n	pro Kopf Einkommen

The GDP

GDP = consumption + gross investment + government spending + (exports – imports)
BIP = Konsum + Bruttoinvestitionen + Staatsausgaben + (Exporte – Importe)

urbanisation *BE* / urbanization *AE* [ˌɜːbnaɪ'zeɪʃn] n	Verstädterung / Urbanisierung
literacy rate ['lɪtrəsiˌreɪt] n	Alphabetisierungsgrad
infant mortality rate [ˌɪnfəntmɔː'tælətiˌreɪt] n	Kindersterblichkeitsrate
population n	Bevölkerung
population growth rate [ˌpɒpjə'leɪʃngrəʊθˌreɪt]	Bevölkerungswachstumsrate
urban population	Stadtbevölkerung
rural population	Landbevölkerung
farming population	Landwirtschaft betreibende Bevölkerung
birth rate n	Geburtenrate
death rate n	Sterberate
natural increase n	natürlicher Zuwachs
natural increase rate	natürliche Zuwachsrate
calorie supply ['kælrisəˌplaɪ] n	Kalorienversorgung
calorie intake n	Kalorienaufnahme
wealth n	Wohlstand / Reichtum
health care n	medizinische Versorgung
primary health care	medizinische Grundversorgung

3 Human environment › 3.7 World development: stages and indicators

Statistics

GDP per capita BIP pro Kopf	**The total value of the goods and services produced in a country in a year divided by the population.** Der Gesamtwert der Güter und Dienstleistungen, die in einem Land in einem Jahr produziert werden, geteilt durch die Bevölkerung.
Birth rate Geburtenrate	**The number of births per 1,000 people per year.** Die Anzahl der Geburten im Jahr pro 1000 Einwohner.
Death rate Sterblichkeitsrate	**The number of deaths per 1,000 people per year.** Die Anzahl der Todesfälle im Jahr pro 1000 Einwohner.
Natural increase Natürliches Wachstum	**The birth rate minus the death rate for a place, given as a percentage of the total population.** Die Geburtsrate minus der Sterblichkeitsrate für einen Raum, als Prozentsatz an der gesamten Bevölkerung angegeben.
Infant mortality Kindersterblichkeit	**The number of babies out of every 1,000 born alive who die before their first birthday.** Die Anzahl aller Neugeborenen unter 1000 Lebendgeburten, die vor dem ersten Geburtstag sterben.
Life expectancy (at birth) Lebenserwartung	**How many years a newborn can expect to live, on average.** Jahre, die ein Neugeborenes im Durchschnitt zu leben erwarten kann.
People per doctor / Access to health care Einwohner pro Arzt / Zugang zum Gesundheitssystem	**The number of people who have to share one doctor. The percentage of the population with access to health care.** Anzahl der Menschen, die sich einen Arzt teilen. Prozentzahl der Bevölkerung mit Zugang zum Gesundheitssystem.
Adult literacy Erwachsenen- alphabetisierungsrate	**The percentage of persons aged 15 and over who can read and write.** Prozentsatz der Bevölkerung ab dem 15. Lebensjahr, die lesen und schreiben können.
Farming population In der Landwirtschaft tätige Bevölkerung	**The percentage of population having agricultural jobs.** Prozentualer Anteil der Bevölkerung mit landwirtschaftlichen Berufen.
Urban population Stadtbevölkerung	**The percentage of population living in urban areas.** Prozentualer Anteil der Bevölkerung, die in städtischen Gebieten lebt.

» people per doctor | Anzahl der Menschen pro Arzt

Factors

history n	Geschichte
colony n	Kolonie
colonisation BE [ˌkɒlənaɪˈzeɪʃn] / colonization AE n	Kolonialisierung
slave n	Sklave
slave trade	Sklavenhandel
triangular trade [traɪˈæŋgjələˌtreɪd] n	Atlantischer Dreieckshandel

labour BE / labor AE [ˈleɪbə] n	Arbeitskräfte
strong adj	stark
capable [ˈkeɪpəbl] adj	fähig / geeignet
goods n pl	Waren
exchange n	Austausch
gun n	Gewehr / Pistole
alcohol n	Alkohol
textiles [ˈtekstaɪlz] n	Textilien
regional development [ˈriːdʒnldɪˌveləpmənt] n	regionale Entwicklung
raw materials [ˌrɔːməˈtɪəriəlz] n	Rohstoffe / Rohmaterialien
self-sufficient [ˌselfsəˈfɪʃnt]	unabhängig / autark
provision [prəˈvɪʒn] n	Bereitstellung / Versorgung
provide with v	mit etwas versorgen

» have a detrimental effect on sth | einen schädlichen Einfluss auf etw. haben

debt [det] n	Schulden
debtor [ˈdetə] n	Schuldner
indebted [ɪnˈdetɪd] adj	verschuldet
deeply indebted / heavily indebted	hochverschuldet
indebtedness n	Verschuldung
state indebtedness / government indeptedness / national dept	Staatsverschuldung

»
state indebtedness of developing countries	Staatsverschuldung von Entwicklungsländern
HIPC – heavily indebted poor countries	HIPC – hochverschuldete Entwicklungsländer

borrow v	leihen
money n	Geld
(foreign) currency [ˌfɒrɪnˈkʌrnsi] n	Devisen
loans n	Darlehen
government n	Regierung
international bodies n pl	internationale Organisationen
International Monetary Fund (IMF) n	Internationaler Währungsfonds (IWF)
World Bank n	Weltbank
bilateral [baɪˈlætrl] adj	bilateral *(zwischen zwei Ländern oder Gruppen)*
multilateral [ˌmʌltiˈlætrl] adj	multilateral *(zwischen mehr als zwei Ländern oder Gruppen)*
high street bank / commercial bank n	Geschäftsbank *(überall präsente Bank)*
credit n	Kredit
credit write off / credit reduction	Kredittilgung
interest rate n	Zins
interest repayment	Tilgung von Zinsen
debt reduction n	Schuldenabbau
owe v	schulden
amount (to) v	sich belaufen auf / betragen
progress n	Fortschritt
improve v	verbessern

»
at high / low rate of interest	zu hohen oder niedrigen Zinsen
keep up with payments	mit den Zahlungen nachkommen
owe a bank money	einer Bank Geld schulden

mountain of debts n	Schuldenberg
remission of debts / release from debts n	Schuldenerlass
equity gearing [ˈekwɪtiˌɡɪərɪŋ] n	Verschuldungsgrad
measure [ˈmeʒə] / action n	Maßnahme
infrastructure [ˈɪnfrəˌstrʌktʃə] n	Infrastruktur
education n	Bildung
education spending	Bildungsausgaben
social welfare system n	Sozialsystem

»
related to development policy	entwicklungspolitisch

politics n pl	Politik
politician [ˌpɒlɪ'tɪʃn] n	Politiker
policy n	Politik
government n	Regierung
dictator n	Diktator
dictatorship n	Diktatur
suppress [sə'pres] v	unterdrücken
civil rights n pl	Bürgerrechte
human rights n pl	Menschenrechte
freedom of speech n	Redefreiheit

»
inefficiently-run government	unfähig geführte Regierung
restrict civil rights	die Menschenrechte beschneiden

bureaucracy [bjʊ'rɒkrəsi] n	Bürokratie / Beamtenapparat
bureaucratic [ˌbjʊərə'krætɪk] adj	bürokratisch
bribery ['braɪbri] n	Bestechung
bribe [braɪb] v	bestechen
corruption [kə'rʌpʃn] n	Korruption
corrupt adj	korrupt
incompetent adj	unfähig / inkompetent
vulnerable ['vʌlnrəbl] adj	verwundbar / verletzlich

»
a vast bureaucracy	ein ausgedehnter Beamtenapparat
be in a vulnerable position	in einer prekären Situation sein

trading bloc n	Handelsgemeinschaft / Handelsblock
influence v	beeinflussen
influence n	Einfluss
volume of foreign trade ['vɒljuːmˌɒv'fɒrɪnˌtreɪd] n	Außenhandelsvolumen
volume of sales n	Umsatzvolumen
OPEC ['əʊpek] / Organisation of Petroleum Exporting Countries [ˌɔːgnaɪ'zeɪʃn əv pe'trəʊliəm ɪkˌspɔːtɪŋ 'kʌntriz] n	OPEC / Organisation Erdöl exportierender Länder
OPEC countries	OPEC-Länder
NAFTA ['næftə] / North American Free Trade Agreement n	NAFTA / Nordamerikanisches Freihandelsabkommen
free trade zone n	Freihandelszone

3 Human environment › 3.7 World development: stages and indicators

Warsaw-pact [ˌwɔːsɔː'pækt] n	Warschauer Pakt
NATO ['neɪtəʊ] / North Atlantic Treaty Organization	NATO / Nordatlantikpakt-Organisation
target selling price ['tɑːgɪtˌselɪŋ'praɪs] n	Zielverkaufspreis
production quote n	Produktionsquote
tariff n	Zoll
import tariff	Einfuhrzoll
trade barrier n	Handelsschranke
protectionism [prə'tekʃnɪzm] n	Protektionismus *(Maßnahmen eines Staates in Form von Handelshemmnissen, um die eigene Wirtschaft zu schützen)*

»

former Warsaw-pact countries	Länder des ehemaligen Warschauer Paktes
eliminate trade barriers	Handelsschranken beseitigen

environmental problem n	Umweltproblem
environmental difficulty n	schwierige Umweltbedingung *(extreme Bedingungen der natürlichen Umgebung)*
harsh climate [ˌhɑːʃ'klaɪmət] n	raues Klima
drought [draʊt] n	Dürre
hurricane ['hʌrɪkən] n	Hurrikan / Orkan
flood n	Überflutung / Überschwemmung / Flut

poverty ['pɒvəti] n	Armut
abject poverty	entsetzliche / bittere Armut
plight [plaɪt] n	Not(-lage)
misery n	Elend
needs n	Bedürfnisse
basic human needs	menschliche Grundbedürfnisse

food n	Nahrung
nutrition [njuː'trɪʃn] n	Ernährung
nutrition facts	Nährwertangaben
diet [daɪət] n	Ernährung
healthy diet	gesunde Ernährung
staple diet	Grundnahrungsmittel
sanitation / hygiene [ˌsænɪ'teɪʃn / 'haɪdʒiːn] n	Hygiene
shelter n	Schutz

nourished ['nʌrɪʃt] adj	ernährt
under-nourished	unterernährt
malnutrition [ˌmælnjuːˈtrɪʃn] n	Unterernährung
malnourished [ˌmælˈnʌriːʃt] adj	unterernährt
severe malnutrition	ernsthafte Unterernährung

» improve health and nutrition | Gesundheit und Ernährung verbessern

marasmus [məˈræzməs] n	Marasmus *(ausgelöst durch Protein- und Eiweißmangel)*
kwashiorkor [ˌkwæʃiˈɔːkɔː] n	Kwashiorkor *(ausgelöst durch Eiweißmangel)*
pellagra [pəˈlægrə] n	Pellagra *(ausgelöst durch Vitamin B3 Mangel)*

disease n	Krankheit
epidemic n	Epidemie
cause of death n	Todesursache
diarrhoea [ˌdaɪəˈrɪə] n	Durchfall / Diarrhöe
dysentery ['dɪsntri] n	Ruhr / Dysentrie
pneumonia [njuːˈməʊniə] n	Lungenentzündung
respiratory infection [rɪˌspɪrətriɪnˈfekʃn] n	Atemwegsinfektion
respiratory disease [rɪˌspɪrətrɪdɪˈziːz] n	Atemwegserkrankung
tuberculosis [tjuːˌbɜːkjəˈləʊsɪs] n	Tuberkulose
malaria [məˈleəriə] n	Malaria
diphtheria [dɪfˈθɪəriə] n	Diphterie
typhoid ['taɪfɔɪd] n	Typhus
measles ['miːzlz] n	Masern
degenerative disease [dɪˈdʒenrətɪvdɪˌziːz] n	degenerative Krankheit
stroke n	Schlaganfall
cancer ['kænsə] n	Krebs
epidemiological transition [ˌepɪˌdiːmiəˈlɒdʒɪkltrænˈzɪʃn]	epidemiologischer Übergang

antibody n	Antikörper
immune [ɪˈmjuːn] adj	immune
vaccination [ˌvæksɪˈneɪʃn] / inoculation n	Impfung
vaccine ['væksiːn] n	Impfstoff
vaccinate v	impfen

»
infectious and parasitic diseases	infektiöse und parasitäre Krankheiten
develop antibodies against a disease	Antikörper gegen eine Krankheit entwickeln
be immune from sth	gegen etwas immun sein
vaccinate sb (against sth) / inoculate sb (against sth)	jmdn. (gegen etw.) impfen

education n — Bildung / Ausbildung
 basic education — Grundbildung
 primary education — Grundbildung / Primarstufe
 secondary education — weiterführende Bildung / Sekundarstufe
 higher education — Hochschulbildung
 substandard education — unzulängliche / mangelhafte Bildung
educate v — ausbilden
enrolment rate [ɪnˈrəʊlmənˌreɪt] n — Einschulungsrate *(Anteil der Kinder, die an einer Schule angemeldet werden)*

bring up / raise v — erziehen / aufziehen
upbringing n — Erziehung
drop out v — die Schule abbrechen
chance n — Möglichkeit / Chance
school-aged adj — im schulpflichtigen Alter
illiteracy [ɪˈlɪtrəsi] n — Analphabetismus
illiterate [ɪˈlɪtrət] n — Analphabet
education of girls n — Mädchenbildung
education of boys n — Jungenbildung
educational attainment [ˌedʒʊˈkeɪʃnləˈteɪnmənt] n — Bildungserrungenschaft

»

Education is believed to be the most important factor for achieving human development worldwide.
Man geht davon aus, dass Bildung der wichtigste Faktor für die weltweite menschliche Entwicklung ist.

Explaining inequalities

model n — Modell / schematische Darstellung
sector model n — Sektorenmodell
level of analysis [əˈnæləsɪs] n — Analyseebene
illustrate [ˈɪləstreɪt] v — veranschaulichen

crude level of analysis | grobe Analyseebene

progress n	Fortschritt
transition [træn'zɪʃn] n	Transition / Übergang
agricultural society [ˌægrɪˌkʌltʃrlsə'saɪəti] n	Landwirtschaftsgesellschaft
industrial society [ɪnˌdʌstriəlsə'saɪəti] n	Industriegesellschaft
service economy n	Dienstleistungsgesellschaft

primary sector n	primärer Sektor
secondary sector n	sekundärer Sektor
tertiary sector [ˌtɜːʃri'sektə] n	tertiärer Sektor

success n	Erfolg
surplus ['sɜːpləs] n	Überschuss
surplus revenue [ˌsɜːpləs'revnjuː] n	Mehrertrag / Überschussertrag
invest v	investieren
new technologies n	neue Technologien
new industries n	neue Industrien
range of industries n	Spektrum an Industrien

a wide range of industries | ein breites Spektrum an Industrien

industrialisation BE / industrialization AE [ɪnˌdʌstriəlaɪ'zeɪʃn] n	Industrialisierung
industrial workforce [ɪnˌdʌstriəl'wɜːkfɔːs] n	Industriearbeiter
manufacturing [ˌmænjə'fæktʃərɪŋ] n	Herstellung
manufacturing industry [ˌmænjə'fæktʃərɪŋ'ɪndəstri] n	verarbeitendes Gewerbe
utilities [juː'tɪlətiz] n pl	Leistungen der öffentlichen Versorgungsbetriebe / Versorgungswirtschaft
utilities sector n	industrieller Sektor / industrieller Bereich
industrial sector n	Industrieproduktion
industrial output n	Industrieproduktion
employed adj	beschäftigt
unemployed adj	arbeitslos

189

3 Human environment › 3.7 World development: stages and indicators

manufacturing industry predominates	verarbeitendes Gewerbe herrscht vor
manufacturing industry is weak	verarbeitendes Gewerbe ist schwach (ausgeprägt)
industrial sector is based on ...	industrieller Sektor basiert auf ...
industrial sector affects ...	industrieller Sektor beeinflusst ...
industrial sector leads to an increase in ...	industrieller Sektor führt zu einer Zunahme an ...
level of development	Stand der Entwicklung
describing the level of development	den Stand der Entwicklung beschreiben

subsistence economy [səbˈsɪstnsɪˌkɒnəmi] n
   traditional subsistence economy
agricultural basis [ˌægrɪˈkʌltʃrlˌbeɪsɪs] n
urban system n
primate city [ˈpraɪmeɪtˌsɪti] n
transport infrastructure [ˈtrænspɔːtˌɪnfrəˈstrʌktʃə] n
core n
   growing core
periphery [pəˈrɪfri] n
   underdeveloped periphery

sustained growth [səˌsteɪndˈɡrəʊθ] n

Subsistenzwirtschaft / Bedarfsdeckungswirtschaft
   traditionelle Subsistenzwirtschaft
landwirtschaftliche Basis
Stadtsystem / städtisches System
Primatstadt
Verkehrsinfrastruktur

Kern (z. B. einer Stadt)
   wachsender Kern
Peripherie / Umland
   unterentwickelte Peripherie / Umland
nachhaltiges Wachstum

Aid

AID – Agency for International Development n
aid n
   aid organisation
   relief organisation BE / relief organization AE [rɪˈliːfˌɔːɡnaɪˈzeɪʃn] n
fund-raising [ˈfʌndˌreɪzɪŋ] n
   fund-raising organization

   fund-raising campaign

Agentur für internationale Entwicklung
Hilfe / Unterstützung
   Hilfsorganisation
   Hilfsorganisation

Fundraising
   Wohltätigkeitsverein / Wohltätigkeitsorganisation
   Wohltätigkeitsveranstaltung

non-profit organisation [ˌnɒnprɒfɪtˌɔːgnaɪˈzeɪʃn] n	Non-Profit-Unternehmen *(nicht gewinnorientiertes gemeinnütziges Unternehmen)*
NGO (non-governmental organisation)	Nicht-Regierungsorganisation / regierungsunabhängige Organisation

goods n pl	Güter / Waren
money n	Geld / Finanzmittel
know-how n	Wissen / Know-how
services n pl	Dienstleistung

donor [ˈdəʊnə] n	Spender / Geld- und Kreditgeber
donor country	Geberland
bilateral aid n	bilaterale Hilfe
multilateral aid n	multilaterale Hilfe
tied aid n	gebundene Entwicklungshilfe
tied-aid credit n	gebundener Entwicklungshilfekredit
charity [ˈtʃærɪti] n	Barmherzigkeit
charity organisation n	Wohlfahrtsorganisation

Types of development

top-down development – Top-Down Entwicklung
Hierarchische Entwicklung – einer Region wird von außerhalb geholfen, Entscheidungen werden auch von außerhalb getroffen.
bottom-up development – Bottom-Up Entwicklung
Die Entwicklung wird regional organisiert.
sustainable development – nachhaltige Entwicklung
multi-purpose scheme – Mischprogramm

large-scale adj	umfangreich / weitreichend
small-scale adj	in begrenztem Umfang
impose upon [ɪmˈpəʊzəˌpɒn] v	aufdrängen / aufzwingen
carry out sth v	(etw.) durchführen
well founded adj	fundiert / gut durchdacht
appropriate adj	angemessen
inappropriate adj	unangemessen
labour-intensive adj	arbeitsintensiv
efficient [ɪˈfɪʃnt] adj	effizient / wirksam
safeguard (sb from sth) [ˈseɪfgɑːd] v	(jdn. vor etw.) schützen

»

safeguard the environment	die Umwelt schützen
culturally acceptable	kulturell annehmbar
technologically understandable	technologisch verständlich
economically affordable	wirtschaftlich tragbar, leistbar

local community n hiesige / örtliche Gemeinschaft
local people n hiesige Bevölkerung
local government n Bezirksverwaltung / Stadtverwaltung / örtliche Verwaltung

decision-making process n Entscheidungsprozess
future generations n nachfolgende Generationen

Examples

logging n Holzgewinnung / Holzfällen
  sustainable logging nachhaltige Holzgewinnung
  logging operation Abholzung
sawmill ['sɔːmɪl] n Sägewerk
timber ['tɪmbə] n Holz / Bauholz
rate of removal [ˌreɪtɒvrɪ'muːvl] n Abholzungsgeschwindigkeit

»

  process timber | Holz verarbeiten

hydroelectric power station n Wasserkraftwerk / Wasserkraftanlage
dam [dæm] n Damm / Staudamm
flood control n Flutkontrolle
flood zone n Hochwassergebiet / Überschwemmungszone

flood wave n Flutwelle
generation of energy n Energiegewinnung
profit n Profit / Gewinn
sustainable method n nachhaltige Methode

earthquake relief ['ɜːθkweɪkrɪˌliːf] n Erdbebenhilfe
blanket n Decke
tent n Zelt
temporary shelter ['tempriˌʃeltə] n Übergangsunterkunft

locating equipment [lə'keɪtɪŋgɪˌkwɪpmənt] n	Suchgerät
tracker device ['trækədɪˌvaɪs] n	Suchgerät
fireman n	Feuerwehrmann

well-building n	Brunnenbau
potable water ['pəʊtəblˌwɔːtə] n	Trinkwasser
drinking-water n	Trinkwasser
ground water n	Grundwasser
water table n	Wasserspiegel / Grundwasserspiegel

economic reason n	wirtschaftlicher Grund
political reason n	politischer Grund
moral reason n	moralischer Grund

market n	Markt
market	Absatzmarkt
manufactured goods [ˌmænjə'fæktʃədˌgʊdz] n pl	produzierte Waren
large population n	große Bevölkerung
purchase n	Kauf / Erwerb

» | further purchase of goods | weiterer Erwerb von Handelswaren |

bonds n	Bindungen
close bonds	enge Bindungen
strengthen bonds	Bindungen stärken
ally ['ælaɪ] n	Verbündeter
gap n	Kluft / Abstand
bridge a gap	eine Kluft überbrücken
narrow a gap	eine Kluft verengen
global stability [ˌgləʊblstə'bɪləti] n	globale Stabilität
global instability n	globale Instabilität / Unsicherheit
maintain [meɪn'teɪn] v	fortführen / aufrechterhalten

duty n	Pflicht
obligation [ˌɒblɪ'geɪʃn] n	Verpflichtung
compensation [ˌkɒmpən'seɪʃn] n	Wiedergutmachung
colonial past [kə'ləʊniəlˌpɑːst]	koloniale Vergangenheit
colonial region	Kolonialgebiet
exploitation [ˌeksplɔɪ'teɪʃn] n	Ausbeutung

3.8 Globalisation

globalisation *BE* / globalization *AE* [ˌgləʊblaɪˈzeɪʃn] n	Globalisierung
global adj	global / weltweit
global player	Global Player
transnational corporation (TNC) n	multinationales Unternehmen
international trade relations n pl	Weltwirtschaftsbeziehungen
international economic order n	Weltwirtschaftsordnung
economic power	Wirtschaftskraft
asset [ˈæset] n	Wirtschaftsgut
combine [kəmˈbaɪn] v	vereinen
facilitate [fəˈsɪlɪteɪt] v	erleichtern / ermöglichen

» The economic power of large TNCs comes from the ownership of assets such as plants, warehouses, mines, tankers or forests.
Die Wirtschaftskraft großer transnationaler Unternehmen entsteht durch den Besitz von Wirtschaftsgütern wie Fabriken, Lagerhäusern, Minen, Tankern oder Wäldern.

Multinational corporations

MNC / transnational corporation n	multinationales Unternehmen
operation n	Geschäftstätigkeit / Unternehmen
operate	tätig sein / agieren / betreiben
extensive [ɪkˈstensɪv] adj	aufwendig / weitreichend
production facility [prəˈdʌkʃnfəˌsɪləti] n	Produktionsstätte / Produktionsanlage
core area [ˈkɔːˌeərɪə] n	Kerngebiet
peripheral region [pəˈrɪfrlˌriːˌdʒn] n	Randgebiet / Peripherregion
operational division [ˌɒprˈeɪʃnldɪˈvɪʒn] n	Geschäftsbereich
research and development (R&D)	Forschung und Entwicklung (F&E)
decision-making	Beschlussfassung / Entscheidungsfindung
planning	Planung
coordination	Koordination / Abstimmung
human resources management (HRM) n	Personalwesen
personnel [ˌpɜːsnˈel] n	Personal / Belegschaft
assembly [əˈsembli] n	Herstellung / Zusammenbau
production	Fertigung / Produktion

» Large MNCs require extensive planning and coordination in order to supply their production facilities with raw materials, component parts and personnel.
Große multinationale Unternehmen erfordern aufwendige Planung und Koordination, um ihre Produktionsstätten mit Rohstoffen, Bauteilen und Personal zu versorgen.

economic transaction n	wirtschaftliche Unternehmung
host country [ˌhəʊstˈkʌntri] n	Gastgeberland
developing country n	Entwicklungsland
newly industrialising country (NIC) n	Schwellenland

Benefits and disadvantages of host countries

Benefits	**Vorteile**
employment	Beschäftigung, Arbeit
investment	Investition
development of resources	Gewinnung von Rohstoffen
manufacturing	verarbeitende Industrie, Fertigung
provision of capital	Bereitstellung von Geldmitteln
improvement of technical skills	Verbesserung von technischen Fähigkeiten
taxes and levies	Steuern und Abgaben
Disadvantages	**Nachteile**
exploitation of labourers	Ausbeutung von Arbeitern
export of resources	Ausfuhr von Rohstoffen
outflow of profits	Abfluss von Erträgen
increased imports lead to increased national debt	steigende Einfuhr führt zu steigender Staatsverschuldung

Consequences of globalisation

consequences of globalisation [ˌkɒnsɪkwənsɪzəvˌgləʊbəlaɪˈzeɪʃn] n	Folgen der Globalisierung
political consequences n	politische Folgen
incentive by the government [ɪnˈsentɪv] n	Anreiz durch die Regierung
subsidies [ˈsʌbsɪdiz] n pl	Subvention / Fördermittel
export processing zone (EPZ) n	Export Processing Zone (EPZ)
free trade zone n	Freihandelszone
special economic zone n	Sonderwirtschaftszone
customs zone n	Zollzone
bonded warehouse n	Lagerhaus für unverzollte Ware / Freilager
free port n	Freihafen

maquiladora [ˌmækɪl'ədɔːrə] n   Fabrik einer amerikanischen Firma in Mexiko
provision of infrastructure n   Bereitstellung von Infrastruktur

» EPZ: industrial zones with special incentives set up to attract foreign investors, in which imported materials undergo some degree of processing before being re-exported again.
EPZ: Industriegebiet mit speziellen Anreizen, um ausländische Investoren anzulocken, in welchen importierte Güter eine Form der Weiterverarbeitung durchlaufen, bevor sie wieder exportiert werden.

Economic

economic consequences n pl   wirtschaftliche Folgen
rationalisation [ˌræʃnlaɪ'zeɪʃn] n   Rationalisierung
lean management   schlankes Management *(im Hinblick auf Effizienz)*
lean production   schlanke Produktion
workforce   Belegschaft / Personal / Arbeiterschaft

»
| slimming down the workforce | Belegschaftsabbau / Verschlankung der Belegschaft |
| sifting of the workforce | Aussieben der Belegschaft |

reorganisation   Neuordnung / Umstrukturierung / Sanierung
subcontracting [ˌsʌbkən'træktɪŋ] n   Vergabe an Sub-Unternehmen oder Zulieferer
outsourcing ['aʊtsɔːsɪŋ] n   Ausgliederung / Fremdvergabe / Fremdbeschaffung

»
| subcontract sb | an jmdn. einen Untervertrag vergeben |

	production		Produktion
outsourcing of	administration	Ausgliederung der	Verwaltung
	marketing		Vermarktung

diversification [daɪˌvɜːsɪfɪ'keɪʃn] n   Diversifizierung / Sortimentserweiterung / Streuung

new international division of labour (NIDL) n
repetitive task [rɪˌpetətɪvˈtɑːsk] n

Neue internationale Verteilung der Arbeit
monotone Arbeit

» relocation of repetitive tasks to low-wage countries | Verlagerung von monotoner Arbeit in Niedriglohnländer

Geographical

geographical consequence n
increase n
increasing adj
business travel n
telecommunications [ˌtelɪkəˌmjuːnɪˈkeɪʃnz] n pl
information processing
cosmopolitan city [ˌkɒzməˈpɒlɪtnsɪti] / metropolitan city [ˌmetrəˈpɒlɪtnsɪti] n

geographische Folge
Anstieg / Zunahme
ansteigend / anwachsend
Geschäftsreise
Telekommunikation / Fernmeldewesen
Informationsverarbeitung
Weltstadt

» congregation of offices in cosmopolitan cities | Ansammlung von Niederlassungen in Weltstädten

property market n
gentrification [ˌdʒentrɪfɪˈkeɪʃn] n
gentrified housing [ˌdʒentrɪfaɪdˈhaʊzɪŋ]
service sector n

Immobilienmarkt / Grundstücksmarkt
Gentrifizierung
Gentrifizierung der Wohnbebauung

Dienstleistungssektor

» Gentrification (also "urban gentrification") describes the changes in an urban residential area associated with the movement of more affluent individuals into a lower-class neigbourhood.
Gentrifizierung (auch „städtische/urbane Gentrifizierung") beschreibt den Wandel in einem städtischen Wohnviertel, der mit dem Umzug von wohlhabenderen Individuen in ein Unterschichtwohnviertel einhergeht.

trade n
favourable [ˈfeɪvrəbl] / favorable AE adj
unfavourable / unfavorable AE adj

Handel
günstig / vorteilhaft

ungünstig / unvorteilhaft / negativ

3 Human environment › 3.8 Globalisation

boundary ['baʊndri] / limit n	Grenze
trading limit	Handelsgrenze
border / boundary n	Grenze / Landesgrenze
economic tie [ˌiːkənɒmɪk'taɪ] n	Wirtschaftsverbindung
merger ['mɜːdʒə] n	Fusion / Zusammenschluss
merge v	fusionieren
capital n	Kapital
investment n	Investition
promote [prə'məʊt] v	fördern
competition n	Wettbewerb
competitiveness [kəm'petɪtɪvnəs] n	Wettbewerbsfähigkeit
improve v	verbessern

interdependence [ˌɪntədɪ'pendəns] n	gegenseitige Abhängigkeit / Interdependenz
trade war ['treɪdˌwɔː] n	Handelskrieg
free trade [ˌfriː'treɪd] n	Freihandel
terms of trade n	Handelsbedingungen / Terms of Trade
trade barrier ['treɪdˌbæriə] n	Handelsschranke / Handelshemmnis
impose [ɪm'pəʊz] v	auferlegen / errichten
remove v	entfernen / beseitigen
accelerate [ək'seləreɪt] v	beschleunigen

tariff ['tærɪf] n	Zolltarif / Zoll
duty-free [ˌdjuːti'friː] adj	zollfrei
rigid ['rɪdʒɪd] adj	starr / fest
quota [ˌkwəʊtə] n	Quote / Kontingent
preferential [ˌprefr'enʃl] adj	bevorzugt / Vorzugs~ / Präferenz~
deny [dɪ'naɪ] v	verweigern
prohibit [prə'hɪbɪt] v	verbieten / untersagen
protectionism [prə'tekʃnɪzm] n	Protektionismus
protectionist adj	protektionistisch
low-wage country n	Niedriglohnland / Billiglohnland
restraint [rɪ'streɪnt] n	Beschränkung
voluntary export restraint (VER) ['vɒləntriˌekspɔːtrɪ'streɪnt]	freiwillige Exportbeschränkung
restrain [rɪ'streɪn] v	hemmen / hindern
non-tariff trade barrier [ˌnɒntærɪf'treɪdˌbæriə] n	nichttarifäres Handelshemmnis
red tape n	(übermäßige) Bürokratie
retaliate [rɪ'tælieɪt] v	zurückschlagen / kontern / Gegenmaßnahmen ergreifen

embargo [ɪm'bɑːgəʊ] n	Embargo
sanctions ['sæŋʃnz] n pl	Sanktionen

exchange control n	Devisenkontrolle / Devisenbewirtschaftung
transfer pricing n	Transferpreissystem
indigenous [ɪnˈdɪdʒɪnəs] adj	einheimisch / heimisch

» The USA subsidize their indigenous farm products.
Die USA subventionieren ihre einheimischen Agrarprodukte.

job security n	Arbeitsplatzsicherheit
ILO (International Labour Organization) n	Internationale Arbeitsorganisation
raise (sth) v	(etw.) anheben
living standard / standard of living n	Lebensstandard
purchasing power n	Kaufkraft

Communication and Internet

communication n	Kommunikation
interconnection [ˌɪntəkəˈnekʃn] n	Verbindung
the Internet n	das Internet
the World Wide Web (www) n	das World Wide Web
global village n	globales Dorf
cosmopolitan city [ˌkɒzməˈpɒlɪtnˌsɪti] / world city / global city n	Weltstadt

»
cultural exchange	Kulturaustausch
exchange of information	Informationsaustausch

Globalisation goes hand in hand with the increased and accelerated exchange of information via the Internet.
Die Globalisierung geht mit dem verstärkten und beschleunigten Informationsaustausch über das Internet Hand in Hand.

networking n	Vernetzung
e-commerce [ˈiːˌkɒmɜːs] n	E-Commerce / elektronischer Handel
electronic marketplace n	elektronische Märkte
auction [ˈɔːkʃn] n	Versteigerung / Auktion
bid [bɪd] v	bieten
link n	Verknüpfung / Link
link v	verknüpfen / verlinken
electronic shopping mall n	virtuelles Einkaufszentrum

3 Human environment › 3.8 Globalisation

returns policy / right of return n   Rückgaberecht
forum ['fɔːrəm] n   (Online-)Forum
hit n   Treffer / Zugriff

» The term "Internet" represents the global network of computers.
Der Begriff „Internet" steht für das weltweite Computernetzwerk.

The site's webmaster says it has over 100,000 hits a day.
Der Webmaster der Seite sagt, sie habe täglich über 100.000 Zugriffe.

track v   verfolgen
information overload n   Informationsüberfluss
search-engine n   Suchmaschine
   search-engine registration   Registrierung bei einer Suchmaschine

e-mail based marketing   E-Mail-Werbung
junk mail / spam n   unerwünschte E-Mail-Sendung
banner ad [ˌbænəˈæd] n   Werbebanner *(im Internet)*
appeal v   ansprechen / anziehen / einen Anreiz bieten

direct v   lenken / richten

Englisches Stichwortregister

A horizon-197 62
ablation 14, 79
abolish 140
aborigine 130
abortion 134
abrasion 14, 84
abrasion platform 86
abroad 136
absentee landowner 124
absolute numbers 29
absorb 66
absorption 66
abstract sign 20
abundance of species 178
abyssal 91
acacia 73
accelerate 198
acceptance 137
access 141, 150
accessibility 150
accumulate 56
acid 59
acid dumping 96
acid rain 96
acid soil 60
acidic 60
acidification 96
Aconcagua 41
action 23
activate 31
activity 177
adit 109
adjust to 95
administration 148, 172
Adriatic Sea 38
adult 131
adult literacy 180
advance warning 56
advection rain 68
adventure 50
advertising 148
aeolian 84
aerate 61
aeration 61
aerial photograph 21
aerial root 72
aeronautical industry 112
aerosol 66
aerosol propellant 96
aerospace 112
affluence 150
affluence model 162

affluent 150
afford sth 152
Africa 38
African city 172
after-sales service 154
aftershock 56
age group 134
age structure 134, 178
age-sex pyramid 134
agent 143
agglomeration economy 102
agrarian structure 123
agree 25
agreement 141
agribusiness 126
agricultural 113
agricultural basis 190
agricultural cooperative 125
agricultural geography 12
agricultural machinery store 116
agricultural product 118
agricultural service supply
  agency 124
agricultural society 189
agriculture 20, 44, 113, 127, 163
agro-industrial farm 126
agroforestry 123
aid 190
AID – Agency for International
  Development 190
air 84
air mass 67
air motion 69
air pressure 67
air stream 69
airplane 169
airport 163, 169
alarming 179
albedo 66
alcohol 183
Aletsch Glacier 41
alfalfa grass 121
algal bloom 90
alienation 157
alkaline 60
alloy smelting works 110
alluvial deposits 34
alluvial fan 82
alluvium 82
ally 193
almond 121
along 22

alongside 22
Alpine folding 53
Alpine Foreland 44
alpine herdsmen's hut 125
alpine meadow 125
Alpine system 43
alpine zone 76
Alps 43, 44
Altai Mountains 47
alternate 73
alternative energies 158
altitudinal vegetation zone 76
aluminium 105
aluminium oxide 60
Amazon 39
amount 26
amount 141, 184
Amur 39
Amur River 48
anaerobic 61
analyse 31
analysis 15
ancient world 170
Andaman Sea 38
animal husbandry 128
announcement 170
anorganic 92
Antarctic Circle 67
Antarctica 38, 41
antecedent valley 83
anthracite 104
antibody 187
anticline 53
anticyclone 67
antimony 105
apartheid 130, 172
apartment building 173
Apennines 44
Appalachian Highlands 48
Appalachian Mountains 50
appeal 200
apple 120
applicant 137
appropriate 191
appropriate technology 116
apricot 120
aquaculture 127
aquifer 87
Arabian Desert 40
Arabian Sea 38
arable 113
Arafura Sea 38

201

Aral Sea 40, 48
Archimedes' screw 118
archipelago 36
Arctic Circle 67
arctic fox 76
arctic hare 76
Arctic Ocean 38
Ardennes 43
area 36, 166
area of ecological regeneration 99
area of settlement 162
arête 81
arid 68
arid region 74
aridity 68
armourer 171
arrangement 141
artesian 88
artesian basin 88
artificial insemination 117
asbestos 106
ascend 71
Asia 38
Asian city 173
asparagus 120
aspect 24, 82
assembly 194
assembly line 101
assembly plant 100
assert 137
assess 152
asset 194
assortment 145
asthenosphere 51
asylum 136
at a right angle 22
Atacama Desert 40
Athabasca Glacier 41
Atlantic Ocean 38
atlas 16, 34
atmosphere 13, 266
atmospheric boundary layer 13
atmospheric circulation 69
atoll 36, 54
attain 137
auction 199
Australia 38
author 23
automation 101
avalanche 80, 93
average 13, 180
avian flu 122
axis 26

azonal soil 61
B horizon 62
back-office 151
background 22
Baden-Wurttemberg 45
Baffin Bay 39
baker 172
Balkan Mountains 44
Baltic Ridge 43
Baltic Sea 38, 45
banana 121
Banda Sea 38
banking 149
banner ad 200
baobab 73
bar chart 28
barchan 84
Barents Sea 38
barley 119
barn 116
barrage 89, 108
barrier 139
barrier beach 35
barrier reef 85
barter trade 140
bartering 140
basalt 55, 58
base level 82
base load power 106
basic industry 100
basin 49, 89
battery farming 125
battery-caged 125
bauxite 105
Bavaria 45
Bavarian Forest 44
bay 35, 79, 85
Bay of Bengal 39
Bay of Biscay 39
bazaar 173
beach 35, 79, 85
beach replenishment 86
bean 120
bedrock 57
beef 122
beer 121, 126
behaviour 177
behavioural geography 12
bend 82
bergschrund 80
Bering Strait 39
Berlin 45
berm 85
beverages 126

bias 153
biased 153
bid 199
big farmer 124
bilateral 184
bilateral aid 191
biocapacity 127
biocide 96
biodegradable 97, 98, 160
biodiesel 158
biodiversity 127
bioenergy 108
biofuel 108
biogas 108
biogeography 12
biological weathering 60
biomass 15, 108, 158
biome 71
biosphere 71
biotechnology 112
birch 76
birth control 134
birth rate 134, 181
birth surplus 134
bison 75
bituminous coal 104
Black Forest 43, 44
Black Sea 38
blacksmith 172
blanket 192
blast furnace 110
blizzard 70
block field pattern 114
block of flats 168
blow 84
blowhole 86
bluff 83
body language 24
body of water 88
bog 47, 78
Bohemian Forest 43
bomb 54
bonded warehouse 195
bonds 193
boom 141
Bora 71
border 18, 137, 198
bordering sea 91
boreal 75
boreal coniferous forest 75
borrow 184
bottom 22
boulder 82
boundary 37, 198

brackish water 92
braided stream 82
branch of industry 100
brand loyalty 155
Brandenburg 45
branding 154
brandy 126
break 85, 91
breakers 79, 85
breakwater 86
breccia 58
breed 117
breeze 64
Bremen 45
brewery 113, 126
bribe 185
bribery 185
bridge 168
bring up 188
briquette 158
briquette factory 109
broadleaved 72
brook 34
brown coal 158
brown earth 61
browse 152
bucket wheel excavator 109
Buddhism 133
Buddhist 133
buffalo grass 75
build up 96
building industry 111
bulb 121
buoyancy 91
bureaucracy 185
bureaucratic 185
Burgess' concentric model 175
burial ground 173
bush savanna 73
business district 163
business enterprise 101
business marketing 31
business travel 197
butcher 172
butte 83
buttress root 72
C horizon 62
caatinga 73
cabbage 120
cable factory 110
cactus 74
cadmium 105
calcareous 61
calcification 61

calcium 57
caldera 54
Caledonian folding 53
Caledonian mountain-building
 episode 42
calm 70
calorie intake 181
calorie supply 181
calve 80
camel 122
can 127
Canadian Shield 48
canal 89
cancer 187
canning factory 113, 127
canopy 72
canyon 34, 49, 83
capable 183
cape 35
capillary action 62
capital 156, 198
capital city 164, 165
capital goods 102
capital goods industry 100
capital intensity 148
capital intensive 102
caption 22, 26
capture 31
car assembly plant 111
car manufacturer 111
car supply industry 111
carbon dioxide 66, 96, 160
carbonation 59
Caribbean Sea 38
caribou 76
carnivore 74
Carpathian Mountains 43
carpenter 171
carry dust 71
carry out 152
carry out sth 191
carrying capacity 127, 134
cartoon 21
cartoonist 23
cascade 83
cash crop farm 123
Caspian Depression 47
Caspian Sea 38
caste 133, 173
castle 172
castle gate 172
castle siege 172
castle tower 172
cataract 83

catch crop 119
catch size 126
catchment area 174
category 153
cathedral 164
cathedral town 165
Catholic 133
cattle 122
cattle farmer 116
cattle grazing 123
cattle market 126
cattle pen 117
cattle trough 117
cause of death 187
Celebes Sea 38
cellulose 106
cellulose factory 111
cement 106
cement manufacturing 111
cemetery 164
census 129, 154
central business district 163,
 166, 173
Central German Uplands 44
Central Plateaus 43
central plaza 172
central reservation 169
Central Siberian Plateau 46
central-place theory 174
centre 22, 174
ceramics industry 113
chalk 58
chance 188
Chang Jiang 39
change 164
changing the spatial structure
 177
channel 78, 88
chaparral 74
charity 191
charity organisation 191
chart 26
cheese factory 126
cheese spread plant 126
chemical industry 110
chemical products 110
chemical weathering 59
chequered pattern 172, 173
Chernozem 61
cherry 120
chicken 122
chili 120
Chinook 71
chips 108

203

chlorine plant 111
chlorofluorocarbon 96, 160
Christian 133
Christianity 133
chrome 105
chromite 47
Chuckchi Peninsula 48
church 164, 171
cinders 54
cinema 164
circle graph 28
circular catchment area 174
circulation pattern 13
cirque 81
cirrus 64
CIS 46
citadel 173
citizen 129
citrus fruit 120
city 164, 174
city centre 163
city wall 173
civil rights 185
classification 166
clay 61, 106
clay mineral 60
clean 161
cleaning 149
clear 97
clearance rate 97
cliff 35, 85
climate 13, 14, 65
climatic 65
climatic change 95
climatic region 71
climatologist 65
climatology 12, 13, 65
climb 179
clints and grykes 83
clothing 112
cloud 64
cloud cover 64
cloud forest 76
cloud formation 64
cloudy 64
clover 121
cluster 36
co-operative 125
CO_2 emission 14
coal 58, 104, 109
coal conversion 109
coal field 104
coal gasification 109
coal measure 104

coal milling plant 109
coal district 109
coal-bearing 104
coast 35, 79, 84, 85
coastal defence 93
coastal dune 85
coastal flooding 95
coastal geography 12
coastal protection 86
coastal sandy heathland 86
coastline 15
cobalt 105
cocoa 73
cocoa 121
coconut palm 121
coexist 37
coexistence 37
coffee 73, 121
cognitive geography 12
coherence 36
coherent 36
cohort 134
coke 109
col 77
cold storage 116
collapse 178
collective farming 125
college 132
collision margin 53
collision zone 53
Cologne 45
colonial 129
colonial past 193
colonial region 193
colonisation 183
colonise 129
colonist 129
colony 129, 183
Colorado beetle 119
Colorado River 50
colour 29
coloured person 131
colouring 17
Columbia River 50
column 29
combine 194
combustion efficiency 107
commerce 146, 172
commercial farming 123, 126
commercial zone 163
commission 143
commodity 144
common glasswort 93
common land 114

common pricing 155
Commonwealth of
    Independent States 46
communication 199
communications 149
communications engineering
    112
communications infrastructure
    170
community 37
commute 175
commuter 136
commuter stream 178
commuting zone 175
comparison 20, 21
compensation 193
competition 141, 153, 198
competitive 153
competitiveness 142, 198
competitor 153
component 29
composed of 51
composition 13, 15
compost 128
composting plant 97
compulsive buying 152
computer software 31
condensation 68
condense 68
cone 54
cone-bearing 75
conflict 138
confluence 34, 82
conglomerate 58
Congo 39
coniferous 72
connecting canal 90
connection 20
consequences of globalisation
    195
conservation 99, 161
conservative margin 53
conserve 98
consider 22
consist of 51
consist of 28
consolidate 124
Constance 44
constant heat 72
constructive margin 53
consultancy 149
consultant 149
consume 104, 138
consumer 112, 151, 156

consumer profile 154
consumer protection 155
consumer research 153
consumer services 147
consumerism 151
consumption 15, 104, 138, 153,
  159, 162, 181
contain 31
container terminal 163
contaminated land 97
contamination 95, 160
context 24
continental climate 71
continental drift 53
continental shelf 53, 91
continental slope 53
continentality 71
contour ploughing 128
contraception 134
contraceptive 134
contract 59
contract cultivation 123
control rods 107
convection 66
convection current 52
convectional rain 68
convective 13
convenience store 145
convention centre 163
converge 82
conversion into electricity 110
convert 176
conveyor system 101
cooking banana 120
cool 54
cool off 69
coolant 107
cooling 59
cooling tower 107
cooper 171
coordination 194
copper 47, 105
coral reef 36, 85
Coral Sea 38
core 51, 172, 190
core area 194
core melt-down 107
Coriolis force 69
cork oak 123
corn 119
corner shop 145
corporation 101
corrosion 83
corrugated-iron hut 164

corrupt 185
corruption 185
cosmopolitan city 165, 199
cost 146
cost of living 152, 181
cost of sales 146
cottage industry 101
cotton 122
council flat 132
counter urbanisation 176
counterurbanisation 151
country 162
country estate 115
country life 163
country of destination 137
country of origin 136
countryside 162
course 78
course of a river 78
courthouse 163
cover 146
cow shed 116
craftsman 171
crag 77
craggy 77
crash 178
crash barrier 168
crater 54
create 31
credit 184
creek 78
crest 35, 91
crevasse 80
crevice 59
crop 113, 118
crop rotation 114
crossroads 167
crown 72
crumb structure 61
crust 51
crustal movement 52
crystal 57
crystalline 57
crystalline rock 46
cultivate 113
cultivated land 114
cultivated plant 119
cultivation 15, 113
cultivation in hot houses 124
cultivation of cash crops 123
cultura mista 115
cultural environment 170
cultural geography 12
cultural landscape 163

culture 36
cumulonimbus 64
cumulus 64
currency 184
current 82, 88
curve 29
cushion plant 76
custom 37
customer 151
customer proximity 150
customs zone 195
cut flower 121
cut through 83
cut-off canal 90
cut-off meander spur 83
cyclone 67
dairy 126
dairy farming 125
dairy industry 113, 126
dam 108, 192
Danube 39, 46
data 17, 26
data set 31
data-based information 31
date palm 121
daub 171
dead 72
deal with 22
dealer 145
death rate 134, 181
Death Valley 50
debt 183
debt reduction 184
debtor 183
decentralisation 150
decentralise 150
deciduous 72
deciduous forest 49, 75
deciduous tree 75
decision 149
decision-making 194
decision-making process 192
decline 176, 178
decomposition 62
decrease 26, 63, 178
deep 18, 60, 78
deep 91
deep water current 91
deep-sea trench 53
define 148
deflation 84
deflect 69
deflection 69
deforest 97

205

deforestation 97
deform 51
degenerative disease 187
degradable 160
degradation 62
deindustrialisation 100, 147
delivery costs 146
delta 34, 49, 78
Delta Scheme 93
demand 138, 151, 157
demand for space 162
demographic 129
demographic transition 134
demography 12, 129
density 91, 166
denudation 14
deny 142, 198
department store 144
deplete 103
depletion 103
depopulation 129
deposit 103
deposition 14, 82
depression 52
deprived 132
depth 18
deregulation 159
derelict land 97, 176
desalinisation 92
descend 71
descent 130
description 22
desert 49, 74
desert pavement 84
desert varnish 84
desertification 49, 73, 96
desire 151
desk research 153
destitute 155
destructive margin 53
detached house 168
detail 22
detergent 97
developing country 178, 195
development 16, 150, 178
development geography 12
development planning 31
device 23
dew 64
dewpoint 68
diamond 106
diarrhoea 187
dictator 185
dictatorship 185

die 90
diesel 111, 158
diet 114, 186
digital data 31
dike 86, 93
dink 131
dip slope 77
diphtheria 187
direct 200
direct distribution 143
direction of flow 88
direction of mining 109
dirigible 169
disagree 25
disastrous 179
discharge 89, 160
discipline 12
discount 154
discovery 50
discrimination 130
discuss 24
disease 187
displaced person 137
display 31
disposable income 152
disposal 96
disrupt 94
dissolve 59, 83
distance 174
distinct 152
distributary 78
distribution 20, 142, 148, 157, 166
distribution of customers 150
distributive 147
distributor 142
district heating 107, 158
disused industrial site 101
diurnal climate 67
divergent plate 53
divide 37
division of labour 156
divorced 131
Dnieper 39
doldrums 69
doline 84
Dolomites 43
domestic 147
domestic cleaner 97
domestic market 139
domestic work 149
Don River 48
donor 191
doorstep selling 143

dormitory town 165
double 134
double-glazing 99
down-market 154
downstream 78
downtown 173
drain 89
drain of land resources 162
drainage 61, 89
drainage of ground water 90
drainage pattern 89
drainage system 17
drained 89
draining ditch 89
draper 171
drawbridge 172
drift 81
drift ice 75
drifting ice 80
drifting sand 84
drilling device 105
drinking water 88
drinking-water 193
dripstone cave 84
drizzle 65
drop 26, 178
drop out 188
drought 46, 68, 96, 186
drought-resistant 74
drumlin 81
dry farming 115
dry out 92
dry savanna 73
dry season 73
dry valley 83
dumping 92, 160
dune 35, 84
dung 117, 128
dungeon 172
dust devil 70
duty 193
duty-free 198
dwarf willow 76
dweller 129
dying of the woods 96
dysentery 187
e-commerce 199
e-mail based marketing 200
early industrialisation 155
early-warning system 93
earth structure 51
earthquake 55, 93
earthquake area 56
earthquake belt 56

206

earthquake relief 192
earthquake victim 56
earthquake-prone 56
earthquake-proof 56
East China Sea 38
East European Plain 43
East Friesland 45
East Frisian Islands 45
Easterlies 69
eastern margin climate 74
eave 171
eco-friendly 98
ecological 98, 159
ecological barrier 162
ecological restriction 161
ecological viability 162
ecology 98, 159
economic 156
economic activity 16
economic bloc 141
economic consequences 196
economic determinism 174
economic geography 12, 15
economic migrant 136
economic power 194
economic reason 193
economic structure 167
economic tie 198
economic transaction 195
economical 159
economically active population 134
economist 156
economy 20, 138, 156, 169, 180
ecosystem 71, 161
edaphic 60
eddy 88
edge city 173
educate 188
educated 132
education 132, 149, 184, 188
education of boys 188
education of girls 188
educational attainment 188
educational institution 164
effect 24
effective energy 158
efficient 162, 191
effluent 160
effusive rock 57
eggplant 120
Eifel 43
eject 54
elderly people 131

electric potential energy 158
electric power 106
electrical 112
electricity 106, 157
electricity cable 169
electronic 112
electronic marketplace 199
electronic shopping mall 199
electronics 112
element 13
elevated railway 168
elevation 18, 77
elite 172
eluviate 15
embankment 82
embargo 142, 198
embroider 171
emergency services 149
emergency shelter 138
emergent 72
emigrant 136
emigrate 136
emigration 135
emission 96, 107, 160
emission of waste heat 96
emit 96
emphasise 24
employed 189
employee 167, 178
employment structure 178
end terrace 168
energy 106, 157
energy crop 108
energy infrastructure 169
energy production 110
energy source 104, 158
energy-efficient 98
energy-saving 161
engine manufacturing 111
engineer 101
English Channel 42
enhance 31
enrolment rate 188
entertainment industry 149
entrepôt trade 140
environment 20, 98, 150
environment minister 161
environmental 159
environmental crisis 161
environmental damage 161
environmental difficulty 186
environmental geography 12
environmental monitoring 98
environmental movement 98

environmental policy 161
environmental problem 186
environmental protection 98, 161
environmentalist 98, 161
environmentally friendly 161
epicentre 56
epidemic 156, 187
epidemiological transition 187
epiphyte 72
equator 18
equatorial climate 72
equatorial low 69
equinox 67
equity gearing 184
equivalent 141
erg 74
erode 42, 82
erosion 14, 43, 82
erratic block 81
erupt 54
eruption 54
eruption plume 93
escarpment 77
ESDP 177
esker 81
estuary 34, 78
ethanol 108
ethnic 130
ethnic minority 167
eucalyptus 73
Euphrates 39
Europe 38, 41
European Plain 46
European Spatial Development Perspective 177
European Union 41
eustatic change in sea-level 80
eutrophication 90, 96
evaporate 68
evaporation 68
evapotranspiration 68
Everglades 50
evergreen 72
ewe 122
exaggerate 24
exaggerated 24
examine 177
exceed 94
exchange 183
exchange control 199
execution 171
exfoliation 59
exhaust fumes 160

207

exhaustion 103
exhibition centre 163
exogenous river 74
exosphere 66
expand 59, 69
explain 24
exploit 103
exploitation 50, 103, 159, 193
exploration 50, 103
export 139, 147
export processing zone 195
expulsion 137
extend 18
extension 18
extensive 194
extensive farming 123
external 147
externalisation of services 147
extinction 98
extract 103
extraction 103
extraordinary 49
extravagance 152
extrusive rock 57
fabric of a building 177
face 35
facial expression 24
facilitate 194
facilities 169
facility 164
factor 13, 149
factor of production 102
factory 101, 155, 163, 166
factory farming 125
fall 63, 178
fallow 115
family 131
family farm 124
family planning 134
farm 113, 115, 163
farm building 115
farm hand 114
farm size 115
farm-gate price 125
farmer 114
farming activity 116
farming system 123
fast breeder reactor 107
fathom sth 177
fattening 116
fattening of bulls 125
fattening of calves 125
fault line 56
faulting 52

fauna 71
favourable 197
feather grass 75
feature 17, 24
feed 114, 117
feed crop farm 123
feed in 107
Feldberg 46
feldspar 57
female 131
fence 117
ferralitic soil 61
ferry 169
fertile 43, 60
fertiliser factory 111
fertility 133
fertility behaviour 134
fetch 91
fibre 110
fibre plant 122
Fichtel Hills 44
field 114
field research 153
Filchner-Ronne Ice Shelf 41
film industry 149
filter 66, 160
finance 148
finances 140
finger lake 81
finished 100
finishing industry 100
fir 75
fire hydrant 169
fire station 164
fireman 193
firewood 108
firn 80
first-order settlement 174
fish meal 127
fish meal production 127
fish population 127
fish processing industry 113, 126
fishing capacity 126
fishing grounds 127
fishing industry 126
fishmonger 172
fissure 54, 59
fjord 35, 42, 81
fjord landscape 42
flash flood 95
flat 168
flatten out 179
flax 122
flee 137

flight 137
flood 46, 78, 89, 186
flood barrier 93
flood control 192
flood wave 192
flood zone 192
flooded field 119
flooding 81, 89, 94
floodplain 34, 81
flora 71
Flores Sea 38
flow 54, 78
flow into 78
flower plantation 121
fluctuate 134
fluvial 81
focus 56
foehn 46, 64, 71
fog 65
fold mountains 53
folding 52
food 186
food canning industry 127
food industry 126
food industry and semi-luxury
  industry 113
food market 173
food processing 126
food production 114
food security 114
food shortage 114
food supply 114
food surplus 114
footloose 102
footwear industry 112
forced migration 137
foreground 22
foreign 130, 147
foreign trade 138
foreigner 130
forest clearance 97
forest fire 97
forest-clad 43
forge 110
form 164
form of employment 148
fort 173
fortress town 165
forum 200
fossil fuel 158
foundry 110
fracture 51
fragmentation 124
fragmentation of land 124

208

fragmented land 114
franchise 145
franchisee 145
franchising 145
franchisor 145
free gift 154
free port 195
free trade 140, 198
free trade zone 185, 195
free-port 140
free-port trade 140
free-range 122
freedom of speech 185
freehold apartment 168
freeze 63
freeze-thaw 80
fresh water 88
friction 69
frictional drag 91
front 65
frontier 50
frost 63
frost heaving 79
frost shattering 59, 79
frozen 75
frozen food 127
fruit 120
fruit plantation 120
fuel 104
fuel oil 105, 158
fuel rods 107
fuelwood 97
full-time farmer 123
full-time farming 123
fumarole 55
fumes 159
function 150, 164, 166, 169
fund-raising 190
fungicide 117
fungus 73
furniture 112
furrier 171
further away 22
Furtwängler Glacier 41
future generations 192
gable 171
gain 179
gain heat 71
gale 64
gallery 109
gap 193
garden 171
garden city 165
Garden City Movement 176

garigue 74
gas 54, 105
gas deposit 47
gas pipe 169
gas pipeline 111
gas supply 169
gas-liquefying plant 111
gaseous 54
gasometer 111
gasworks 111
gate 170
gated community 173
gazetteer 17
GDP – gross domestic product 181
generate 158
generation 162
generation of energy 192
generator 107
genetically modified 126
genetically modified food 126
gentle 77
gentrification 177, 197
geodesy 12
Geographic Information System 31
geographical consequence 197
geography 12, 31
geography of religion 13
geological era 53
geology 14, 31, 41
geomorphology 12, 14, 76
geostrophic wind 70
geosyncline 52
geothermal energy 108, 158
geothermal heat 108
geothermal power station 55
geyser 55
ghetto 130
glacial debris 46
glacial deposit 47
glacial stream 80
glaciation 42
glacier 42, 44, 49, 80
Glacier Bay 41
glaciology 12
glass industry 113
glasshouse 116
gley 61
gleying 61
global 194
global energy budget 67
global financial market 162
global grid 18

global instability 193
global stability 193
global village 199
global warming 14, 95, 160
globalisation 159, 194
glover 171
gneiss 58
GNI – gross national income 181
GNP – gross national product 181
goat 122
Gobi Desert 40
gold 47, 106
gold mining town 165
golf course 163
Gondwanaland 37, 53
goods 15, 139, 156, 171, 183, 191
goods depot 163
goose 122
gorge 34, 83
government 172, 184, 185
government sector 172
government spending 181
gradual 179
graduate 132
grafting 114
grain 119
grain cultivation 115
granary 116
Grand Canyon 50
granite 57
grant 125
grapes 120
graph 26
graphics 26
graphite 47, 106
gravel 61, 82
gravity 66
graze 117
grazing 115
Great Bear Lake 40
Great Lakes 50
Great Plains 48
Great Salt Lake 50
Great Sandy Desert 40
Great Slave Lake 40
Great Victoria Desert 40
green belt 176
green consumerism 152
green issues 161
green landscape 44
green revolution 114
greenhouse effect 66, 96, 160

209

greenhouse gas 66, 96, 160
grid plan 172
grid square 18
grid system 26
gridiron street pattern 172
grind 121
grocer 172
grocery store 145
gross 181
gross investment 181
gross selling price 146
ground water 88, 193
ground water pump 90
ground-breaking 159
grove 120
grow 119
growing season 67
growth industry 101
growth of services 147
growth pole 102
growth rate 141
groyne 86
guano 117
guest worker 136
guest-worker 130
guideline 139
gulf 35, 49
Gulf of Aden 39
Gulf of Bothnia 42
Gulf of Finland 42
Gulf of Guinea 39
Gulf of Mexico 39
Gulf of Riga 42
Gulf of Sidra 39
Gulf of Thailand 39
Gulf of Tonkin 39
Gulf Stream 46
Gulf-Atlantic Coastal Plain 48
gully 83
gullying 83
gun 183
gust 64
habitat 71
habitat density 178
habitat 127
Hadley cell 69
hail 64
halophyte 74
halophyte bush 93
Hamburg 45
hamlet 164, 174
hammada 74
hangar 169
Hanseatic town 165

harbour 168
harbour city 165
hard coal 109, 158
hard discount store 145
hard water 88
hardwood 73
Harmattan 71
harmful 160
Harris and Ullman's multiple
  nuclei model 175
harsh climate 186
harvest 116
harvester 116
Harz Mountains 44
hazardous materials 160
haze 65
HDI – human development index 180
HDR – human development report 180
head of the valley 83
headland 35, 85
headquarters 178
health 132
health care 149, 181
health geography 12
heat energy 94
heat transfer 13, 67
heather 76
heating 59
heatwave 63
heavy 179
heavy industry 100
heavy metal 96, 105
height 18
Heligoland 45
Heligoland Bay 45
hemp 122
herbicide 117
herbivore 74
herd 116
Hesse 45
hexagon 174
hide 114
hierarchy 164
high 18, 63
high humidity 72
high pressure 67
high street bank 184
high technology industry 101
high yield variety 114
high-rise 173
highland 77
hill 77

hilly 77
Hindu 133
Hinduism 133
hinterland 173
historical geography 12
history 183
hit 200
hoar frost 63
hoard 152
hoarding 152
hoe culture 115
hog cholera 122
hold steady 179
hollow 83
home country 136
home shopping 143
home trade 138
home-work 101
hop 121
horn 81
horse latitudes 69
horticulture 124
hosier 171
hospital 164
host country 137, 195
hot spot 55
hotel and restaurant sector 149
hotel business 149
household 131
household goods 113
household waste 96
Hoyt's sector model 175
Huang Ho 39
hub 167
Hudson Bay 39
Hudson Bay Lowlands 48
Hudson Strait 39
human geography 12
human labour 156
human resources management
  194
human rights 185
humic acid 60
humid 68
humidity 68
humification 60
humus 60
Hungarian Plain 44
Hunsrück 43
hurricane 64, 70, 94, 186
hybridisation 117
hydration 59
hydro-electricity 108
hydroelectric power station 192

210

hydrological cycle 87
hydrology 12, 87
hydrolysis 59
hydropower 158
hypermarket 145
Iberian Peninsula 43
ice 15
Ice Age 44, 53, 79
ice sheet 42, 80
ice wedge 81
iceberg 80
identity 37
igneous rock 55, 57
illiteracy 132, 188
illiterate 132, 188
illustrate 26, 188
illuviate 15
illuviation 62
ILO 199
image 150
immigrant 136
immigrate 136
immigration 136
immune 187
import 139, 147
impose 140, 198
impose upon 191
improve 142, 177, 184, 198
improved grassland 115
impulse buyer 152
impulse buy 152
in bulk 143
in front of 22
in principle 25
in stock 145
in the distance 22
inappropriate 191
incentive by the government 195
incineration 97
income 131
incompetent 185
increase 26, 63, 134, 179
increase 197
increasing 197
increment 27
indebted 183
indebtedness 183
independence 170
index 16
India rubber 106
Indian Ocean 38
indigenous 130, 172, 199
indigenous people 130

individual information 31
industrial 16, 100
industrial area 101, 163
industrial concern 101
industrial density 101
industrial estate 166
industrial inertia 103
industrial linkage 102
industrial location 101
industrial monostructure 101
industrial output 189
industrial park 101
industrial plant 101
industrial production 100
industrial region 101
industrial restructuring 103
industrial sector 189
industrial society 189
industrial village 165
industrial water 88
industrial worker 101
industrial workforce 189
industrialisation 100, 189
industrial country 178
industry 20, 100
industry structure 178
inequality 157
infant mortality rate 181
infertile 60
infiltration pool 89
influence 185
information overload 200
information processing 197
information technology 112
infrastructure 169, 184
inhabit 129
inhabitant 129, 166
injustice 157
innovation 101
insecticide 117
insert 31
insight 32
insolation 66
insolation weathering 59
insulate 99
insulation 99
insurance 149
integrate 130
integrated 130
integration 130
intensification 115
intention 24
interconnection 199
interdependence 198

interdependency 167
interest 37
interest rate 184
interglacial 53
interior of the earth 51
intermediary 142
intermittent river 88
intermittent spring 84
international bodies 184
international economic order 194
International Monetary Fund 184
international trade relations 194
interrelationship 16
intertropical convergence zone 69
intervention 177
interview 153
interviewer 153
intrazonal soil 61
inversion 65
invest 189
investment 181, 198
invisibles 139
ionosphere 66
iron and steel industry 110
iron and steel production 110
iron and steel works 110
the Iron Curtain 37
iron 105
iron oxide 60
iron pan 62
irony 24
irrigation 118
irrigation farming 115
Irtysh River 48
Islam 133
Islamic city 173
island 36
island arc 53
islet 85
isobar 67
isotherm 67
isotropic surface 174
issue 22
isthmus 35
Java Sea 38
jet stream 70
Jew 133
jewellery 113
Jewish 133
Jewry 133

211

job security 199
judge 25
jump 179
jungle 72
junk mail 200
just-in-time 144
just-in-time production 102
jute 122
Kalahari Desert 40
Kamchatka Peninsula 48
kame 81
kampong 173
kaolin 106
Kara Sea 38
karst 83
karst weathering 60
Kattegat 42
keep 172
kerb 168
key industry 100
Khingan Mountains 47
kibbutz 125
Kiel Bay 45
Kiel Canal 45
Kilimanjaro 41
knick point 82
know-how 191
Kola Peninsula 47
kolkhoz 125
Kolyma River 48
kwashiorkor 187
label 26
labour 148, 167, 183
labour cost 102
labour intensive 102
labour supply 102
labour-intensive 191
labourer 171
lack of oxygen 90
lagoon 35, 85
lake 17, 34, 78
Lake Baikal 40, 48
Lake Balaton 40
Lake Constance 40, 44
Lake Erie 40
Lake Garda 40
Lake Geneva 40
Lake Huron 40
Lake Ladoga 48
Lake Michigan 40
Lake Nyasa 40
Lake Ontario 40
Lake Superior 40
Lake Tanganyika 40

Lake Victoria 40
lamb 122
Lambert Glacier 41
land breeze 70
land consolidation 124
land reclamation 86
land reform 124
land surface 13
land tenure 124
land use 114, 177
land use pattern 166
landed property 156
landfill 79, 97, 163
landform 41, 76
landless 114
landlord 175
landowner 114
landscape 14, 36, 76
landscape ecology 12
landscape reserve 99
landslide 95
language 36
lapilli 54
Lapland 42
larch 75
large farm animals 122
large population 193
large town 164, 165
large-scale 191
late-night shopping 144
latent 13
laterite 61
latifundium 124
Latin American city 172
latitude 18
Laurasia 37, 53
lava 54
law firm 149
lawyer 149
layer 15, 31, 51
layer of air 66
layer of vegetation 72
leaching 62
lead 105
leaf 72
lean management 196
lean production 102
lean production 196
leather goods 112
leek 120
leeward 70
left 22
legal adviser 149
legal services 149

legend 16
legume 120, 121
leisure industry 149
lemon 121
Lena 39
Lena River 48
length 18
length of day 67
lentil 120
less demanding plant 117
lessivé 61
lettuce 120
levée 82
level of analysis 188
level of education 180
level off 179
liana 72
liberalisation 159
library 164
lichen 76
life expectancy 131, 134, 180
lifestyle 152
lifestyle group 167
light industry 100
light manufacturing 175
light metal 105
lighthouse 93
lightning 65
lignite 58, 105, 109
limestone 44, 58
line 18
line graph 27
linear village 165
linguistic cluster 173
link 199
liquefaction 56
liquid 54
liquid gas 158
literacy rate 181
lithology 57
lithosphere 51
litter 62
livelihood 155
livestock 116, 122
livestock breeding 113
livestock farming 123
living conditions 131
living space 132
living standard 199
load 89
loam 61
loans 184
local community 192
local government 149, 192

local market 173
local people 192
locate 18, 102
locating equipment 193
location 20, 102, 149
location factor 102
locational triangle 101
lock 85
locksmith 171
loess 58, 61
Lofoten 42
logging 97, 192
long 18
long profile 88
long-term 13
longitude 18
longshore current 85
loop 175
loss leader pricing 154
lot 124
low 26, 27, 63
low pollution 98
low pressure 67
low-class residential 175
low-density housing 175
low-wage country 198
lower course 78
Lower Saxony 45
lowering of the ground water table 90
lowland 17, 77
lowlands 42
lush 72
Luzon Strait 39
maar 54
machine and instrument producing industry 111
machinery 156
MacKenzie 39
mad cow disease 122
madrasah 173
maglev 168
magma 54
magnitude 56
mahogany 73
mail order 143
mail order catalogue 143
mail order company 143
mail shot 143
Main 46
main crop of cultivation 119
main industry 100
main topic 20
mainland 49

maintain 193
maize 119
Makassar Strait 39
malaria 187
male 131
malnourished 187
malnutrition 132, 187
manganese 105
mango 121
mangrove 73
manioc 119
mantle 51
manufacture 100
manufactured goods 142, 193
manufacturer 142
manufacturing 189
manufacturing industry 100, 189
manufacturing process 100
manufacturing zone 175
manure 117, 128
map title 18
maquiladora 196
maquis 74
marasmus 187
marble 58, 106
marginalised 132
marina 169
marine 90
marine deposit 79
marine ecosystem 90
maritime air mass 70
maritime climate 45, 72
market 193
market area 174
market economy 157
market gardening 123
market gardening firm 124
market place 170
market research 149, 153
market segment 153
market-orientated 155
marketable 153
marketing 148, 153
marketing mix 154
marketing principle 174
marl 58
married 131
marsh 61, 78
mass production 102, 157
massif 34
Massif Central 43
massive 179
Matterhorn 41

maximise 153
maximum data 27
meadow 115
meander 70, 83
meaning 24
means of production 102
measles 187
measure 147, 177, 184
measurement 26
meat 122
meat products 126
mechanical engineering 111
mechanisation 101, 116
Mecklenburg Lake District 45
Mecklenburg-Western Pomerania 45
medieval 170
mediterranean climate 74
Mediterranean Sea 38
medium-class residential 175
medium-sized town 165
Mekong 39
melon 120
melting pot 130
meltwater 88
Mercalli scale 56
merchandise 145
merchant 143, 171
mercury 105
merge 198
merger 198
meridian 18
mesh opening 127
mesosphere 66
message 24
mestizo 131
metabolism 60
metal alloy 105
metal goods 110
metal industry 110
metal production 110
metamorphic rock 58
meteorology 63
methane 96, 160
metropolis 165
metropolitan area 165
mica 57
micro-electronics 112
micro-organism 73
microchip 112
Mid-Atlantic Ridge 53
Mid-Ocean Ridge 53
Middle Ages 170
middleman 143

213

migrant 175
migrant worker 136
migrate 135
migration 135
mild 46
milk 116
milk processing plant 125
milking parlour 116
millet 119
mine 103, 108, 109
mine dump 109
mineral 15, 57
mineral substance 60
mineral water spring 55
minimum data 27
mining area 109
mining 108
mining town 165
ministry for the environment 161
misery 155, 186
Mississippi 50
mist 65
Mistral 70
mixed 172
mixed farming 123
mixed fuelling 107
MNC 194
moat 172
mobility 135
model 188
Mohorovičić discontinuity 51
molten 51
molybdenum 105
monastery 171
money 184, 191
monoculture 123
monopolies commission 155
monsoon 69
montane 76
montane tree line 76
moor 75, 78
moose 76
moraine 44, 80
moral reason 193
mortality 134
mosaic 36
Moselle 46
mosque 173
moss 76
motorway 168
motorway intersection 168
Mount Cameroon 41
Mount Everest 41

mountain 17, 34, 76
mountain of debts 184
mountain pasture 115
mountain range 17, 49, 77
mountain ridge 77
mountain threshold 44
mountain wind 71
mountainous 17, 76
mountains 34, 77
mouth 78, 80
Mozambique Channel 39
mud flats 85, 92
mud flow 93
mudflow 54
mudslide 94
mudstream 81
mulatto 131
mulberry tree 122
mulch 128
multi-person-household 167
multicultural 130
multilateral 184
multilateral aid 191
multiple store 144
multiple-family dwelling 168
multiracial 130
Munich 44
museum 164
mushroom rock 84
Muslim 133
mycorrhiza 73
NAFTA 185
name 23
Namib 40
nanotechnology 112
nation 37
nation-state 37
national government 149
National Park 50, 99
nationalisation 125
Native American 131
NATO 186
natural arch 35, 84
natural disaster 93
natural environment 13
natural gas 158
natural gas reserves 47
natural hazard 93
natural increase 181
natural landscape 163
natural religion 133
natural vegetation 71
nature 20
nature reserve 99

near 22
Neckar 46
need 132, 156
needs 186
negative 24
negative spiral 176
neglect 156
neo-liberalism 159
net foreign investment 181
net price 146
networking 199
neutral 24
new industries 189
new technologies 189
New Towns 176
newly industrialising country 195
NGO 191
Niagara Falls 50
niche 152
nickel 47, 105
Niger 39
Nile 39
nimbus 64
nitrogen 117
nitrous oxide 96
nivation 79
nocturnal 74
nomad 125
non-ferrous metal 105
non-polluting 161
non-profit organisation 191
non-renewable 158
non-tariff trade barrier 142, 198
North America 37
North American city 173
North European Plain 42
north face 35
North Friesland 45
North Frisian Islands 45
North German Plain 45
North Rhine-Westphalia 45
North Sea 38, 45
North-east trade wind 69
north-south divide 178
Norther 70
Northern Limestone Alps 44
Northwestern Uplands 42
nourished 187
nuclear accident 108
nuclear energy 107
nuclear fission 107
nuclear industry 110
nuclear power 158

nucleated village 165
nucleus 175
number 26
nunatak 80
nursery school 132
nutrient 60
nutrient cycle 73, 92
nutrient-demanding plant 117
nutrition 186
oasis 34, 74
oasis agriculture 123
oats 119
Ob River 48
Ob-Irtysh 39
obligation 193
occurence 93
ocean 13, 35, 79
ocean conveyor 91
ocean current 91, 158
ocean depth 91
ocean circulation 91
oceanography 12
office building 163
office space 151
office work 150
offshore wind 70
oil 105, 158
oil company 111
oil deposit 47
oil industry 111
oil palm 120
oil platform 105
oil pollution 92
oil refinery 111
oil reserves 47
oil rig 105
oil spill 105
oil-bearing crops 120
oilfield 105
oilseed rape 108, 120
Oka River 48
old age 134
old-age dependency ratio 134
olive 120
on the horizon 22
one-child policy 134
one-way street 168
onion 120
onshore wind 70
OPEC 185
open fields 114
open-pit mining 109
opening hours 144
opera 164

operate commercially 123
operate 194
operation 194
operational area 166
operational division 194
opinion 25
optical industry 112
optics 112
optimisation 156
optimise 16, 153
opulent society 162
orange 121
orchid 73
ore 47, 105, 110
Ore Mountains 43, 44
organic material 60
organic matter 15, 92
organic product 161
organic weathering 60
organically 127
orientation 17
originate 94
orogenesis 44
orthophoto 32
orthorectify 32
out-migration 176
outflow 140
outgoings 140
outpouring 54
outsourcing 147, 196
outwash plain 81
overburden 109
overcast 64
overcrowded 129, 176
overcultivation 96
overexploitation of forests 97
overfish 127
overfishing 127
overgrazing 96
overheads 146
overheating of water 90
overpopulation 129
overproduction 102
overseas trade 138
oversupply 157
owe 184
own brand 145
ownership 124
ox-bow lake 83
oxidation 59
oxygen 57, 66
oxygen steel converter 110
ozone 66, 160
ozone concentration 66

ozone hole 66, 96
ozone layer 66, 96
P-wave 55
Pacific Coast Ranges 48
Pacific Ocean 38
pack ice 95
paid work force 156
palaeoclimatology 12
palaeogeography 12
Palatine Forest 44
Pamir Mountains 47
pampas 75
Pangaea 37, 53
papaya 121
paper mill 111
paper processing 111
paper production 111
paprika 120
parent material 62
Paris Basin 42
parking area 163
part-time agent 143
part-time farming 123
pass 35
passport 137
Pasterze Glacier 41
pastoral farming 123
pasture 115
path 94
pattern 36, 164
patterned ground 81
pauperism 155
pavement 168, 169
pea 120
peach 120
peak 27, 35, 49, 77
peanut 120
pear 120
peat 58, 61
peat bog 78
pedestrian crossing 169
pedestrian precinct 168
pedology 12, 15
pellagra 187
pellets 108
peninsula 36, 49
people's commune 125
pepper 120
per capita income 178, 181
percentage 26, 28, 29
percolate 87
percolation 87
percolation plant 89
perennial stream 88

215

perilous 179
period of time 29
peripheral region 194
periphery 190
Perito Moreno Glacier 41
permafrost 75
permanent agriculture 115
permanent crop 119
permanent grassland 115
permeability 37
permeable 37, 87
persecute 137
persecution 137
Persian Gulf 39
person of mixed parentage 131
personnel 150, 194
pervious 87
pest 117
pesticide 96, 117
petrochemical industry 111
petrol 158
petroleum 111
pH value 60
pharmaceutical industry 111
Philippine Sea 38
phosphate 106, 117
photograph 21
photovoltaic 108
physical features 17
physical geography 12
physical map 17
physical-geographical region 41, 48
physiographic subregion 47
physiography 14
picture 21
pie chart 28
piece 28
Piedmont 48
pig 122
pig iron 110
pigsty 116
pillory 170
pilot survey 154
Pindus Mountains 44
pine 75
pineapple 121
pingo 81
pipeline 111
plain 35, 77
planetary circulation 69
planetary winds 70
plankton 92
planned city 170

planning 194
plant 116
plant disease 117
plant protection 117
plantation farming 123
plastics 110
plate 52
plate boundary 53
plate tectonics 52
plateau 35, 49, 77
platinum 106
plight 186
plot 29, 114
plough 116
plum 120
plummet 178
plunge 178
plunge line 91
plunge pool 83
plutonite 57
plywood factory 112
pneumonia 187
podzol 61
podzolization 61
point bank 83
point of view 25
polar bear 76
polar front 69
polar high 69
polar regions 72
polder 86
police station 164
policy 185
Polish Plain 43
political consequences 195
political geography 12
political landscape 41
political reason 193
politician 185
politics 31, 185
polity 170
polje 84
pollutant 95, 160
pollute 95, 159
pollution 13, 95, 159
pollution control 98
pollution-free 98
polytunnel 116
pond 78
poor 131, 178
poorhouse 156
poppy 121
populate 129
populated 129

population 20, 129, 181
population change 134
population concentration 176
population development 133
population explosion 134, 155
population geography 12
population growth 133
population pyramid 134
population structure 134, 167
populous 129
porcelain 113
porcelain industry 113
pork 122
porous 54, 61
port 163, 193
position of the sun 67
positioning 24
positive 24
post office 163
potable water 193
potash 106, 117
potash salt 106
potato 119
potential market 153
pothole 82
potter 171
poulterer 172
poultry farming 125
poverty 131, 155, 176, 186
power cut 106
power line 106
power station 107, 157
power supply 157, 169
prairie 49, 75
precious metal 105
precious stone 106
precious timber 73
precious wood 122
precipitation 46, 68
precision engineering 112
precision mechanics 112
predator 74
predict 94
preferential 142, 198
present 29
press 118
pressure 56
pressure gradient 91
pressure release 59
pressure wave 55
pressurised water reactor 107
prestige 150
prevailing wind 64
price 141, 146

price agreement 155
price discrimination 155
price drop 157
price leadership 154
price mechanism 157
price plateau 155
price war 154
price-cutting 154
pricing process 157
primary industry 100
primary product 144
primary production 92
primary school 132
primary sector 189
primary energy 158
primate city 164, 190
principal 143
printing industry 112
privatisation 159
process 14, 26
process 126
processing 100
processing industry 100
produce 16, 100, 114, 141
producer 156
producer services 146
product 141
product placement 155
product quality 148
production 138, 156
production area 105
production costs 102
production facility 194
production 194
production planning 148
production quote 186
productivity 162
profit 157, 192
profit motive 157
progress 184, 189
prohibit 142, 198
projection 16, 34
promote 198
promotion 139, 154
promotion scheme 154
property market 197
prospecting 103
prosperity 131
protection 161
protectionism 142, 186, 198
protectionist 142, 198
protective containment vessel 107
protective forest strip 128

protective plantation 128
protein 92
Protestant 133
protractor 29
provide with 183
provision 183
provision of infrastructure 196
proximity 177
public authorities 177
public bath 173
public expense 156
public transport 169
publish 23
published 23
publishing 149
pumice 55
puna 76
punishment 170
purchase 193
purchase price 146
purchaser 151
purchasing power 152, 180, 199
purify 160
push and pull factor 136
pygmy 131
Pyrenees 44
pyroclastic fall 54
quality of life 131
quantify 147
quantity 29
quantity of fish caught 127
quartz 57
quarzite 58
quay 163
quicksand 82
quince 120
quota 125, 142, 198
race 130
radiation 66
radiation deficit 67
radiative 13
radioactive contamination 108
radioactive waste 107
raging 78
rail vehicle production 111
railway bridge 168
railway line 18
railway network 18
railway station 163
rain 64
rainfall 64
rainfed agriculture 115
rainforest 72
rainshadow 68

rainstorm 64
rainy 64
raise 199
raised beach 86
raisin 120
rally 179
ranch 125
range of industries 189
rapid 78, 83, 179
rapid growth 72
rapid urbanisation 176
rate of removal 192
rationalisation 147, 196
ravine 83
raw material 103
raw material oriented 102
raw materials 183
re-export 140
re-import 140
reactor core 107
ready-made meal 127
rear 116
receipts 140
receiving water 34
recover 179
recoverable 103
recreation 167
recruit 136
recultivation 109
recycle 98
recycling 98, 169
Red Sea 38
red tape 142, 198
redistribute 124
refer 24
refine 111
refinery 163
reflect 24, 66
reflection 66
refrigerant 96
refuge 137
refugee 137
refuse 96, 160
refuse incineration plant 97
reg 84
region 18, 36, 170
regional development 183
regional development planning 177
regional distribution of farm size 123
regional planning 177
regionalism 37
register 16

217

registration 137
regolith 62
regulated river course 90
reindeer 76
rejuvenation 82
relation 20
relative humidity 68
relative numbers 29
release 95
relief 17, 41, 76
relief organisation 190
relief rainfall 68
religion 133
religious enclave 173
relocation 109, 115
remission of debts 184
remove 198
rendzina 61
renewable 158
renewable energy 108
rent 124
reorganisation 196
reprocessing plant 107
reptile 74
resale price maintenance 146
research and development 101, 148
research and development 194
reservation 130
reserve 103
reservoir 17, 34, 89, 108
resettle 109
resettlement 137
residential 166
residential building 166
residential district 162, 166
residential zone 172, 175
resistance to earthquakes 56
resistant 119
resource 15, 103
resource management 31
resources 98
respiratory disease 187
respiratory infection 187
restaurant sector 149
restore 177
restrain 142, 198
restraint 198
restrict 162
restrict access 37
restrict contact 37
resurgence 84
retail 144
retail trade 144

retailer 144
retailing 148
retaining basin 89
retaliate 198
retirement age 131
return migration 136
returns policy 200
reurbanisation 176
revetment 86
Rheinish Massif 45
Rhine 39, 46
Rhineland-Palatinate 45
Rhodope Mountains 44
Rhön 45
ria 86
rias 35
rice 119
rich 178
Richter scale 56
ridge 35, 77
riffle 82
rift valley 53
rifting 52
right 22
rigid 51, 142, 198
Ring of Fire 55
ring road 168
Rio Grande 50
rise 26, 63, 179
rise 78
rise in sea level 95
river 15, 17, 34, 78
river bank 78
river capture 89
river gorge 47
river oasis 74
river profile 88
river regime 88
river terrace 82
riverbed 78
rivulet 78
road 18
roadway 169
roast 121
roche moutonnée 81
rock 57
rock joint 59
rock salt 58
rock type 15, 57
rocky 77
Rocky Mountains 48
rolling hill 43
rolling mill 110
Roman Empire 170

roof 171
root crops 119
rooting depth 61
rosewood 73
Ross Ice Shelf 41
rot 72
rotation with grass period 123
round village 165
rounded 77
routeway 175
routine task 150
rubber 73, 122
rubbish dump 96
rubbish railway 110
rugged 77
running expenses 146
runoff 87
runway 169
rural 162
rural area 176
rural geography 13
rural region 174
rural settlement 163
ruralise 163
Russian Federation 46
rye 119
S-wave 55
Saarland 45
saddle 77
safeguard 191
Sahara Desert 40
Sahel 73
sales 146, 148
sales forecast 153
sales gimmick 155
sales tax 146
salination 118
salinisation 62, 97
salt 106
salt content 91
salt marsh 86
salt meadow 93
salt pan 74
salt water 88, 92
salt water biotope 92
saltpetre 106
salty soil 92
sample 154
San Andreas fault 56
sanction 142
sanctions 198
sand 61
sandbank 85
sandstone 58

sanitation 132, 186
satellite image 21
satellite town 165
satire 24
saturated 68
savanna 73
savings ratio 152
sawmill 192
Saxony 45
Saxony-Anhalt 45
Sayan Mountains 47
scale 17, 27
Scandinavian Peninsula 42
scarcity 157
scarp slope 77
scattered settlement 165
scattering 66
scavenger 74
scenic hilly area in Franconia 44
schistosomiasis 118
Schleswig-Holstein 45
school 164
school-aged 188
scientific investigation 31
Scirocco 71
sclerophyllous 74
scorch 97
scree 61, 81
scrub vegetation 74
sea 35
sea breeze 70
sea level 18
Sea of Azov 38
Sea of Japan 38
Sea of Marmara 38
Sea of Okhotsk 38
sea-floor spreading 52
sea-water pollution 92
seam 105
search-engine 200
season 67
seasonal climate 67
seasonal worker 114
second-order settlement 174
secondary energy 158
secondary industry 100
secondary school 132
secondary sector 189
section 17
sectionalism 37
sector 28, 146, 167
sector model 188
sediment 14
sedimentary material 46

sedimentary rock 58
seed 117
segment 28
segregate 130
segregation 130
seif 84
seismic wave 55
seismograph 56
seismological station 56
seismology 55
seismometre 56
self-sufficiency 124
self-sufficient 183
Selva 73
semi-arid 74
semi-desert 74
semi-detached house 168
semi-nomad 125
semiconductor 112
separated 131
serir 74, 84
service 16, 146, 156
service economy 189
service industry 101
service sector 148
service sector 197
services 139, 169, 191
set-aside system 128
setting 23
settle 129
settlement 37, 47, 129, 162, 174
settlement geography 13
settlement hierarchy 164
settlement system 166
sewage 90, 160
sewage disposal 169
sewage plant 90
sewer 170
sex 131
shade 17, 29
shading 20
shaduf 118
shaft 109
shale 58
shallow 60, 73, 78
shallow bay 86
shallow water zone 92
shanty 172
shanty town 138, 164
shape 14, 164
sharp 179
shatter 59
shear 117
shear wave 55

shed 171
sheep 122
sheep shed 116
shelf area 91
shelter 186
shield 46, 53, 77
shifting cultivation 115, 123
shifting dune 84
shipbuilding industry 112
shipping lane 89
shipping lane depth 89
shipyard 112
shoal 85
shock 55
shoemaker 171
shop 166, 171
shopping centre 163
shopping mall 145
shopping precinct 145
shopping spree 152
shore 35, 79
shore cliff 35
shore ice 85
shoreline 35
short grass prairie 75
shortage 103
shower 64
showroom 144
shrivel 73
shrub layer 72
sial 51
side canal 90
Sierra Nevada 44
silage 117
silicon 57
silicon chip 112
silkworm breeding 122
silo 116
silt 61, 82
silting zone 85, 92
silver 106
sima 51
simplification 156
simulation 32
single 131
single family house 168
single-person household 167
sink 63
sisal 122
site 164
situation 164
size 18, 166
size of farm area 115
Skagerrak 42

219

skerry 35
skilled worker 101
skyscraper 173
slag 110
slash-and-burn farming 123
slate 58
slaughterhouse 126
slave 183
sleet 64
slide 178
slight 179
slip zone 53
slip-off slope 83
slope 15, 43, 54, 77, 82, 178
slope formation 15
slow 179
sludge 90
sluice 90
slum 164, 166
small farm animals 122
small town 164, 165
small-scale 191
small-scale industry 101
smallholder 114
smelt 110
smelting of aluminium 110
smelting 110
smelting of non-ferrous metals 110
smith 171
smog 65, 96, 160
smoke 54
snout 80
snow 64
snow line 75
snow storm 64
snowdrift 64
snowfall 46
snowfield 80
soar 179
social 155, 159
social benefit 132
social class 132, 175
social facility 132
social geography 13
social status 132, 153
social structure 132, 167
social welfare 149
social welfare system 184
Social-spatial 166
society 155, 169
soil 15, 41, 60, 128
soil degradation 118
soil fertility 60, 178

soil formation 60
soil moisture 87
soil organism 60
soil profile 62
soil structure 61
soil texture 61
soil type 61
soil horizon 62
solar cell 108
solar constant 66
solar energy 66
solar furnace 108
solar panel 108
solar power 108, 158
sole retailer 145
solfatara 55
solid 51
solidify 54
solifluction 80
soluble 59
solution 59
solvent 96
Sonora 40
sophisticated 151
source 23, 78
South America 37
South China Sea 38
South-east trade wind 69
sovkhozy 125
sow 116
soybean 120
spa town 165
space technology 112
space-oriented 177
sparkling wine 126
spatial 32, 36
spatial analysis 16, 178
spatial compatibility 177
spatial development 177
spatial distribution 15
spatial fragmentation 177
spatial interaction 167
spatial pattern 177
spatial relevance 177
spatial research 177
spatial structure 177
spawning ground 127
special economic zone 195
specialisation 156
specialised crop 119
specialist shop 145
speciality shop 145
species 71
speed hump 168

spirits 126
spit 35
spit 86
splitting up of possessions 124
sports complex 163
spreader 109
spring 34, 87
spring tide 95
sprinkler 118
spruce 75
spur 35, 77
squall 64
squatter settlement 138
St. Lawrence 50
stabilise 176, 179
stable 63
stables 116
stack 35, 86
stadium 163
stalactite 84
stalagmite 84
standard of living 152, 180
standardisation 156
staple 114, 132
state-owned farm 125
status symbol 170
steady 179
steel plant 110
steel production 110
steel stabiliser 106
steep 77
steppe 75
sterilisation 134
stimulate 176
stock 145
stock up 145
stockist 145
stone wall 170
store 31, 87, 166
storm 64, 94
storm surge 95
storm tide 85
storm wave 95
strait 35
Strait of Dover 42
Strait of Malacca 39
strangler 72
stratified 153
stratopause 66
stratosphere 66
stratus 64
stream 78, 82
stream 81
street 170

street light 169
street village 165
strengthen 179
stretch of water 178
striation 80
strip city 165
strip of protective vegetation 128
strip-farming 128
stroke 187
strong 183
study 22
study category 26
sub-contracting 147
subcontinent 37
subcontracting 196
subcontractor 147
subduction zone 53
subject 22
submarine relief 90
subpolar low 69
subset 153
subsidies 195
subsidise 125
subsidy 125, 176
subsistence economy 190
subsistence 124
subsistence level 132
subsoil 15, 62
substance 15
subtropical high pressure belt 69
subtropics 72
suburb 162, 175
suburbanisation 151, 173, 176
success 189
succulent 74
Sudeten Mountains 43
sugar beet 119
sugar cane 119
sugar mill 127
sulfur 106
sulphur dioxide 96
sulphurous gas 54
sultry 63
Sulu Sea 38
summer drought 74
summer solstice 67
summit 35, 77
"sun city" 165
sunflower 120
sunny intervals 64
super store 145
superannuation 134

supercontinent 37
superimpose 32
supermarket 144
supply 132, 138, 151, 157, 166
support 156
support industry 101
suppress 185
surf 35, 79, 85
surface 14
surface circulation 91
surface crusting 62
surface of the sea 91
surface water 88
surface water drain 169
surge 91, 179
surplus 157, 189
surplus of importance 166
surplus of women 134
surplus revenue 189
survey 152
suspension 89
sustainability 98
sustainable 98, 127, 159
sustainable method 192
sustained growth 190
Swabian Alps 43, 44
swallow hole 84
swamp 49, 78
swash 85
swell 91
swine flu 122
symbol 20, 24
symbolism 24
syncline 53
system of land use 123
systematic 153
table 26
table of contents 16
tabular data 32
taiga 75
tailor 172
tangerine 121
tangled roots 72
tank 118
tanker 105
tanner 172
tap 122
target group 153
target selling price 186
tariff 140, 186, 198
taro 119
Tasman Sea 38
Taunus 43
taxi stand 168

Taymyr Peninsula 47
tea 121
teak 73, 122
technology park 112
tectonics 52
telecommunications 150, 197
telephone cable 170
temperate 72
temperate climate 45
temperate rainforest 49
temperate zone 72
temperature 63, 67
temporary shelter 192
tenant 124, 175
tension 56, 130
tent 192
tent camp 138
tenure 124
termite 74
terms of trade 141, 198
terra rossa 61
terrace agriculture 115
terraced house 168
territory 37, 137
tertiarisation 146
tertiary 146
tertiary sector 146, 189
textile industry 112
textiles 183
texture 20
Thames 39
Thames Barrier 93
thaw 75
The Great Belt 42
the Internet 199
The Little Belt 42
The Pennines 42
the sea 79
theatre 164
thematic map 17, 20
theme 20, 22
thermocline 91
thermohaline circulation 91
thermosphere 66
thick bark 73
third-order settlement 174
thorny 74
thoroughfare 168
three-field rotation 123
thrift 152
throughflow 87
thunder 65
thunderstorm 65
Thuringia 45

221

Thuringian Basin 45
Thuringian Forest 43, 45
tidal inlet 85
tidal power 108, 158
tidal range 85
tidal wave 85, 91
tide 79
tides 85
tied aid 191
Tien Shan 47
till 81
timber 122, 192
timber frame 171
timber-framed 171
time horizon 161
Timor Sea 38
tin 105
titanium 106
title 23
tobacco 121
tobacco products 113
tolerance 130
tolerant 130
toll 170
tomato 120
tombolo 35
top 22
topical event 24
topography 42
topsoil 15, 60, 62
tornado 70, 94
torrential rain 94
total melt-down 107
tourism 44, 140, 149
tourism geography 13
tower 170
town 174
town hall 163
town wall 170
township 173
townspeople 170
toxic 95
toxic waste 96
toxic waste dumping 96
track 200
tracker device 193
tract 43
tractor 116
trade 100, 138, 146, 197
trade balance 139
trade barrier 140, 186, 198
trade deficit 139
trade surplus 139
trade war 140, 198

trade wind 69
trading bloc 185
trading city 165
trading estate 101
trading links 138
traffic infrastructure 150
traffic lights 169
Transcaucasus 47
transfer pricing 199
transformation 158
transhumance 123
transition 189
transition zone 173, 175
transnational 137
transnational corporation 194
transpiration 68
transport 141, 149
transport costs 174
transport infrastructure 169, 190
transport route 175
transportation geography 13
transportation route 18
Transylvanian Alps 44
travel agency 149
travel agent 149
trawl 127
trawler fleet 127
treatment 161
tree line 75
tree nursery 121, 124
tremor 55, 93
triangular trade 183
tribalism 138
tribe 130
tributary 34, 78
Tropic of Cancer 67
Tropic of Capricorn 67
tropical 72
tropical climate 49
tropical cyclone 94
tropical fruit 121
tropical rainforest 72
tropics 72
tropopause 66
troposphere 66
trough 91
tsunami 56, 94
tube mill 110
tuberculosis 187
tuff 55
tundra 49, 75
tungsten 105
tunnel 168

turf 37
turkey 122
turnover 146
24/7 144
twister 70
two-family house 168
type of farm 123
typhoid 187
typhoon 70, 94
ultraviolet 66
Uluru 41
unbiased 153
uncontrolled chain reaction 107
undercut 86
underdevelopment 16
underground 109
underground mining 109
underground stream 83
undergrowth 72
undernutrition 132
underpopulation 129
undulating 42
unemployed 189
unfavourable 197
unit 27
unit price 146
university 164
unleaded 161
unskilled 101
unspiked water 88
unsustainable 159
untouchable 133
up-market 153
upbringing 188
upland 47
uplift 42, 52
upper town 165
upper-class residential area 166
uproot 94
upstream 78
uptown 173
Ural Mountains 47
uranium 105
urban 162
urban area 176
urban geography 13
urban sprawl 176
urban system 190
urbanisation 181
Urstromtal 81
usage 20
use 166
utilisation 166
utilities 189

utilities sector 189
V-shaped valley 83
vaccinate 187
vaccination 187
vaccine 187
valley 17, 34, 42, 43, 77, 81
valley wind 71
value 27, 141, 181
vanadium 105
variable 27
Variscian Folding 44
VAT 146
Vatnajökull 41
vegetables 120
vegetation 41
vegetation zone 71
vehicle exhausts 96
vein 103
velocity 88, 95
vent 54
village 164, 174
village built around a green 165
vine 121
vineyard 118
vintage 118
vintner 172
viscous 54
visibility 65
visibles 139
visual 21
visualisation 26
visualise 26
viticulture 118
volcanic 54
volcanic ash 54
volcanic eruption 93
volcanic plug 54
volcanism 53
volcano 47, 53
volcanology 54
Volga 39
Volga River 48
volume of foreign trade 185
volume of sales 185
voluntary export restraint 142
Vosges 43
vulnerable 185
wadi 74
walkway 170
walnut 121
want 151
warehouse 144, 163
warehousing 149
Warsaw-pact 186

washing out of salt 93
Wasserkuppe 46
waste 160
waste disposal 167
waste dump 97
waste heat 90
waste management 97
waste management
  infrastructure 169
waste of space 177
waste reduction 97
waste water 88
water buffalo 122
water conduit 88
water cycle 87
water disposal 87
water distribution sluice 89
water exchange 87
water infrastructure 169
water main 169
water management 87
water pipe 88
water pollution 90, 96
water production 87
water reserve 90
water retention capacity 61
water rights 87
water supply 87, 169
water supply and distribution
  87
water table 87, 193
water vapour 68
water withdrawal 87
waterfall 34, 83
watering place 117
waterlogging 61
watershed 89
waterway 89
waterworks 88
wattle 171
wave 79, 91
wave energy 108
wave length 91
wave power 158
wave-cut notch 86
wave-cut platform 86
waxy 74
weaken 178
wealth 170, 181
weather 13, 59, 63
weather conditions 13
weather forecast 13, 63
weather map 63
weather record 13

weather report 63
weathering 14, 44, 59
weathering by root pressure 60
weaver 172
weighbeam 170
weir 89
well 171
well founded 191
well-being 162
well-building 193
wells in a row 118
Weser 46
West Frisian Islands 42
West Siberian Plain 46
Westerlies 69
western margin climate 74
wet savanna 73
wet season 73
wet-dry climate 72
wetland 45, 47
whaling 127
wheat 119
Wheeler Peak 50
whirlwind 70
wholesale 142
wholesale market 173
wholesale trade 142
wholesaler 143
wide 18
wide strip field pattern 114
width 18
wilderness 50
wildlife sanctuary 99
wind 63
wind direction 63
wind energy 158
wind farm 108
wind force 64
wind power 108
wind speed 63
windbreak 128
windmill 108
windward 70
wine 121
wine grower 118
winepress 118
winter solstice 67
wood 122
wood industry 112
wood pellet 158
work the land 115
worker 167
workers' housing estate 165
workforce 102

223

workforce 196
working poor 156
working-class town 165
world 37
World Bank 184
world region 170
world religion 133
world trade 138
the World Wide Web 199
xenophobic 130

xerophyte 74
xerophytic 74
Yablonovy Range 47
yam 119
yardang 84
Yellow Sea 38
Yenisey 39
Yenisey River 48
yield 115
yuppie 131

zinc 105
zone of ablation 80
zone of accumulation 80
zone of eluviation 62
zone of illuviation 62
zone of working people's
  homes 175
zucchini 120
Zugspitze 41, 46

Deutsches Stichwortregister

A-Horizont 62
Aasfresser 74
Abbau 103
abbaubar 160
abbauen 103, 109
Abbaufläche 109
Abbaurichtung 109
abbrennen 97
Abenteuer 50
Abfall 160
Abfallbeseitigung 97
abfallen 63
Abfallentsorgungsinfrastruktur 169
Abfluss 87, 140
Abflusssystem 17
Abgase 159, 160
abgeben 95, 96
abgestorben 72
Abhang 54
abholzen 97
Abholzung 97
Abholzungsgeschwindigkeit 192
Abholzungsrate 97
abkühlen 54
Abkühlung 59
Abladen von Müll 160
Ablagerung 14, 82
Ablagerungsgestein 58
ablandiger Wind 70
Ablation 14, 79
ablenken 69
Ablenkung 69
Abmessung 26
Abnahme 26
abnehmen 26
Abrasion 14
Abrasionsplatte 86
Abrasionsplattform 86
Abraum 109
Abraumbahn 110
Abraumhalde 109
abrutschen 178
Absatz 146
Absatzgebiet 174
Absatzkosten 146
Absatzprognose 153
Abschnitt 17
Absetzer 109
Absicht 24
absolute Zahlen 29

absorbieren 66
Absorption 66
Abstand 174
absteigen 71
abstraktes Zeichen 20
abstürzen 178
Abtragung 14
Abtreibung 134
Abwanderung von Industrie aus den Zentren 176
Abwärme 90
Abwärme-Emission 96
Abwasser 88, 90, 160
Abwasserentsorgung 169
Abwasserkanal 170
abwechseln 73
Abwicklungsstelle 151
Achse 26
Ackerbausystem 123
Aconcagua 41
Ader 103
Adriatisches Meer 38
Aerosol 66
Afrika 38
afrikanische Stadt 172
Agentur für internationale Entwicklung 190
Agglomerationsvorteil 102
Agrargeografie 12
Agrarstruktur 123
Agribusiness 126
Agroforstwirtschaft 123
agroindustrieller Betrieb 126
aktivieren 31
Aktivität 177
aktuelles Ereignis 24
Akzeptanz 137
Albedo 66
Aletschgletscher 41
Algenblüte 90
Alkohol 183
alleinstehend 131
Allmende 114
Alluvion 34
Alm 125
Almhütte 125
Alpen 43, 44
Alpenvorland 44
alphabetisches Ortsverzeichnis 17
Alphabetisierungsgrad 181
Alpidische Faltung 53

alpine Stufe 76
alpines System 43
Altai Gebirge 47
Altarm 83
Altenquotient 134
ältere Menschen 131
alternative Energiequellen 158
Altersgruppe 134
Alterspyramide 134
Altersstruktur 134, 178
Aluminium 105
Aluminiumoxid 60
Aluminiumverhüttung 110
am Horizont 22
Amazonas 39
Amerikanische Ureinwohner 131
Amur 48
Amut 39
an den Rand gedrängt 132
an Trockenheit angepasst 74
anaerob 61
Analphabet 132, 188
Analphabetismus 132, 188
Analyse 15
Analyseebene 188
analysieren 31
Ananas 121
Anbau 15, 92
anbauen 113, 119
Anbaufolge 114
Anbauprodukt 118
Andamanensee 38
Angebot 138, 151, 157
Angebotsüberhang 157
angemessen 191
angepasste Technologie 116
Angerdorf 165
Angestellte 167
anheben 199
Anmeldung 137
anreichern 15, 31
Anreicherung 62
Anreicherungshorizont 62
Anreiz durch die Regierung 195
Ansicht 25
ansprechen 200
anstehendes Gestein 57
ansteigen 26, 179
ansteigend 197
Anstieg 26, 134, 197
Antarktis 38, 41

225

Anthrazitkohle 104
Antike 170
Antikörper 187
Antimon 105
Antizyklone 67
Anwaltskanzlei 149
anwerben 136
anzapfen 122
äolisch 84
Apartheid 130, 172
Apenninen 44
Apfel 120
Apfelsine 121
Appalachen 50
Appalachen-Plateau 48
Aprikose 120
Aquakultur 127
Äquator 18
äquatoriale Tiefdruckrinne 69
Äquatorialklima 72
Arabische Wüste 40
Arabisches Meer 38
Arafurasee 38
Aralsee 40, 48
Arbeit 148
Arbeiter 167, 171
Arbeitersiedlung 165
Arbeiterstadt 165
Arbeiterwohnzone 175
arbeitsintensiv 102, 191
Arbeitskosten 102
Arbeitskräfte 102, 167, 183
Arbeitskräftepotential 102
arbeitslos 189
Arbeitsplatzsicherheit 199
Arbeitsteilung 156
archimedische Schraube 118
Archipel 36
Ardennen 43
Arktisches Meer 38
arm 131, 178
Ärmelkanal 42
Armenhaus 156
Armut 131, 155, 176, 186
Art 71
Artenvielfalt 178
artesisch 88
artesisches Becken 88
Asbest 106
asiatische Stadt 173
Asien 38
Asowsches Meer 38
Asthenosphäre 51
Asyl 136

Atakama Wüste 40
Atemwegserkrankung 187
Atemwegsinfektion 187
Athabasca-Gletscher 41
Äthanol 108
Atlantik 38
Atlantischer Dreieckshandel 183
Atlas 16, 34
Atmosphäre 13, 66
atmosphärische Grenzschicht 13
atmosphärische Zirkulation 69
Atoll 36, 54
Atomindustrie 110
Aubergine 120
auf und ab verlaufend 42
Aufbau 20
aufbauen 96
aufbereiten 26
aufbrauchen 103
aufdrängen 191
auferlegen 140, 198
Aufgabe 150
aufgelassenes Land 97
Aufheiterung 64
auflandiger Wind 70
Auflistung 26
auflösen 59, 83
Aufnahmeland 137
Aufschüttung 79
aufsteigen 71
auftauen 75
Auftraggeber 143
Auftragnehmer 143
Auftrieb 91
aufwendig 194
aufziehen 116
Ausbeutung 50, 159, 193
ausbilden 188
Ausblasung 84
ausbrechen 54
Ausbruch 54
Ausbruchsschlot 93
ausdehnen 59
Ausdehnung 18
Ausfuhr 139
Ausgaben 140
Ausgangsgestein 62
Ausgliederung 147, 196
Auskommen 155
Auslagerung von Dienstleistungen 147
Ausländer 130

ausländerfeindlich 130
ausländisch 130
Auslandshandel 138
Auslands~ 147
auslaufende Welle 85
Außenhandelsvolumen 185
außergewöhnlich 49
Aussiedlung 115
Ausstellungsraum 144
Aussterben 98
Ausströmen 54
Aussüßung 92
Austausch 183
Australien 38
austrocknen 73, 92
Auswanderer 136
auswandern 136
Auswanderung 135
auswaschen 15
Auswaschung 62
Auswaschungshorizont 62
Auswurfmaterial 54
Autoabgase 96
Autobahn 168
Autobahnkreuz 168
Autohersteller 111
Automatisierung 101
Automobilmontagewerk 111
Autor 23
azonaler Boden 61
B-Horizont 62
Bach 34, 78
Bächlein 78
Bäcker 172
Baden-Württemberg 45
Baffin Bay 39
Bahnhof 163
Bahnlinie 18
Bahnnetz 18
Baikalsee 40, 48
Balkendiagramm 28
Baltischer Landrücken 43
Banane 121
Bandasee 38
Bandstadt 165
Bankgeschäft 149
Baobab 73
Barackensiedlung 138
Barchan 84
Barentssee 38
Barmherzigkeit 191
Barriereriff 85
Basalt 55, 58
Basar 173

basisch 60
Basisdienstleistungen 147
Bauer 114
Bauernhof 115, 163
Bauindustrie 111
Baumgrenze 75
Baumkrone 72
Baumriese 72
Baumschule 121, 124
Baumwolle 122
Bausubstanz 177
Bauxit 105
Bayern 45
Bayrischer Wald 44
beachten 22
Beben 55
Becken 49
Bedarf 156
bedeckt 64
Bedeutung 24
Bedeutungsüberschuss 166
Bedürfnis 132, 151
Bedürfnisse 186
beeinflussen 185
Befangenheit 153
begradigter Flusslauf 90
behandeln 22, 24
Behandlung 161
Bekanntmachung 170
Bekleidung 112
Belastung 95
Belegschaft 196
belüften 61
Benzin 111, 158
Berater 149
Beratung 149
Bereitstellung 183
Bereitstellung von Infrastruktur 196
Berg 17, 34, 76
Bergbau 108
Bergbaustadt 165
Bergfried 172
Berggipfel 77
Berghang 77
bergig 76
Bergrücken 77
Bergschrund 80
Bergspitze 77
Bergwerk 108
Bergwind 71
Berieselungsanlage 118
Beringstraße 39
Berlin 45

beschäftigt 189
Beschäftigte 178
Beschäftigtenstruktur 178
Beschäftigungsart 148
beschleunigen 198
Beschlussfassung 194
beschränken 142
Beschränkung 198
Beschreibung 22
Beschriftung 26
besiedeln 129
Besiedlung 129
Besitzparzelle 124
Besitzverhältnis 124
Besitzzersplitterung 124
besorgniserregend 179
Bestand 145
bestechen 185
Bestechung 185
bestehen aus 28, 51
Bestrafung 170
betonen 24
Betrag 26
Betriebsfläche 115
Betriebsgröße 115
Betriebsgrößenstruktur 123
Betriebssystem 123
beurteilen 25
bevölkern 129
bevölkert 129
Bevölkerung 20, 129, 181
Bevölkerungsentwicklung 133
Bevölkerungsexplosion 134, 155
Bevölkerungsgeografie 12
Bevölkerungskonzentration 176
Bevölkerungspyramide 134
Bevölkerungsstruktur 134, 167
Bevölkerungsveränderung 134
Bevölkerungswachstum 133
Bevölkerungs~ 129
bevorzugt 198
bewachtes Wohnviertel 173
Bewässerung 118
Bewässerungsfeldbau 115
Bewegung der Erdkruste 52
Beweidung 115
Bewerber 137
bewirtschaften 113
bewohnen 129
Bewohner 129
bewölkt 64
beziehen auf 24
Bezirksverwaltung 192

Bezug 20
Bibliothek 164
Bier 121, 126
bieten 199
bilateral 184
bilaterale Hilfe 191
Bild 21
Bildmaterial 21
Bildung 132, 184, 188
Bildungseinrichtung 164
Bildungserrungenschaft 188
Bildungsgrad 180
Bildunterschrift 22
Bims 55
Bindungen 193
Binnenhandel 138
Binnenmarkt 139
Binnen~ 147
Biodiesel 158
Biodiversität 127
Bioenergie 108
Biogas 108
Biogeografie 12
Biokapazität 127
Biokraftstoff 108
biologisch 127
biologisch abbaubar 97, 98, 160
biologische Verwitterung 60
Biomasse 15, 108, 158
Bioprodukt 161
Biosphäre 71
Biotechnologie 112
Biozid 96
BIP – Bruttoinlandsprodukt 181
Birke 76
Birne 120
Bison 75
blasen 84
Blatt 72
Blätterdach 72
Blei 105
bleifrei 161
Blitz 65
Blockflur 114
Blowhole 86
Blumenanbau 121
Blumenzwiebel 121
BNE – Bruttonationaleinkommen 181
Bodden 86
Boden 15, 41, 60, 128
Bodenbildung 60
Bodenfeuchtigkeit 87
Bodenfließen 80

227

Bodenfruchtbarkeit 60, 178
Bodenhorizont 62
Bodennutzungssystem 123
Bodenorganismus 60
Bodenprofil 62
Bodensee 40, 44
Bodenstruktur 61
Bodentextur 61
Bodentyp 61
Bodenzerstörung 118
boden~ 60
Böe 64
Böhmerwald 43
Bohne 120
Bohrgerät 105
Bohrplattform 105
Boom 141
boomen 141
Bora 71
Bordstein 168
boreal 75
borealer Nadelwald 75
Böschung 82
Botschaft 24
Bottnischer Meerbusen 42
Brache 115, 176
brachliegend 115
Brackwasser 92
Branchenstruktur 178
Brandenburg 45
Brandrodungsfeldbau 123
Brandung 35, 79, 85
Brandungshohlkehle 86
Brandungspfeiler 35, 86
Brandungsströmung 85
Brandungstor 35
Branntwein 126
Brauchwasser 88
Brauerei 113, 126
Braunerde 61
Braunkohle 58, 105, 109, 158
Breccie 58
brechen 51, 85, 91
Brechpunkt der Welle 91
breit 18
Breite 18
Breitstreifenflur 114
Bremen 45
Brennholz 108
Brennstäbe 107
Brennstoff 104
Brettwurzel 72
Briefwerbung 143
Brikett 158

Brikettfabrik 109
Brise 64
Bruchlinie 56
Brücke 168
Brunnen 171
Brunnenbau 193
Brunnengalerie 118
brutto 181
Bruttoinvestition 181
Bruttoverkaufspreis 146
BSP – Bruttosozialprodukt 181
Bucht 35, 79, 85
Buddhismus 133
Buddhist 133
buddhistisch 133
Büffelgras 75
Buhne 86
Bullenmast 125
Buntmetall 105
Buntmetallverhüttung 110
Burg 172
Burgbelagerung 172
Bürger 129
Bürgerrechte 185
Bürgersteig 168, 169
Burgess Modell der
   konzentrischen Ringe 175
Burggraben 172
Burgtor 172
Burgturm 172
Büroarbeit 150
Bürofläche 151
Bürogebäude 163
Bürokratie 142, 185, 198
bürokratisch 185
C-Horizont 62
Caatinga 73
Calcium 57
Caldera 54
Canyon 34, 49, 83
Celebessee 38
Chaparral 74
Chemieprodukte 110
chemische Industrie 110
chemische Verwitterung 59
Chinook 71
Chlorwerk 111
Christ 133
Christentum 133
Chrom 105
Chromit 47
Cluster 36
CO_2-Emission 14
Colorado 50

Columbia River 50
Computerprogramme 31
Containerterminal 163
Corioliskraft 69
Dach 171
Damm 108, 192
Darlehen 184
das Internet 199
Daten 17, 26
datengestützte Information 31
Datensatz 31
Dattelpalme 121
Dauerfeldbau 115
Dauerfrost 75
Dauergrünland 115
Dauerkultur 119
dazu gewinnen 179
Decke 192
-decken 146
definieren 148
degenerative Krankheit 187
Degradierung 62
Deich 86, 93
Deindustrialisierung 147
Delta 34, 49, 78
Deltaplan 93
Demografie 12, 129
demographischer Übergang
   134
den Preis festsetzen 146
Deponie 97
der Eiserne Vorhang 37
Deregulierung 159
Desertifikation 73, 96
Desurbanisierung 176
Detail 22
Deutsches Mittelgebirge 44
Devisen 184
Devisenkontrolle 199
dezentralisieren 150
Dezentralisierung 150
Diagramm 26
Diamant 22
dicht besiedelt 129
Dichte 166
Dichte 91
dicke Rinde 73
die Großen Seen 50
die Pasterze 41
die Schule abbrechen 188
die See 79
Dienstleistung 16, 139, 146, 156,
   169
Dienstleistungen 139, 191

Dienstleistungsbereich 148
Dienstleistungsbranche 101
Dienstleistungsgesellschaft 189
Dienstleistungssektor 197
Diesel 111, 158
digitale Daten 31
Diktator 185
Diktatur 185
Dink 131
Diphterie 187
Direktvertrieb 143
Discountgeschäft 145
Diskriminierung 130
Distribution 166
divergierende Platte 53
Diversifizierung 196
Dnjepr 39
Doline 84
Dolomiten 43
Dom 164
Domstadt 165
Don 48
Donau 39, 46
Donner 65
Doppelhaushälfte 168
Doppelverglasung 99
Dorf 164, 174
dornig 74
Dornsavanne 73
Drehscheibe 167
Dreifelderwirtschaft 123
Druchbruchstal 83
Druck 56
Druckentlastung 59
Druckgewerbe 112
Druckunterschied 91
Druckwasserreaktor 107
Druckwelle 55
Drumlin 81
Dschungel 72
Düne 35, 84
Dung 117, 128
Düngemittelfabrik 111
düngen 128
Dünger 117, 128
Dunst 65
durch Wasserkraft gewonnene Energie 108
Durchfall 187
Durchfluss 87
durchführen 152, 191
Durchgangsstraße 168
durchlässig 37, 87
Durchlässigkeit 37, 61

Durchlüftung 61
Durchschnitt 13, 180
durchschnittlich 13, 180
durchstoßen 83
Durchwurzelung 61
Dürre 46, 68, 96, 186
E-Commerce 199
E-Mail-Werbung 200
Ebene 31, 35, 77
Edelholz 73, 122
Edelmetall 105
Edelstein 106
Edge City 173
effizient 162, 191
Eifel 43
Eigentumswohnung 168
ein Überangebot erzeugen 157
Ein-Kind-Politik 134
Einbahnstraße 168
Einblick 32
einen akademischen Grad erwerben 132
Einfamilienhaus 168
Einfluss 185
Einfrieren und Auftauen 80
einfügen 31
Einfuhr 139
Eingriff 177
einheimisch 172, 199
Einheit 27
Einkaufspassage 145
Einkaufstour 152
Einkaufszentrum 163
Einkaufszone 145
Einkommen 131
einleiten 160
einmachen 127
Einnahmen 140
einpendeln 179
Einpersonenhaushalt 167
Einrichtung 169
einschätzen 152
einschränken 162
Einschulungsrate 188
einspeisen 107
Einstrahlung 66
Einstrahlungsdefizit 67
Einwanderer 136
einwandern 136
Einwanderung 136
Einwohner 129, 166
einzeichnen 29
Einzelhandel 144, 148

Einzelhandelsunternehmen 144
Einzelhandels~ 144
Einzelhändler 144
Einzugsbereich 174
Eis 15
Eisbär 76
Eisberg 80
Eisdrift 80
Eisen 105
Eisen- und Stahlindustrie 110
Eisen- und Stahlproduktion 110
Eisenbahnbrücke 168
Eisenoxid 60
Eiskeil 81
Eisschild 42
Eiszeit 44, 53, 79
Eiweiß 92
Elch 76
elektrisch 112
elektrische Energie 158
Elektrizität 106, 157
Elektronik 112
elektronisch 112
elektronische Märkte 199
Element 13
Elend 155, 186
Elendssiedlung 164
Elite 172
Embargo 142, 198
Emission 96, 107, 160
Energie 106, 157
energieeffizient 98
Energieerzeugung 110
Energiegewinnung 192
Energieinfrastruktur 169
Energiepflanze 108
energiesparend 161
Energieträger 104, 158
Energieversorgung 157
Entdeckung 50
entfernen 140, 198
Entfremdung 157
enthalten 31
Entindustrialisierung 100
entlang 22
Entscheidung 149
Entscheidungsprozess 192
Entsorgung 96, 167
entspringen 78
entstehen 94
Entvölkerung 129
entwässern 89
entwässert 89

229

Entwässerung 89
Entwässerungskanal 89
Entwässerungssystem 89
Entwicklung 16, 150, 178
Entwicklungsgeografie 12
Entwicklungsland 178, 195
Entwicklungsplanung 31
entwurzeln 94
Epidemie 156, 187
epidemiologischer Übergang 187
Epiphyt 72
Epizentrum 56
Erbse 120
Erdaufbau 51
Erdbeben 55, 93
Erdbebengebiet 56
erdbebengefährdet 56
Erdbebengürtel 56
Erdbebenherd 56
Erdbebenhilfe 192
Erdbebenmessgerät 56
Erdbebenopfer 56
erdbebensicher 56
Erdbebensicherheit 56
Erdbebenwarte 56
Erdbebenwelle 55
Erdgas 158
Erdgasleitung 111
Erdgasspeicher 111
Erdgasvorräte 47
Erdinneres 51
Erdkern 51
Erdkruste 51
Erdkruste aufschiebender Rand 53
Erdkruste bewahrender Rand 53
Erdkruste bildender Rand 53
Erdkruste verbrauchender Rand 53
Erdmantel 51
Erdnuss 120
Erdöl 105, 158
Erdölfeld 105
Erdölgesellschaft 111
Erdölraffinerie 111
Erdölverarbeitung 111
Erdrutsch 95
Erdstoß 55
Erdwärme 108, 158
Erdzeitalter 53
erfassen 31
Erfolg 189

Erg 74
ergründen 177
Ergussgestein 57
Erhaltung 99
erhärten 54
Erhöhung 27
Eriesee 40
erklären 24
Erkundung 50
erleichtern 194
ernähren 114
ernährt 187
Ernährung 114, 186
Ernährungssicherheit 114
erneuerbar 158
erneuerbare Energie 108
Erntemaschine 116
ernten 116
erodieren 42, 82
Erosion 14, 43, 82
Erosionsbasis 82
erreichen 137
Erschöpfung 103
Erschütterung 93
Erstarrungsgestein 57
erstellen 31
Ertrag 115
Erwachsenenalphabetisierungsrate 180
Erwachsener 131
Erwärmung 59
Erwerbsarme 156
Erz 47, 110
erzeugen 158
Erzeugerpreis 125
Erzeugnis 141
Erzeugnisse 114
Erzgebirge 43, 44
erziehen 188
Erziehung 149, 188
erzwungene Migration 137
ethnisch 130
ethnische Minderheit 167
Eukalyptus 73
Euphrat 39
EUREK 177
Europa 38, 41
Europäische Union 41
Europäisches Flachland 46
Europäisches Raumentwicklungskonzept 177

eustatische Meeresspiegelschwankung 80
Eutrophierung 90, 96
Evaporation 68
Everglades 50
Exfoliation 59
Existenzminimum 132
exklusiv 153
Exosphäre 66
Export Processing Zone 195
Export~ 147
Exposition 82
extensive Bewirtschaftung 123
extern 147
Fabrik 101, 155, 163, 166
Fabrik einer amerikanischen Firma in Mexiko 196
Facharbeiter 101
Fachgeschäft 145
Fachhandel 145
Fachwerk 171
Fachwerk~ 171
fähig 183
Fahrbahn 169
Fähre 169
Fahrrinne 89
Fahrwassertiefe 89
Faktor 13, 149
Fall 26
fallen 26, 63, 178
Fallkolk 83
Faltengebirge 53
Faltung 52
Familie 131
Familienplanung 134
Fangmenge 126, 127
färben 29
Farbgebung 17, 20
Farbiger 131
Farbton 17
Faser 110
Faserpflanze 122
Federgras 75
Fehlernährung 132
Feinmechanik 112
Feld 114
Feldberg 46
Feldfrucht 113
Feldgraswirtschaft 123
Feldspat 57
Fels 77
Felsblock 82
Felsbogen 84

felsig 77
Felssäule 35
Fernwärme 107, 158
ferralitischer Boden 61
fertig 100
Fertiggericht 127
Fertigung 194
fest 51
fest werden 54
Festland 49
Festung 173
Festungsstadt 165
feucht 68
Feuchtgebiet 47
Feuchtigkeit 68
Feuchtsavanne 73
Feuerholz 97
Feuerwache 164
Feuerwehrmann 193
Fichte 75
Fichtelwald 44
Filchner-Ronne-Schelfeis 41
Filmindustrie 149
filtern 66, 160
Finanzen 140
Finanzwesen 148
Findling 81
Finnischer Meerbusen 42
Firma 101
Firmenhauptsitz 178
Firn 80
Fischbestand 127
Fischereiwirtschaft 126
Fischfangkapazität 126
Fischgrund 127
Fischhändler 172
Fischmehl 127
Fischmehlproduktion 127
Fischverarbeitung 113, 126
Fjord 35, 42, 81
Fjordlandschaft 42
flach 60, 73, 77, 78
Fläche 36
Flächennutzung 166
Flächenverbrauch 162
Flachs 122
Flachwasserzone 92
Flechte 76
Flechtwerk 171
Fleisch 122
Fleischfresser 74
Fleischwaren 126
Fließband 101
fließen 78

Fließgeschwindigkeit 88
Fließgewässer 81, 88
Fließrichtung 88
Floressee 38
Flöz 105
Flucht 137
flüchten 137
Flüchtling 137
Flughafen 163, 169
Flugsand 84
Flugzeug 169
Flugzeugindustrie 112
Fluorchlorkohlenwasserstoff 96, 160
Flur 114
Flurbereinigung 124
Flurzersplitterung 124
Fluss 15, 17, 34, 78, 82
Fluss mit zahlreichen Seitenarmen 82
Flussanzapfung 89
Flussbett 78
Flusseinzugsgebiet 89
Flusshaushalt 88
flüssig 51, 54
Flüssiggas 158
Flusslauf 78
Flussoase 74
Flussschlucht 47
Flusssediment 82
Flussufer 78
Fluss~ 81
flutartige Überschwemmung 95
Flutkontrolle 192
Flutwelle 85, 91, 95, 192
Föhn 46, 64, 71
Folgen der Globalisierung 195
Folienhaus 116
Förderbandanlage 101
förderbar 103
Fördergebiet 105
fördern 103, 198
Förderung 103, 139
Form 14, 164
Forschung und Entwicklung 101
Forschung und Entwicklung 148, 194
fortführen 193
Fortschritt 184, 189
Forum 200
fossiler Brennstoff 158
Fotografie 21
Franchise 145

Franchisegeber 145
Franchisenehmer 145
Franchising 145
Fränkische Alb 44
Frauenüberschuss 134
frei verfügbares Einkommen 152
Freihafen 140, 195
Freihandel 140, 198
Freihandelszone 185, 195
freistehendes Einfamilienhaus 168
freiwillige Exportbeschränkung 142
Freizeitindustrie 149
Fremdenverkehrsgeografie 13
Fremdlingsfluss 74
Friedhof 164, 173
Front 65
Frost 63
Frosthub 79
Frostmusterboden 81
Frostsprengung 59, 79
fruchtbar 43, 60
Fruchtbarkeit 133
Frühindustrialisierung 155
Frühwarnsystem 93
Fumarole 55
fundiert 191
Funktion 164, 166
funktionieren 169
Funktionsraum 166
Furtwängler-Gletscher 41
Fusion 198
fusionieren 198
Fußbekleidungsindustrie 112
Fußgängerübergang 169
Fußgängerweg 170
Fußgängerzone 168
Futterbaubetrieb 123
Futtermittel 117
Futtertrog 117
Ganggestein 57
Gans 122
Gardasee 40
Garigue 74
Garten 171
Gartenbau 124
Gartenbaubetrieb 124
Gartenstadt 165
Gartenstadtbewegung 176
Gas 54, 105
Gasrohr 169
Gastarbeiter 130, 136

231

Gastgeberland 195
Gastgewerbe 149
Gastronomiebereich 149
Gasverflüssigungsanlage 111
Gasversorgung 169
Gasvorkommen 47
Gaswerk 111
Gas~ 54
Gebiet 43, 166
Gebiet mit geringer
  Wohndichte 175
gebildet 132
Gebirge 34, 77
gebirgig 17
Gebirgsbildung 44
Gebirgskette 17, 49
Gebirgsketten der
  nordamerikanischen Pazifik-
  küste 48
Gebirgsweide 115
Gebirgszug 77
Gebirgs~ 76
gebundene Entwicklungshilfe
  191
Geburtenkontrolle 134
Geburtenrate 134, 181
Geburtenüberschuss 134
Geburtsjahrgang 134
Geest 86
gefährlich 179
Gefälle 82
Gefällskurve 88
Geflügelhaltung 125
Geflügelhaltung in
  Legebatterien 125
Geflügelhändler 172
gefrieren 63
gefroren 75
gegenseitige Abhängigkeit 167,
  198
Gegenstand 20, 22
Gegenurbanisierung 151
Gegenwert 141
gehobener Strand 86
Gelbes Meer 38
Geld 184, 191
Fundraising 190
geltend machen 137
gemäßigt 72
gemäßigte Breiten / gemäßigte
  Zone 72
gemäßigter Regenwald 49
gemäßigtes Klima 45
Gemeinkosten 146

Gemeinschaft unabhängiger
  Staaten 46
Gemengelage 114
gemischt 172
Gemüse 120
Generation 162
generatives Verhalten 134
Generator 107
Genfer See 40
Genossenschaft 125
gentechnisch verändert 126
gentechnologisch veränderte
  Lebensmittel 126
Gentrifizierung 177, 197
Geodäsie 12
Geografie 12
Geografie des ländlichen
  Raumes 13
Geografie 31
geographische Folge 197
Geografisches Informationssys-
  tem 31
Geologie 14, 31, 41
Geomorphologie 12, 14, 76
geostrophischer Wind 70
Geosynklinale 52
geothermale Energie 108
geothermische Energie 158
geothermisches Kraftwerk 55
geplante Stadt 170
Gerätebau 111
Gerber 172
Gerichtsgebäude 163
Geröll 61
Gerste 119
gerundet 77
Gesamtwert ausländischer
  Investitionen 181
gesättigt 68
Geschäft 171
Geschäftsbank 184
Geschäftsbereich 194
Geschäftsreise 197
Geschäftstätigkeit 194
Geschäftsviertel 163
Geschichte 183
geschichtet 153
Geschiebe 81
Geschiebelehm 81
geschieden 131
Geschlecht 131
Geschwindigkeit 95
Gesellschaft 155, 169
Gesellschaftsklasse 132

Gesellschaft~ 155
Gesichtsausdruck 24
Gesichtspunkt 24
Gestein 57
Gesteinsart 15, 57
Gesteinsbrocken 54
Gesteinshorizont 62
Gesteinskunde 57
Gesteinsspalte 59
Gesundheit 132
Gesundheitsgeografie 12
Gesundheitspflege 132
gesundheitsschädliche
  Materialien 160
Gesundheitswesen 149
Getränke 126
Getreide 119
Getreideanbau 115
Getreidespeicher 116
getrennt 131
gewähren 125
Gewässer 88, 178
Gewässerbelastung 90
Gewässerüberwärmung 90
Gewässerverschmutzung 96
Gewehr 183
Gewerbebetrieb 101
Gewerbefläche 101
Gewerbegebiet 163, 166
gewerbliche Landwirtschaft
  123
Gewinn 157
Gewinnmotiv 157
Gewitter 65
Gewitterwolke 64
Gewohnheit 37
Geysir 55
Gezeiten 79, 85
Gezeitenkraft 108, 158
Ghetto 130
Giebel 171
Gießerei 110
Gipfel 35, 49
Gittersystem 26
Glacier Bay 41
Glashauskultur 124
Glasindustrie 113
Glazialablagerung 47
glazialer Schutt 46
Glaziologie 12
gleichbleibende Hitze 72
gleichmäßig 179
Gleis 18
Gleithang 83

Gletscher 42, 44, 49, 80
Gletscherbach 80
Gletscherschliff 80
Gletscherspalte 80
Gletschertor 80
Gletscherzunge 80
Gliederung 166
Glimmer 57
global 194
globale Erwärmung 14, 95, 160
globale Instabilität 193
globale Stabilität 193
globaler Finanzmarkt 162
globaler Wärmehaushalt 67
globales Dorf 199
globales Förderband 91
Globalisierung 159, 194
Gneis 58
Gold 47, 106
Goldgräberstadt 165
Golf 35, 49
Golf von Aden 39
Golf von Bengalen 39
Golf von Biscaya 39
Golf von Guinea 39
Golf von Mexiko 39
Golf von Siam 39
Golf von Tonking 39
Golf-Atlantische Küstenebene 48
Golfplatz 163
Golfstrom 46
Gondwanaland 37, 53
Grabenbruch 53
Gradnetz der Erde 18
graduell 179
Grand Canyon 50
Granit 57
Grafik 26
Graphit 47, 106
Grat 35
Grat zwischen benachbarten Karen 81
Graupel 64
Grenze 18, 37, 50, 137, 198
grenzüberschreitend 137
Großbauer 124
Größe 18, 166
große Bevölkerung 193
Große Sandwüste 40
Große Sytre 39
Große Viktoriawüste 40
Großer Bärensee 40
Großer Belt 42

Großer Hinggan 47
Großer Salzsee 50
Großer Sklavensee 40
Großgrundbesitz 124
Großhandel 142
Großhandelsmarkt 173
Großhandels~ 142
Großhändler 143
Großstadt 164, 165
Großvieh 122
Grundbesitz 156
Grundlast 106
Grundnahrungsmittel 114, 132
Grundschule 132
Grundstoffindustrie 100
Grundwasser 88, 193
Grundwasserableitung 90
Grundwasserabsenkung 90
Grundwasserpumpe 90
Grundwasserspiegel 87
Grüne Revolution 114
Grüngürtel 176
Grünlandlandwirtschaft 123
Grünlandschaft 44
Guano 117
Gummi 73, 122
günstig 197
GUS 46
Güter 15, 139, 191
Güterbahnhof 163
Hackbau 115
Hackfrüchte 119
Hadleyzelle 69
Hafen 163, 168, 173
Hafenstadt 165
Hafer 119
Hagel 64
Hain 120
Halbinsel 36, 49
Halbinsel Kola 47
Halbinsel Taimyr 47
Halbleiter 112
Halbnomade 125
Halbwüste 74
Hallig 85
Halophyten 74
Hamada 74
Hamburg 45
Hammada 84
Hammerwerk 110
Hamstern 152
Handel 138, 146, 172, 197
handeln 146
Handelsbedingungen 141, 198

Handelsbilanz 139
Handelsdefizit 139
Handelsgemeinschaft 185
Handelskrieg 140, 198
Handelsschranke 140, 186, 198
Handelsstadt 165
Handelsüberschuss 139
Handelsverbindungen 138
Handelsware 145
Händler 143, 145
Handlung 23
Handschuhmacher 171
Handwerk 100
Handwerker 171
Hanf 122
Hang 15, 43
Hangar 169
Hangbildung 15
Hangneigung 178
Hansestadt 165
Harmattan 71
hartes Wasser 88
Hartholz 73
Hartlaub~ 74
Harz 44
Haufendorf 165
Hauptanbauart 119
Hauptgeschäftszentrum 166, 173
Hauptgeschäftszentrum 163
Hauptindustrie 100
Hauptstadt 164, 165
Hausarbeit 149
Haushalt 131
Haushaltsmüll 96
Haushaltsreiniger 97
Haushaltswaren 113
Hausmarke 145
Haustürverkauf 143
HDI – Index der menschlichen Entwicklung 180
HDR – Bericht zur menschlichen Entwicklung 180
heben 42
Hebung 52
Heide 76
Heimarbeit 101
Heimatland 136
Heimindustrie 101
Heizöl 105, 158
Helgoland 45
Helgoländer Bucht 45
hemmen 198
herausschleudern 54

Herde 116
Herkunft 130
Herkunftsland 136
Hersteller 142
Herstellung 189, 194
Hessen 45
Hexagon 174
Hierarchie 164
hiesige 192
hiesige Bevölkerung 192
High-Tech-Branche 101
Hilfe 190
Hilfsmittel 23
Hilfsorganisation 190
Hindu 133
Hinduismus 133
hinduistisch 133
Hinrichtung 171
Hintergrund 22
Hirse 119
Historische Geografie 12
Hitzewelle 63
hoch 18, 63
Hochbahn 168
Hochdruck 67
Hochebene 35, 49, 77
hochentwickelt 151
Hochhaus 173
Hochland 47, 77
Hochleistungssorte 114
Hochofen 110
Hochschulabsolvent 132
Hochschule 132
Hochspannungsleitung 106
Höchstwert 27
Hochwassergebiet 192
Höhe 18
hohe Luftfeuchtigkeit 72
Hoheitsgebiet 137
Höhenlage 77
Höhenstufe der Vegetation 76
Hoher Balkan 44
Holz 122, 192
Holzeinschlag 97
Holzgewinnung 192
Holzindustrie 112
Holzpellet 158
Holzpellets 108
Holzraubbau 97
Homeshopping 143
Hopfen 121
horten 152
Hot Spot 55
Hotelgewerbe 149

Hoyt'sches Sektorenmodell 175
Huang He 39
Hudson Bay 39
Hudsonbai 48
Hudsonstraße 39
Hufe 114
Hufschmied 172
Hügel 77
hügelig 77
Huhn 122
Hülsenfrucht 120
Humangeografie 12
Humifizierung 60
Huminsäure 60
Humus 60
Humusauflage 62
Hunsrück 43
Huronsee 40
Hurrikan 64, 94, 186
Hüttenwerk 110
Hydrant 169
Hydration 59
Hydrologie 12, 87
Hydrolyse 59
Hygiene 186
Iberische Halbinsel 43
Identität 37
illegale Siedlung 138
im Ausland 136
im Käfig gehalten 125
im rechten Winkel 22
im schulpflichtigen Alter 188
Image 150
immergrün 72
Immobilienmarkt 197
immune 187
impfen 187
Impfstoff 187
Impfung 187
Import~ 147
in begrenztem Umfang 191
in der Ferne 22
in Freilandhaltung 122
in Mengen 143
indigen 130
Indischer Ozean 38
individuelle Information 31
Industrialisierung 100, 189
Industrie 20, 100
Industrieanlage 101
Industriearbeiter 189
Industriebeschäftigter 101
Industriebrache 101
Industriedichte 101

Industriedorf 165
Industriegebiet 101, 163
Industriegesellschaft 189
Industrieland 178
industriell 16, 100
industrielle Monostruktur 101
industrielle Produktion 100
industrielle Verflechtung 102
industrieller Sektor 189
industrieller Strukturwandel 103
Industrieproduktion 189
Industrieregion 101
Industriestandort 101
Industrieunternehmen 101
Industriewaren 142
Industriezone 175
Industriezweig 100
Informationstechnologie 112
Informationsüberfluss 200
Informationsverarbeitung 197
Infrastruktur 169, 184
Ingenieur 101
Inhaltsverzeichnis 16
Inlandeis 80
Innenstadt 163, 173
innertropische Konvergenzzone 69
Innovation 101
Insektenvernichtungsmittel 117
Insel 36
Inselbogen 53
Insolationsverwitterung 59
Integration 130
integrieren 130
integriert 130
Intensivierung 115
Interesse 37
Internationale Arbeitsorganisation 199
internationale Organisationen 184
internationaler Handel 140
Internationaler Währungsfonds 184
Interview 153
Interviewer 153
Inversion 65
investieren 189
Investition 181, 198
Investitionsgüter 102
Investitionsgüterindustrie 100
Ionosphäre 66
Ironie 24

Irtysch 48
Islam 133
Isobare 67
isolieren 99
Isolierung 99
Isotherme 67
Jablonowy Gebirge 47
Jahreszeit 67
Jahreszeitenklima 67
Jams 119
Jangtsekiang 39
Japanisches Meer 38
Javasee 38
Jenissei 48
Jenissej 39
Jetstream / Strahlstrom 70
Jude 133
Judentum 133
jüdisch 133
Jungenbildung 188
just-in-time 144
Just-in-time-Produktion 102
Jute 122
Kabelwerk 110
Kadmium 105
Kaffee 73, 121
Kaianlage 163
Kakao 73, 121
Kaktus 74
Kalahari 40
kalben 80
Kälbermast 125
Kaledonische Faltung 53
kaledonische Gebirgsbildung 42
Kali 106
Kalisalz 106
kalkhaltig 61
Kalkstein 44, 58
Kalmen 69
Kalorienaufnahme 181
Kalorienversorgung 181
Kame 81
Kamel 122
Kamerunberg 41
Kamm 35, 77, 91
Kampung 173
Kamtschatka Halbinsel 48
Kanadischer Schild 48
Kanal 89
Kaolin 106
Kap 35
Kapillarwirkung 62
Kapital 156, 198

Kapitalintensität 148
kapitalintensiv 102
Kar 81
Karasee 38
Karbonisierung 59
Karibisches Meer 38
Karibu 76
Karikatur 21
Karikaturist 23
Karpaten 43
Karren 83
Karst 83
Karstquelle 84
Karstverwitterung 60
Kartellamt 155
Kartentitel 18
Kartoffel 119
Kartoffelkäfer 119
Käserei 126
Kaskade 83
Kaspische Senke 47
Kaspisches Meer 38
Kaste 133, 173
Katarakt 83
katastrophal 179
Kategorie 153
Katholik 133
katholisch 133
Kattegat 42
Kauf 193
Käufer 151
Kaufhaus 144, 166
Kaufkraft 152, 180, 199
Kaufmann 171
Kaufpreis 146
Kaufzwang 152
Kaukasus 47
Kautschuk 106, 122
Kegel 54
Kelter 118
keltern 118
Kennzeichen 24
Keramikindustrie 113
Kerbtal 83
Kerker 172
Kern 172, 175, 190
Kernenergie 158
Kernernergie 107
Kerngebiet 194
Kernschmelze 107
Kernspaltung 107
Kette 144
Kibbuz 125
Kiefer 75

Kieler Bucht 45
Kies 61, 82
Kilimandscharo 41
Kindergarten 132
Kindersterblichkeitsrate 181
Kino 164
Kirche 164, 171
Kirsche 120
Klamm 83
Kläranlage 90
Klärschlamm 90
Klee 121
Kleinbauer 114
Kleinbetrieb 101
Kleine Syrte 39
Kleiner Belt 42
kleiner Wirbelsturm 70
Kleinstadt 164, 165
Kleinvieh 122
Kliff 85
Klima 13, 14, 65
Klimageografie 12
klimatisch 65
Klimatologe 65
Klimatologie 13, 65
Klimawandel 95
Klimazone 71
Klippe 35
Kloster 171
Kluft 193
Knotenpunkt 167
Kobalt 105
Kochbanane 120
Koexistenz 37
koexistieren 37
kohärent 36
Kohärenz 36
Kohl 120
Kohle 104, 109
Kohlefeld 104
kohleführend 104
Kohlendioxid 66, 96, 160
Kohlenstaubanlage 109
Kohleveredelung 109
Kohlevergasung 109
Kokospalme 121
Koks 109
Kolchose 125
Kollektivierung 125
Kollisionszone 53
Köln 45
kolonial 129

235

koloniale Vergangenheit 193
Kolonialgebiet 193
kolonialisieren 129
Kolonialisierung 183
Kolonie 129, 183
Kolonist 129
Kolyma 48
kommerziell bewirtschaften 123
kommerzielle Landwirtschaft 126
Kommune 37
Kommunikation 149, 199
Kommunikationsinfrastruktur 170
Komponente 29
Kompost 128
Kompostierungsanlage 97
Kondensation 68
kondensieren 68
Konflikt 138
Konglomerat 58
Kongo 39
Kongresszentrum 163
Konkurrent 153
konkurrenzfähig 153
Konservenfabrik 113, 127
Konservenindustrie 127
konservieren 98
Konstanz 44
Konsum 15, 151, 153
Konsument 156
Konsument 151
konsumieren 138
Kontakt unterbinden 37
Kontinentalabhang 53
Kontinentalität 71
Kontinentalklima 71
Kontinentalschelf 53, 91
Kontinentalverschiebung 53
Konturpflügen 128
Konvektion 66
Konvektionsniederschlag 68
Konvektionsstrom 52
konvektive 13
Koordination 194
Korallenriff 36, 85
Korallensee 38
Korkeiche 123
Körnermais 119
Körpersprache 24
Korrosion 83
korrupt 185
Korruption 185

Kosten 146
Kraftwerk 107, 157
Krankenhaus 164
Krankheit 187
Krater 54
Krebs 187
Kredit 184
Kreide 58
Kreisdiagramm 28
Kreuzung 117
Kristall 57
kristallin 57
kristallines Gestein 46
Krümelstruktur 61
Krümmung 82
Küfer 171
Kühlflüssigkeit 107
Kühlhaus 116
Kühlmittel 96
Kühlturm 107
Kuhstall 116
Kultur 36
Kulturgeografie 12
Kulturkreis 170
Kulturland 114
Kulturlandschaft 163
Kunde 151
Kundendienst 154
Kundennähe 150
Kundenverteilung 150
künstliche Befruchtung 117
Kunststoff 110
Kunstweide 115
Kupfer 47, 105
Kürschner 171
Kurstadt 165
Kurve 29
Kurzgrassteppe 75
Küste 35, 79, 84, 85
Küstenaufschüttung 86
Küstendüne 85
Küsteneis 85
Küstenform 35
Küstengeografie 12
Küstenlinie 15, 79
Küstenschutz 86, 93
Küstenüberschwemmung 95
Kwashiorkor 187
Laden 166
Laden an der Ecke 145
Ladogasee 48
Lage 164
Lager 144
Lagerhaltung 149

Lagerhaus 163
Lagerhaus für unverzollte Ware 195
lagern 144
Lagune 35, 85
Laichplatz 127
Lambertgletscher 41
Lamm 122
Land 162
Land bearbeiten 115
Landarbeiter 114
Landbesitz 124
Landbesitzer 114
Landbesitzer, der nicht auf seinem Land lebt 124
Landenge 35
Landfläche 13
Landform 41, 76
Landgewinnung 86
Landgut 115
Landleben 163
ländlich 162
ländliche Region 174
ländliche Siedlung 163
ländlicher Markt 173
ländlicher Raum 176
Landmaschinenhandel 116
Landnutzung 114, 177
Landreform 124
Landregen 68
Landschaft 14, 36, 76
Landschaftsökologie 12
Landschaftsschutzgebiet 99
Landschaftszone 71
Landspitze 35, 85
Landwind 70
Landwirtschaft 20, 44, 113, 127, 163
landwirtschaftlich 113
landwirtschaftlich nutzbar 113
landwirtschaftliche Aktivität 116
landwirtschaftliche Basis 190
Landwirtschaftliche Produktionsgenossenschaft 125
landwirtschaftlicher Familienbetrieb 124
landwirtschaftliches Erzeugnis 118
Landwirtschaftsgesellschaft 189
Landzunge 35
lang 18

Länge 18
langsam 179
Längsdüne 84
Längsprofil 88
längsseits 22
Langzeit~ 13
Lapilli 54
Lappland 42
Lärche 75
lateinamerikanische Stadt 172
latent 13
Laterit 61
laubabwerfend 72
Laubbaum 75
Laubwald 49, 75
Laub~ 72
Lauch 120
laufende Kosten 146
Laurasia 53
Laurasien 37
Lava 54
Lawine 80, 93
Lebensbedingungen 131
Lebenserwartung 131, 134, 180
Lebenshaltungskosten 152, 181
Lebensmittelgeschäft 145, 172
Lebensmittelherstellung 126
Lebensmittelindustrie 126
Lebensmittelknappheit 114
Lebensmittelmarkt 173
Lebensmittelversorgung 114
Lebensqualität 131
Lebensraum 71
Lebensstandard 152, 180, 199
Lebensstil 152
Lebensstilgruppe 167
Lederwaren 112
Lee~ 70
Legende 16
Legierungsmetall 105
Legierungsmetallhütte 110
Leguminose 121
Lehm 61
Lehmbewurf 171
leicht 179
Leichtindustrie 100, 175
Leichtmetall 105
leihen 184
Leistungen der öffentlichen
 Versorgungsbetriebe 189
Leitplanke 168
Lena 39, 48
lenken 200
Leuchtturm 93

Liane 72
Liberalisierung 159
Liniendiagramm 27
linke 22
Linse 120
Lithosphäre 51
Lockangebot 154
Lofoten 42
Lohnarbeiterschaft 156
Lohnunternehmen 124
lokale Regierung 149
löslich 59
Löss 58, 61
Lösung 59
Lösungsmittel 96
Luft 84
Luft- und Raumfahrttechnik 112
Luftbewegung 69
Luftbild 21
Luftdruck 67
Luftmasse 67
Luftschicht 66
Luftschiff 169
Luftstrom 69
Luftwurzel 72
Lungenentzündung 187
Luxus 152
Luzerne 121
Luzon Straße 39
Mäander 83
mäandrieren 70, 83
Maar 54
Macchie 74
MacKenzie 39
Mädchenbildung 188
Magma 54
Magnetschwebebahn 168
Magnitude 56
Mahagoni 73
mahlen 121
Main 46
Mais 119
Makassarstraße 39
Malakka Straße 39
Malaria 187
Malawisee 40
Mandarine 121
Mandel 121
Mangan 105
Mangel 103, 157
Mango 121
Mangrove 73
Maniok 119
männlich 131

Marasmus 187
Marginalsiedlung 166
marines Ökosystem 90
maritime Luftmasse 70
maritimes Klima 72
Markenkennzeichnung 154
Markentreue 155
Marketing 153
Marketing-Mix 154
Marksegment 153
Markt 193
marktfähig 153
Marktforschung 149, 153
Marktfruchtbetrieb 123
Marktgemüseanbau 123
marktorientiert 155
marktorientierter Anbau 123
Marktort 174
Marktplatz 170
Marktprinzip 174
Marktwirtschaft 157
Marmarameer 38
Marmor 58, 106
Marschboden 61
Maschenweite 127
Maschinen 156
Maschinenbau 111
Masern 187
Maßeinteilung 27
Massenproduktion 102, 157
Massentierhaltung 125
Massen~ 154
Massiv 34, 179
Maßnahme 177, 184
Maßstab 17
Mast 116
Matterhorn 41
Maulbeerbaum 122
maximieren 153
Mechanisierung 101, 116
Mecklenburg-Vorpommern 45
Mecklenburgische Seenplatte
 45
mediterrane Vegetation 74
medizinische Versorgung 181
Medrese 173
Meer 35, 79
Meerenge 35
Meeresablagerung 79
Meeresboden 90
Meeresoberfläche 91
Meeresspiegelanstieg 95
Meeresströmung 91, 158
Meerestiefe 91

237

Meeres~ 90
Meerwasserverschmutzung 92
Mehrertrag 189
Mehrfamilienhaus 168
Mehrkernemodell nach Harris und Ullman 175
Mehrpersonenhaushalt 167
Mehrwertsteuer 146
Meinung 25
Mekong 39
melken 116
Melkkammer 116
Melone 120
Menge 29
mengenmäßig messen 147
Menschenrechte 185
menschliche Arbeitskraft 156
Mercalli-Skala 56
Mergel 58
Meridian 18
meritimes Klima 45
Merkmal 17
Mesosphäre 66
messen 147
Messezentrum 163
Mestize 131
Metallerzeugung 110
Metallindustrie 110
metallisches Erz 105
Metallwaren 110
Methan 96, 160
Metropole 165
Metropolraum 165
Metzger 172
Michigansee 40
Mieter 175
Migrant 175
Mikrochip 112
Mikroelektronik 112
Mikroorganismus 73
Milchproduktion 125
milchverarbeitender Betrieb 125
Milchverarbeitungsindustrie 113, 126
mild 46
Mineral 15, 57
mineralische Substanz 60
Mineralquelle 55
Minimalwert 27
Mischbetrieb 123
Mischfeuerung 107
Mischling 131
Mississippi 50

Mistral 70
mit etwas versorgen 183
mit Schleppnetz fischen 127
mit Zapfen 75
Mittelalter 170
mittelalterlich 170
Mittelatlantischer Rücken 53
Mittelgebirgsschwelle 44
Mittelmeer 38
Mittelmeerklima 74
Mittelozeanischer Rücken 53
Mittelpolnisches Tiefland 43
Mittelschicht-Wohnzone 175
Mittelsibirisches Bergland 46
Mittelstadt 165
Mittelstreifen 169
Möbel 112
Mobilität 135
Modell 188
Möglichkeit 164, 188
Mohn 121
Mohorovičić-Diskontinuität 51
Molkerei 126
Molybdän 105
Monokultur 123
monotone Arbeit 197
Monsun 69
Montagewerk 100
montane Baumgrenze 76
Moor 47, 75, 78
Moorboden 61
Moos 76
moralischer Grund 193
Moräne 44, 80
Mosaik 36
Moschee 173
Mosel 46
Motorenbau 111
Mount Everest 41
Mulatte 131
mulchen 128
Mulde 53
Müll 96, 160
Mülldeponie 97, 163
Müllhalde 96
Müllreduzierung 97
Müllverbrennungsanlage 97
multikulturell 130
multilateral 184
multilaterale Hilfe 191
multinationales Unternehmen 194
multirassisch 130
München 44

münden 78
Mündung 34, 78
Mure 81
Museum 164
Muslim 133
muslimisch 133
Muster 164
Mutterboden 60
Mutterschaf 122
Mykorrhiza 73
Nachbeben 56
nachfolgende Generationen 192
Nachfrage 138, 151, 157
nachhaltig 98, 127
nachhaltige Methode 192
nachhaltiges Wachstum 190
Nachhaltigkeit 98
Nachrichtentechnik 112
nächtlich 74
Nadel~ 72
NAFTA 185
nahe 22, 177
Naherholung 167
Nährgebiet 80
Nährstoff 60
Nährstoffhaushalt 92
Nährstoffkreislauf 73
Nahrung 186
Nahrungs- und Genussmittelindustrie 113
Nahrungsmittelproduktion 114
Nahrungsmittelüberschuss 114
Namib 40
Nanotechnologie 112
Nassfeld 119
nationale Regierung 149
Nationalpark 50, 99
Nationalstaat 37
NATO / Nordatlantikpakt-Organisation 186
Natur 20
Naturgefahr 93
Naturkatastrophe 93
Naturlandschaft 163
natürliche Vegetation 71
natürlicher Damm 82
natürlicher Zuwachs 181
Naturpark 99
Naturreligion 133
Nebel 65
Nebelwald 76
Nebenarm 78
Nebenerwerbsbetrieb 123

Nebenfluss 78
Neckar 46
negativ 24
Negativspirale 176
Nehrung 35, 86
nennen 23
Neoliberalismus 159
Nettopreis 146
neue Industrien 189
Neue internationale Verteilung der Arbeit 197
neue Technologien 189
Neuordnung 196
neutral 24
New Towns 176
Niagarafälle 50
nicht erneuerbar 158
nicht standortgebunden 102
nicht zustimmen 25
Nicht-Regierungsorganisation 191
nichtorganisch 92
nichttarifäres Handelshemmnis 142, 198
Nickel 47, 105
Niedergang 176
Niedersachsen 45
Niederschlag 46, 64, 68
Niedriglohnland 198
nieseln 65
Nieselregen 65
Niger 39
Nil 39
Nische 152
Nomade 125
Non-Profit-Unternehmen 191
Nord-Ostsee-Kanal 45
Nord-Süd-Gefälle 178
Nordamerika 37
nordamerikanische Langgrassteppe 49
Norddeutsche 45
Norddeutsches Tiefland 42
Nordeuropäisches Tiefland 42
nordfriesische Inseln 45
Nordfriesland 45
Nördliche Kalkalpen 44
Nördlicher Wendekreis 67
Nordostpassat 69
Nordrhein-Westfalen 45
Nordsee 38, 45
Nordwand 35
Nordwestliches Hochland 42
Normalnull 18

Not 186
Notfalldienste 149
Notquartier 138
Nunatak 80
Nutzenergie 158
Nutzholz 122
Nutzpflanze 119
Nutzung 166
Oase 34, 74
Oasenwirtschaft 123
Ob 48
Ob-Irtysch 39
Oberboden 15, 62
oberer Rand 22
Oberer See 40
Oberfläche 14
Oberflächenform 17
Oberflächengestalt 76
Oberflächenwasser 88
Oberflächenzirkulation 91
Oberschichtwohngebiet 166
Oberstadt 165
Obst 120
Obst und Gemüse 114
Obstkultur 120
Ochotskisches Meer 38
öffentliche Badeanstalt 173
öffentliche Hand 177
öffentlicher Transport 169
Öffnungszeiten 144
ohne Landbesitz 114
Oka 48
Ökologie 98, 159
ökologisch 98, 159
ökologische Restriktion 161
ökologische Schranke 162
ökologische Tragfähigkeit 162
ökologischer Regenerationsbereich 99
ökonomischer Determinismus 174
Ökosystem 71, 161
Olive 120
Ölpalme 120
Ölpest 92, 105
Ölplattform 105
Ölsaaten 120
Ölvorkommen 47
Ölvorräte 47
Ontariosee 40
OPEC 185
Oper 164
Optik 112
optimieren 16, 153

Optimierung 156
opulente Gesellschaft 162
Orchidee 73
organische Stoffe 92
organische Substanz 60
organische Verwitterung 60
organisches Material 15
orientalisch-islamische Stadt 173
Orientierung 17
Orkan 70
Ort 20, 149, 164
Ort höherer Ordnung 174
Ort mittlerer Ordnung 174
Ort unterer Ordnung 174
Orthofoto 32
orthorektifizieren 32
Ortstein 62
Os 81
Ostchinesisches Meer 38
Osteuropäische Ebene 43
Ostfriesische Inseln 45
Ostfriesland 45
Ostküstenklima 74
Ostsee 38, 45
Ostwindzone 69
Oxidation 59
Oxygenstahlkonverter 110
Ozean 13, 35
ozeanische Zirkulation 91
Ozeanografie 12
Ozon 66, 160
Ozonkonzentration 66
Ozonloch 66, 96
Ozonschicht 66, 96
Pacht 124
pachten 124
Pächter 124
Packeis 95
Paläogeografie 12
Paläoklimatologie 12
Palisander 73
Pamirgebirge 47
Pampa 75
Pangaea 37, 53
Papaya 121
Papiererzeugung 111
Papierfabrik 111
Papierverarbeitung 111
Paprika 120
Parabraunerde 61
Pariser Becken 42
Parkplatz 163
Partikularismus 37

239

Parzelle 114
Pass 35, 77, 137
Passat 69
Pauperismus 155
Pazifik 38
Pediment 48
Pedologie 12, 15
Pellagra 187
pendeln 175
Pendelstrecke 175
Pendler 136
Pendlerstrom 178
Pendlerzone 175
Pennines 42
Pepperoni 120
periodischer Fluss 88
Peripherie 190
Perito-Moreno-Gletscher 41
permanenter Fluss 88
Persischer Golf 39
Personal 150, 194
Personalwesen 194
petrochemische Industrie 111
Pfad 94
Pfälzer Wald 44
Pfeffer 120
Pfirsich 120
pflanzen 116
Pflanzenfresser 74
Pflanzenkrankheit 117
Pflanzenschutz 117
Pflanzenschutzmittel 96
Pflanzenwelt 71
Pflaume 120
Pflicht 193
Pflug 116
pflügen 116
ph-Wert 60
Pharmaindustrie 111
Philippinensee 38
Phosphat 106, 117
Photovoltaik 108
physiogeografische Region 41, 48
Physiografie 14
physiografische Subregion 47
Physische Geografie 12
physische Karte 17
physische Merkmale 17
Pilotstudie 154
Pilz 73
Pilzfelsen 84
Pilzvernichtungsmittel 117
Pindos 44

Pingo 81
Pipeline 111
planetarische Winde 70
planetarische Zirkulation 69
Plankton 92
Planquadrat 18
Plantagenwirtschaft 123
Planung 194
Platin 106
Platte 52
Plattenrand 53
Plattensee 40
Plattentektonik 52
Platzierung 24
Plaza 172
plötzlich ansteigen 179
Podsol 61
Podsolierung 61
polarer Kaltlufteinbruch in Nordamerika 70
polares Hoch 69
Polarfront 69
Polarfuchs 76
Polarkreis 67
Polarregionen 72
Polder 86
Polis 170
Politik 31, 185
Politiker 185
politische Folgen 195
Politische Geografie 12
politische Landschaft 41
politischer Grund 193
Polizeirevier 164
Polje 84
Polsterpflanze 76
porös 54, 61
Porzellan 113
Porzellanindustrie 113
positiv 24
Postamt 163
Postversand 143
potentieller Markt 153
Pottasche 117
Prallhang 83
Pranger 170
Prärie 75
Präriegebiete im Westen der USA 48
präsentieren 29
Präzisionstechnik 112
Preis 141, 146
Preisabsprache 155
Preisbindung 146

Preisdiskriminierung 155
Preisfindung 157
Preisführerschaft 154
Preiskrieg 154
Preismechanismus 157
Preisniveau 155
Preissenkung 154
Preisverfall 157
Prestige 150
Priel 85
Primärenergie 158
primärer Sektor 189
Primärerhebung 153
Primärindustrie 100
Primärprodukt 144
Primärproduktion 92
Primärwelle 55
Primatstadt 164, 190
prinzipiell 25
Privatisierung 159
pro Kopf Einkommen 181
Pro-Kopf-Einkommen 178
Probe 154
probieren 154
Produkt 141
Produktion 138, 156
Produktionsfaktor 102
Produktionskosten 102
Produktionsmittel 102
Produktionsplanung 148
Produktionsquote 186
Produktionsstätte 194
Produktivität 162
Produktplatzierung 155
Produktqualität 148
Produzent 156
produzieren 16, 100, 141
produzierte Waren 193
Profit 192
Projektion 16, 34
Prospektion 103
Protektionismus 142, 186, 198
protektionistisch 142, 198
Protestant 133
protestantisch 133
Provision 143
Prozentsatz 26, 28, 29
Prozess 14
prüfen 177
Pseudogley 61
Puna 76
Push-und-Pull-Faktor 136
Pute 122
Pygmäen 131

240

Pyramide 81
Pyrenäen 44
Quarz 57
Quarzit 58
Quecksilber 105
Quelle 23, 34, 78, 87
Queller 93
Quellkuppe 54
Quellwolke 64
Quitte 120
Quote 125, 142, 198
Rabatt 154
radioaktive Verseuchung 108
radioaktiver Abfall 107
Raffinerie 163
raffinieren 111
Ranch 125
Randgebiet 194
Randkanal 90
Randmeer 91
Raps 108, 120
Rasse 130
Rathaus 163
Rationalisierung 147, 196
Raubtier 74
Rauch 54
raues Klima 186
Raumanalyse 16, 178
Raumanspruch 162
raumbezogen 177
Raumentwicklung 177
Raumfahrttechnik 112
Raumforschung 177
Raumfragmentierung 177
Raumgefüge 177
räumlich 32, 36
räumliche Verflechtung 167
räumliche Verteilung 15
Raummuster 177
Raumordnung 177
Raumplanung 177
raumverändernd 177
Raumverschwendung 177
Raumverträglichkeit 177
Raumwirksamkeit 177
Raureif 63
Reaktorkern 107
Reaktorsicherheitsbehälter 107
Reaktorunfall 108
Rechtecksmuster 172
rechte 22
Rechtsanwalt 149
Rechtsbeistand 149
Rechtsleistungen 149

recyceln 98
Recycling 98, 169
Redefreiheit 185
Reexport 140
reexportieren 140
reflektieren 24, 66
Reflexion 66
Regen 64
Regenfeldbau 115
Regenschatten 68
Regenwald 72
Regenwasserabfluss 169
Regenwolke 64
Regenzeit 73
Regierung 172, 184, 185
Region 18, 36, 170
regionale Entwicklung 183
Regionalismus 37
Register 16
regnerisch 64
Reibung 69
Reibungswiderstand 91
reich 178
Reihendorf 165
Reiheneinfamilienendhaus 168
Reiheneinfamilienhaus 168
Reimport 140
reimportieren 140
reinigen 160
Reinigung 149
Reis 119
Reisebüro 149
Reiseveranstalter 149
reißend 78
Rekultivierung 109
relative Luftfeuchte 68
relative Zahlen 29
Relief 41
Religionsgeografie 13
Religionszugehörigkeit 133
Rendzina 61
renovieren 177
Rentenalter 131
Rentier 76
Rentnerstadt 165
Reptil 74
Reservat 130
Reserve 103
Ressource 15, 103
Reurbanisierung 176
Revier 37, 109
Rhein 39, 46
Rheinisches Schiefergebirge 45
Rheinland-Pfalz 45

Rhodopen 44
Rhön 45
Ria 86
Riasküste 35
Richter-Skala 56
Richtlinie 139
Riffküste 35
Rifting 52
Rigaischer Meerbusen 42
Rinderwahnsinn 122
Rinderweidewirtschaft 123
Rindfleisch 122
Ringstraße 168
Rinne 83
Rinnsal 78
Rio Grande 50
Rocky Mountains 48
roden 97
Rodung 97
Roggen 119
Roheisen 110
Röhrenwerk 110
Rohstoff 103
Rohstoffe 183
Rohstoffmanagement 31
rohstofforientiert 102
Rohstoffquellen 98
Rohwasser 88
Rollbahn 169
Römisches Reich 170
Rosine 120
Ross-Schelfeis 41
Rossbreiten 69
rösten 121
Roterde 61
Rotes Meer 38
Routinetätigkeit 150
Rückgaberecht 200
Rückhaltebecken 89
Rückwanderung 136
Ruhr 187
Rumpffläche 77
runder Einzugsbereich 174
Rundhöcker 81
Rundling 165
Russische Föderation 46
Saarland 45
Saat 117
Sache 22
Sachsen 45
Sachsen-Anhalt 45
säen 116
Sägewerk 192
Sahara 40

241

Sahel 73
Saisonarbeiter 114
Sajan Gebirge 47
Salat 120
Salpeter 106
Salz 106
Salzausspülung 93
Salzboden 92
Salzbusch 93
Salzgehalt 91
Salzmarsch 86
Salzpfanne 74
Salzwasser 88, 92
Salzwasserbiotop 92
Salzwiese 93
San-Andreas-Linie 56
Sand 61
Sandbank 83, 85
Sander 81
Sandstein 58
sanfter Hügel 43
Sankt-Lorenz-Strom 50
Sanktion 142
Sanktionen 198
Satellitenbild 21
Satellitenstadt 165
Satire 24
Sattel 53, 77
sauber 161
sauer 59, 60
Sauerstoff 57, 66
Sauerstoffmangel 90
Säure 59
Säureeinleitung 96
saurer Boden 60
saurer Regen 96
Savanne 73
schachbrettartiger Plan 172
Schachbrettmuster 172, 173
Schacht 109
schädlich 160
Schädling 117
Schädlingsvernichtungsmittel 117
Schadstoff 95, 160
schadstoffarm 98
Schadstoffeinleitung 96
schadstofffrei 98
Schaf 122
Schafstall 116
Schale 51
scharf 179
schattieren 29
Schauer 64

Schaufelradbagger 109
Schaumwein 126
Schauplatz 23
Scheitelpunkt 82
Schelfgebiet 91
scheren 117
Scherungszone 53
Scherwelle 55
Scheune 116
Schicht 15
Schichtstufe 77
Schichtwolke 64
Schiefer 58
Schienenfahrzeugbau 111
Schiffbau 112
Schild 46, 53
Schirmakazien 73
Schistosomiasis 118
Schlachthof 126
Schlacke 54, 110
Schlafstadt 165
Schlaganfall 187
Schlamm 82
Schlammlawine 54, 93, 94
schlanke Produktion 102, 196
schlankes Management 196
Schleswig-Holstein 45
Schlosser 171
Schlot 54
Schlucht 34, 83
Schluckloch 84
Schluff 61
Schlüsselindustrie 100
Schmelzkäsewerk 126
Schmelztiegel 130
Schmelzwasser 88
Schmied 171
Schmuckwaren 113
Schnee 64
Schnee-Erosion 79
Schneefall 46
Schneefeld 80
Schneegrenze 75
Schneehase 76
Schneesturm 64, 70
Schneewehe 64
Schneider 172
schnell 179
Schneller Brüter 107
schnelles Wachstum 72, 176
Schnittblume 121
Schranke 139
Schuhmacher 171
Schulden 183, 184

Schuldenabbau 184
Schuldenberg 184
Schuldenerlass 184
Schuldner 183
Schule 164
Schuppen 171
Schuttbelastung 89
Schuttkegel 81
Schutz 161, 186
schützen 191
Schutzpflanzung 128
Schutzstreifen 128
Schwäbische Alb 43, 44
schwächen 178
Schwachzehrer 117
schwanken 134
Schwarzerde 61
Schwarzes Meer 38
Schwarzwald 43, 44
Schwebstoffe im Fluss 89
Schwefel 106
Schwefeldioxid 96
Schwefelgas 54
Schwein 122
Schweinefleisch 122
Schweinegrippe 122
Schweinepest 122
Schweinestall 116
Schwellenland 195
Schwemmfächer 82
schwer 179
schwere Niederschläge 64
Schwerindustrie 100
Schwerkraft 66
Schwermetall 96, 105
schwierige Umweltbedingung 186
schwül 63
Scirocco 71
Sea-floor-spreading 52
Sediment 14, 46
See 17, 34, 78
Seewind 70
Segment 28
Segregation 130
seichter Abschnitt 82
Seidenraupenzucht 122
Seismograph 56
Seismologie 55
Sektor 28, 146, 167
Sektorenmodell 188
Sekundärenergie 158
sekundärer Sektor 189
Sekundärerhebung 153

Sekundärindustrie 100
Sekundärwelle 55
selbständige Einzelhändler 145
Selbstversorgung 124
Selvas 73
semi-arid 74
Senkung 52
Serir 74
Shaduf 118
Shanty 172
Sialschicht 51
sich abkühlen 69
sich anpassen an 95
sich ansiedeln 102
sich auf Landleben umstellen 163
sich aufbauen 56
sich ausdehnen 69
sich belaufen auf 141, 184
sich erholen 179
sich erstrecken 18
sich erwärmen 71
sich etw. leisten 152
sich umsehen 152
sich verdoppeln 134
sich wälzen 54
Sichtweite 65
Sickerteich 89
Siedlung 37, 47, 162, 174
Siedlungsdichte 178
Siedlungsgebiet 162
Siedlungsgeografie 13
Siedlungshierarchie 164
Siedlungsstruktur 166
Siel 85
Sierra Nevada 44
Silage 117
Silber 106
Silicium 57
Siliziumchip 112
Silo 116
Simaschicht 51
Simulation 32
sinken 63
sintflutartiger Regenfall 94
Sippe 130
Sisal 122
Skagerrak 42
Skandinavische Halbinsel 42
Sklave 183
Slum 164
Smog 65, 96, 160
Sohle 109
Sojabohne 120

Solarenergie 108
Solarkonstante 66
Solarofen 108
Solarzelle 108
Solfatar 55
Sommersonnenwende 67
Sommertrockenheit 74
Sonderabfall 96
Sonderkultur 119
Sonderwirtschaftszone 195
Sonnenblume 120
Sonnenenergie 66, 158
Sonnenkollektor 108
Sonnenstand 67
Sonora 40
Sortiment 145
Sowchose 125
Sozial 159
sozial benachteiligt 132
soziale Position 153
soziale Schicht 175
sozialer Status 132
Sozialgeografie 13
Sozialhilfe 132
sozialräumlich 166
Sozialstation 132
Sozialstruktur 132, 167
Sozialsystem 184
Sozialwesen 149
Sozialwohnung 132
Spalt 59
Spalte 29, 54, 59
Späne 108
Spannung 56, 130
Sparen 152
Spargel 120
Sparquote 152
spätabendliches Einkaufen 144
speichern 31
Spektrum an Industrien 189
Spender 191
Sperrholzfabrik 112
Sperrwerk 93
Spezialgeschäft 145
Spezialisierung 156
Spirituosen 126
Spitze 27
Spontankauf 152
Spontankäufer 152
Sporn 77
Sportanlagen 163
Sprache 36
springen 179
Springflut 95

sprunghaft ansteigen 179
Staat 37
Staatsausgaben 181
Staatsfarm 125
Staatsgebiet 37
Staatskosten 156
stabil 63
stabil halten 179
stabilisieren 176, 179
Stadion 163
Stadt 164, 174
Stadtbewohner 170
Stadtgeografie 13
städtisch / urban 162
städtischer Raum 176
Stadtmauer 170, 173
Stadtsystem 190
Stadtzentrum 175
Stahlerzeugung 110
Stahlveredler 106
Stahlwerk 110
Stalagmit 84
Stalaktit 84
Stallung 116
Standardisierung 156
Standort 102, 127
Standortdreieck 101
Standortfaktor 102
stark 183
stärken 179
Starkzehrer 117
starr 51, 142, 198
Statussymbol 170
Staub mit sich tragen 71
Staudamm 89, 108
Staunässe 61
Stausee 17, 34, 89, 108
Staustufe 90
steigen 63
Steigungsregen 68
steil 77
Steilhang 35
Steilküste 35
Steinkohle 58, 104, 109, 158
Steinkohleeinheit 104
Steinmauer 170
Steinsalz 58
Steppe 75
Sterberate 134, 181
Sterblichkeit 134
Sterilisation 134
Steuerstab 107
Stichkanal 90
Stichwortverzeichnis 16

243

Sticker 171
Stickoxide 96
Stickstoff 117
stimulieren 176
Stockwerkbau 72
Stockwerkkultur 115
Stoffwechsel 60
Stollen 109
Strahlung 66
Strahlungs~ 13
Strand 35, 79, 85
Strandwall 85
Straße 18, 170
Straße von Dover 42
Straße von Mosambik 39
Straßendorf 165
Straßenlaterne 169
Straßenschwelle 168
Stratopause 66
Stratosphäre 66
Strauch- und Krautschicht 72
Streichlänge 91
Streifenkultur 128
Streusiedlung 165
Streuung 66
Strom 106
stromabwärts 78
stromaufwärts 78
Stromausfall 106
Stromschnelle 78, 83
Strömung 82, 88
Stromversorgung 169
Stromversorgungskabel 169
Strudelloch 82
Struktur 36
Stück 28
Stückpreis 146
Stufenfläche 77
Sturm 64, 94
Sturmflut 85
stürmischer Wind 64
Sturmwelle 95
stürzen 178
Subduktionszone 53
Subkontinent 37
subpolare Tiefdruckrinne 69
Subsistenzwirtschaft 190
Substanz 15
Subtropen 72
subtropischer Hochdruckgürtel 69
Subunternehmer 147
Suburbanisierung 151, 173, 176
Subvention 125, 176, 195

subventionieren 125
Suche 103
Suchgerät 193
Suchmaschine 200
Südamerika 37
Südchinesisches Meer 38
Sudeten 43
Südfrucht 121
Südkarpaten 44
Südlicher Wendekreis 67
Südostpassat 69
Südpolarkreis 67
Sukkulente 74
Sulusee 38
Sumpf 49, 78
Sumpfgebiet 45
Super-Gau 107
Superkontinent 37
Supermarkt 144
Süßwasser 88
Symbol 20, 24
Symbolik 24
systematisch 153
Tabak 121
Tabakwaren 113
tabellarische Daten 32
Tabelle 26
Tag-und-Nacht-Gleiche 67
Tagebau 109
Tageslänge 67
Tageszeitenklima 67
Taifun 70, 94
Taiga 75
Tal 17, 34, 42, 43, 77, 81
Tal des Todes 50
Talkessel 83
Talschluss 83
Talwind 71
Tanganyikasee 40
Tanker 105
Tanne 75
Tante-Emma-Laden 145
Taro 119
Tasmanisches Meer 38
tätig sein 194
Tau 64
Taunus 43
Taupunkt 68
Tauschhandel 140
Taxistand 168
Teak 73
Teakholz 122
Technologiepark 112
Tee 121

Teich 78
Teilmenge 153
Teilzeitvertreter 143
Tektonik 52
Telefonkabel 170
Telekommunikation 150, 197
Temperatur 63, 67
Termite 74
Terrasse 82
Terrassenfeldbau 115
tertiär 146
Tertiärer Sektor 146, 189
Tertiärisierung 146
Textilien 183
Textilindustrie 112
Theater 164
Thema 20, 22
thematische Karte 17, 20
Themse 39
Themse-Barriere 93
Theorie der Zentralen Orte 174
thermische Sprungschicht 91
Thermosphäre 66
Thüringen 45
Thüringer Becken 45
Thüringer Wald 43, 45
Tian Shan 47
Tidenhub 85
tief 18, 26, 27, 63, 78
Tiefbau 109
Tiefdruck 67
Tiefe 18, 91
Tiefengestein 57
Tiefenströmung 91
tiefgründig 60
Tiefkühlkost 127
Tiefland 17, 42, 77
Tiefsee 91
Tiefseegraben 53
Tierwelt 71
Timorsee 38
Titan 106
Titel 23
Todesursache 187
tolerant 130
Toleranz 130
Tomate 120
Ton 61, 106
Tonmineral 60
Töpfer 171
Topografie 42
Tor 170
Torf 58
Torfmoor 78

Tornado 70, 94
Tortendiagramm 28
Tourismus 44, 140, 149
Township 173
toxisch 95
Tragfähigkeit 127, 134
Traktor 116
Transferpreissystem 199
Transition 189
Transpiration 68
Transport 141, 149
Transportkosten 174
Transportweg 18, 175
Trauf 77
Traufrinne 171
Trawler-Flotte 127
Treffer 200
Treibeis 75
Treibgas 96
Treibhaus 116
Treibhauseffekt 66, 96, 160
Treibhausgas 66, 96, 160
Treibsand 82
trennen 130
Tribalismus 138
Trichtermündung 78
Trinkwasser 88, 193
Trinkwasserleitung 169
trocken 68
Trockenfeldbau 115
Trockengebiet 74
Trockenheit 68
trockenheitsresistent 74
Trockensavanne 73
Trockental 83
Trockenzeit 73
Trog 91
Tropen 72
Tropfsteinhöhle 84
tropisch 72
tropischer Regenwald 72
tropischer Wirbelsturm 94
tropisches Klima 49
Tropopause 66
Troposphäre 66
Tschuktschen Halbinsel 48
Tsunami 56, 94
Tuberkulose 187
Tuchhändler 171
Tuff 55
Tundra 49, 75
Tunnel 168
Turm 170
Twister 70

Typhus 187
Überalterung 134
Überangebot 157
überbevölkert 176
Überbevölkerung 129
übereinander lagern 32
Übereinkunft 141
überfischen 127
Überfischung 127
Überflutung 81, 186
Überflutungsebene 81
überfüllt 129
Übergangsbereich 173
Übergangsunterkunft 192
Übergangszone 175
Überkultivierung 96
Überproduktion 102
überschreiten 94
Überschrift 26
Überschuss 189
überschwemmen 78, 89
Überschwemmung 46, 78, 89, 94
Überschwemmungsebene 34
Überseehandel 138
übertreiben 24
übertrieben 24
Überweidung 96
Ufersicherung 86
ultraviolett 66
Uluru 41
umfangreich 191
umkippen 90
Umland 173
Umlaufberg 83
Umsatz 146
Umsatzsteuer 146
Umsatzvolumen 185
umsiedeln 109
Umsiedlung 109, 137
umverteilen 124
umwandeln 176
Umwandlung 158
Umwandlungsgestein 58
Umwelt 13, 20, 98, 150
Umweltbeobachtung 98
Umweltbewegung 98
umweltbewusstes Konsumverhalten 152
Umweltfragen 161
umweltfreundlich 98, 161
Umweltgeografie 12
Umweltkrise 161
Umweltminister 161

Umweltministerium 161
Umweltpolitik 161
Umweltproblem 186
umweltschonend 161
Umweltschutz 98, 161
Umweltschützer 98, 161
Umweltzerstörung 161
Umwelt~ 159
unabhängig 183
Unabhängigkeit 170
unangemessen 191
unbegrenzte und ebene Fläche 174
Unberührbarer 133
Unbeweglichkeit des Industriestandorts 103
unerwünschte E-Mail-Sendung 200
unfähig 185
unfruchtbar 60
Ungarische Tiefebene 44
ungelernt 101
Ungerechtigkeit 157
Ungleichheit 157
ungünstig 197
unhaltbar 159
Universität 164
unkontrollierte Kettenreaktion 107
Unkrautvernichtungsmittel 117
unter Tage 109
Unterbevölkerung 129
Unterboden 15, 62
unterbrechen 94
unterdrücken 185
Unterentwicklung 16
unterer Rand 22
unterernährt 187
Unterernährung 132, 187
Unterhaltungsindustrie 149
unterhöhlen 86
unterhöhlt 86
Unterholz 72
unterirdischer Fluss 83
Unterlauf 78
unternehmensbezogene Dienstleistungen 146
Unterstützung 156
untersuchen 22, 152
Untersuchung 152
Untersuchungskategorie 26
Untervergabe 147
Untiefe 85
ununterbrochen 144

245

unvoreingenommen 153
üppig 72
Uralgebirge 47
Uran 105
Ureinwohner 130
Urstromtal 81
US-Amerikanische Stadt 173
Vanadium 105
Variable 27
variszische Orogenese 44
Vatnajökull 41
Vegetation 41
Vegetationszonen 71
veranschaulichen 26, 188
verarbeiten 126
verarbeitende Industrie 100
verarbeitendes Gewerbe 189
Verarbeitungsprozess 100
verarmt 155
verbessern 142, 177, 184, 198
verbieten 142, 198
Verbindung 20, 199
Verbindungskanal 90
Verbot einer landwirtschaftlichen Nutzung 128
Verbrauch 20, 104, 138, 159, 162, 181
verbrauchen 104
Verbraucher 112
Verbraucherforschung 153
Verbrauchermarkt 145
Verbraucherprofil 154
Verbraucherschutz 155
Verbrennung 97
Verbündeter 193
verdunsten 68
Verdunstung 68
Veredelung 100, 114
Veredelungsindustrie 100
Vereinbarung 141
vereinen 194
Vereinfachung 156
verflachen 179
Verflüssigung 56
verfolgen 137, 200
Verfolgung 137
verformen 51
Vergabe an Sub-Unternehmen oder Zulieferer 196
Vergleich 20, 21
Vergletscherung 42
Vergleyung 61
Vergreisung 134

Verhaltensgeografie 12
Verhaltensweise 177
verheiratet 131
verhütten 110
Verhüttung 110
Verhütung 134
Verhütungsmittel 134
Verjüngung 82
Verkalkung 61
Verkaufsaktion 154
Verkaufstrick 155
Verkehrsampel 169
Verkehrsgeografie 13
Verkehrsinfrastruktur 150, 169, 190
Verkehrsweg 175
Verklappung 92
verknüpfen 199
Verknüpfung 199
verkoken 109
Verkrustung 62
Verlagswesen 149
Verlandungszone 85, 92
Vermarktung 31, 148
Vermieter 175
Vernetzung 199
veröffentlichen 23
veröffentlicht 23
verorten 18
Verpflichtung 193
verrotten 72
Versalzung 62, 97, 118
Versandhaus 143
Versandhauskatalog 143
Versandkosten 146
Versäuerung 96
verschieden 152
verschmutzen 95, 159
Verschmutzung 13, 159
verschuldet 183
Verschuldung 183
Verschuldungsgrad 184
Verseuchung 95, 160
Versicherung 149
versickern 87
Versickerung 87
Versickerungsanlage 89
Versorgung 132, 166
Verstaatlichung 125
Verstädterung 181
Versteigerung 199
Verstromung 110
Verteilung 20, 157
Vertikalkonvektion 91

Vertragsanbau 123
Vertreibung 137
Vertrieb 142, 148
Vertriebene/r 137
Vertriebsagent 142
Vertriebs~ 147
verunreinigtes Land 97
Verwahrlosung 156
Verwaltung 148, 172
Verwaltungssektor 172
verweigern 142, 198
Verwerfung 52
verwittern 59
Verwitterung 14, 44, 59
verwundbar 185
Vieh 116, 122
Viehhalter 116
Viehhaltung 123, 128
Viehmarkt 126
Viehpferch 117
Viehtränke 117
Viehzucht 113
Viertel einer bestimmten Religion 173
Viertel einer bestimmten Sprachgruppe 173
Viktoriasee 40
virtuelles Einkaufszentrum 199
Visualisierung 26
Vogelgrippe 122
Vogesen 43
Volkskommune 125
Volkszählung 154
Vollerwerbsbetrieb 123
Vollerwerbslandwirt 123
vor 22
Vordergrund 22
voreingenommen 153
Vorfluter 34
vorherrschender Wind 64
vorhersagen 94
Vorkommen 93, 103
Vorort 162, 173, 175
vorrätig 145
Vorsprung 35
Vorwarnung 56
Vorzugs~ 142
Vulkan 47, 53
Vulkanasche 54
Vulkanausbruch 93
vulkanisch 54
vulkanisches Gestein 55
Vulkanismus 53
Vulkanologie 54

wächsern 74
Wachstum im
  Dienstleistungsbereich 147
Wachstumsbranche 101
Wachstumsperiode 67
Wachstumspol 102
Wadi 74
Waffenschmied 171
Wahrnehmungsgeografie 12
waldbedeckt 43
Waldfeuer 97
Waldschutzstreifen 128
Waldsterben 96
Walfang 127
Walnuss 121
Walzwerk 110
Wand 35
Wanderarbeiter 136
Wanderdüne 84
Wanderfeldbau 115, 123
wandern 135
Wanderung 135
Wanderweidewirtschaft 123
Waren 139, 156, 171, 183
Wärmeaustausch 13
Wärmeenergie 94
Wärmetransport 67
Warschauer Pakt 186
Waschmittel 97
Wasserausgleichsschleuse 89
Wasseraustausch 87
Wasserbecken 118
Wasserbewirtschaftung 87
Wasserbüffel 122
Wasserdampf 68
Wasserentnahme 87
Wasserentnahmerecht 87
Wasserentsorgung 87
Wasserfall 34, 83
wasserführende Schicht 87
Wasserführung 89
Wassergewinnung 87
Wasserhaltekapazität 61
Wasserhaushalt 87
Wasserkraft 158
Wasserkraftwerk 192
Wasserkreislauf 87
Wasserkuppe 46
Wasserleitung 88
Wasserscheide 37, 89
Wasserschutzgebiet 90
Wasserspeicher 89
Wasserspiegel 193
Wasserversorgung 87, 169

Wasserversorgungsinfra-
  struktur 169
Wasservorrat 87
Wasserweg 89
Wasserwerk 88
Wasserwirtschaft 87
Wasserzuleitung 88
Watt 85, 92
Weber 172
Wechsel 164
Wechselbeziehung 16
wechselfeuchtes Klima 72
Wegegeld 170
Wehr 89
weiblich 131
Weide 115
weiden 117
Weiler 164
Wein 121
Weinbau 118
Weinberg 118
Weinernte 118
Weinhändler 172
Weinrebe 121
Weintrauben 120
weiter weg 22
weiterführende Schule 132
weiterverarbeitende Industrie
  100
Weiterverarbeitung 100
Weizen 119
Wellblechhütte 164
Welle 79, 91
Wellenbrecher 86
Wellenenergie 108
Wellenkraft 158
Wellenlänge 91
Welt 37
Weltbank 184
Welthandel 138
Weltregion 170
Weltreligion 133
Weltstadt 165, 197, 199
Weltwirtschaftsbeziehungen
  194
Weltwirtschaftsordnung 194
Werbebanner 200
Werbegeschenk 154
Werbung 148, 154
Werft 112
Wert 27, 141, 181
Weser 46
Westfriesische Inseln 42
Westküstenklima 74

Westsibirisches Tiefland 46
Westwindzone 69
Wettbewerb 141, 153, 198
Wettbewerbsfähigkeit 142, 198
Wetter 13, 63
Wetteraufzeichnung 13
Wetterbericht 63
Wetterkarte 63
Wetterkunde 63
Wettervorhersage 13, 63
Wheeler Peak 50
widerstandsfähig 119
wieder füllen 145
Wiederaufbereitungsanlage
  107
Wiederauftauchen 84
Wiederausfuhrhandel 140
Wiedergutmachung 193
Wiegebalken 170
Wiese 115
Wildnis 50
Wildschutzgebiet 99
Wind 63
Windenergie 108
Windfarm 108
Windgenerator 108
Windgeschwindigkeit 63
Windhöcker 84
Windkraft 158
Windrichtung 63
Windschliff 84
Windschutzhecke 128
Windstärke 64
windstill 70
Windstille 70
Wind~ 70
Winkelmesser 29
Wintersonnenwende 67
Winzer 118
Wirbel 88
Wirbelsturm 70
Wirkung 24
Wirkungsgrad 107
Wirkwarenhändler 171
Wirtschaft 20, 138, 156, 169, 180
wirtschaftlich 156, 159
wirtschaftlich aktive
  Bevölkerung 134
wirtschaftliche Aktivität 16
wirtschaftliche Folgen 196
wirtschaftliche Unternehmung
  195
wirtschaftlicher Grund 193
Wirtschaftsblock 141

247

Wirtschaftsexperte 156
Wirtschaftsflüchtling 136
Wirtschaftsgebäude 115
Wirtschaftsgeografie 12, 15
Wirtschaftsgut 144, 194
Wirtschaftskraft 194
Wirtschaftsstruktur 167
Wirtschaftsverbindung 198
Wissen 191
wissenschaftliche Disziplin 12
wissenschaftliche
 Untersuchung 31
Witterungsverhältnisse 13
Woge 91
Wohlfahrtsorganisation 191
wohlhabend 150
Wohlstand 131, 150, 162, 170, 181
Wohlstandsmodell 162
Wohnblock 168, 173
Wohngebäude 166
Wohngebiet 162, 166, 172
Wohngebiete der Mittel- und
 Oberschicht 175
Wohngebiete der Unterschicht
 175
Wohnraum 132
Wohnung 168
Wohn~ 166
Wolfram 105
Wolga 39, 48
Wolke 64
Wolkendecke 64
Wolkenformation 64
Wolkenkratzer 173
das World Wide Web 199
Wunsch 151
Würger 72
Wurzelgeflecht 72
Wurzelsprengung 60
Wüste 49, 74
Wüste Gobi 40
Wüstenbildung 49
Steinwüste 84
Xerophyt 74
Yachthafen 169

Yuppie 131
zähflüssig 54
Zahl 26
Zaun 117
Zeche 108
Zehrgebiet 80
zeigen 31
Zeithorizont 161
Zeitspanne 29
Zellulose 106
Zellulosefabrik 111
Zelt 192
Zeltstadt 138
Zement 106
Zementherstellung 111
Zensus 129
zentrale Plateaus 43
Zentralmassiv 43
Zentrum 22, 174
zerklüftet 77
Zerschluchtung 83
Zersetzung 62
Zersiedelung 176
Zersplitterung 124
zertrümmern 59
Zeugenberg 83
Ziege 122
Zielgruppe 153
Zielland 137
Zielverkaufspreis 186
Zimmermann 171
Zink 105
Zinn 105
Zins 184
Zirkulationsmuster 13
Zirkumpazifischer Feuergürtel
 55
Zirren 64
Zitadelle 173
Zitrone 121
Zitrusfrucht 120
Zoll 186
zollfrei 198
Zolltarif 140, 198
Zollzone 195

zonaler Boden 61
Zubehörindustrie 111
Zucchini 120
züchten 117
Zuckerfabrik 127
Zuckerrohr 119
Zuckerrübe 119
Zuflucht 137
Zufluss 34
Zugang 141, 150
Zugang begrenzen 37
Zugänglichkeit 150
Zugbrücke 172
zugreifen 150
Zugspitze 41, 46
zukunftsfähig 159
zukunftsweisend 159
Zuliefererbetrieb 101
Zunahme 26
zunehmen 26
Zungenbecken 81
zurückgehen 178
zurückschlagen 198
zusammenbrechen 178
zusammenfließen 82
Zusammenfluss 34, 82
zusammengesetzt aus 51
Zusammenhang 24
zusammenlegen 124
Zusammensetzung 13, 15
zusammenziehen 59
zustimmen 25
Zuwachsrate 141
Zweifamilienhaus 168
Zwergweide 76
Zwiebel 120
Zwischeneiszeit 53
Zwischenfrucht 119
Zwischenhändler 142
Zwischenhändler 143
Zyklone 67

Übersicht über die Infoboxen

Plants in mediterranean climates ... 75
Trees in mixed forest regions 75
Vegetation zones in tropical mountains 76
The tides 91
Marine species 92
Coastal fauna 93

Industrialisation:
The development of industry 101
Stages in development 180
The GDP 181
Statistics 182
Types of development 191
Benefits and disadvantages of host countries 195

Phonetische Umschrift

['] folgende Silbe hat die stärkste Betonung: geography [ʤi'ɒgrəfi]
[ˌ] folgende Silbe die zweitstärkste Betonung: climatology [ˌklaɪmə'tɒləʤi]

[ɪ] in
[e] yes
[æ] can
[ʌ] sun
[ɒ] job
[ʊ] good
[ə] climate ['klaɪmət]
[i:] meet
[ɑ:] chart
[ɔ:] border
[u:] school
[ɜ:] bird
[eɪ] rain
[aɪ] my
[ɔɪ] toy
[əʊ] ocean
[aʊ] now
[p] pollution
[t] top
[k] climate
[f] far
[θ] thematic

[s] sun
[ʃ] shoulder
[h] horizon
[m] main
[n] near
[ŋ] length
[b] boreal
[d] down
[g] good
[v] vertical
[ð] weather
[z] physical
[ʒ] television
[l] like
[r] red
[j] yes
[w] wet
[tʃ] China
[dʒ] geo
[i] react
[u] visual

Verwendete Abkürzungen

AE	American English – Amerikanisches Englisch
adj	adjective – Adjektiv, Eigenschaftswort
adv	adverb – Adverb
BE	British English – Britisches Englisch
n	noun – Nomen, Substantiv, Hauptwort
pl	plural – Plural, Mehrzahl
sb	somebody – jemand(es/em/en)
sg	singular – Singular, Einzahl
sth	something – etwas
v	verb – Verb, Zeitwort
etw.	etwas – something
jmd.	jemand(es/em/en) – somebody
Pl.	Plural, Mehrzahl – plural
Sg.	Singular, Einzahl – singular

➔ *Abb. 1* Projections

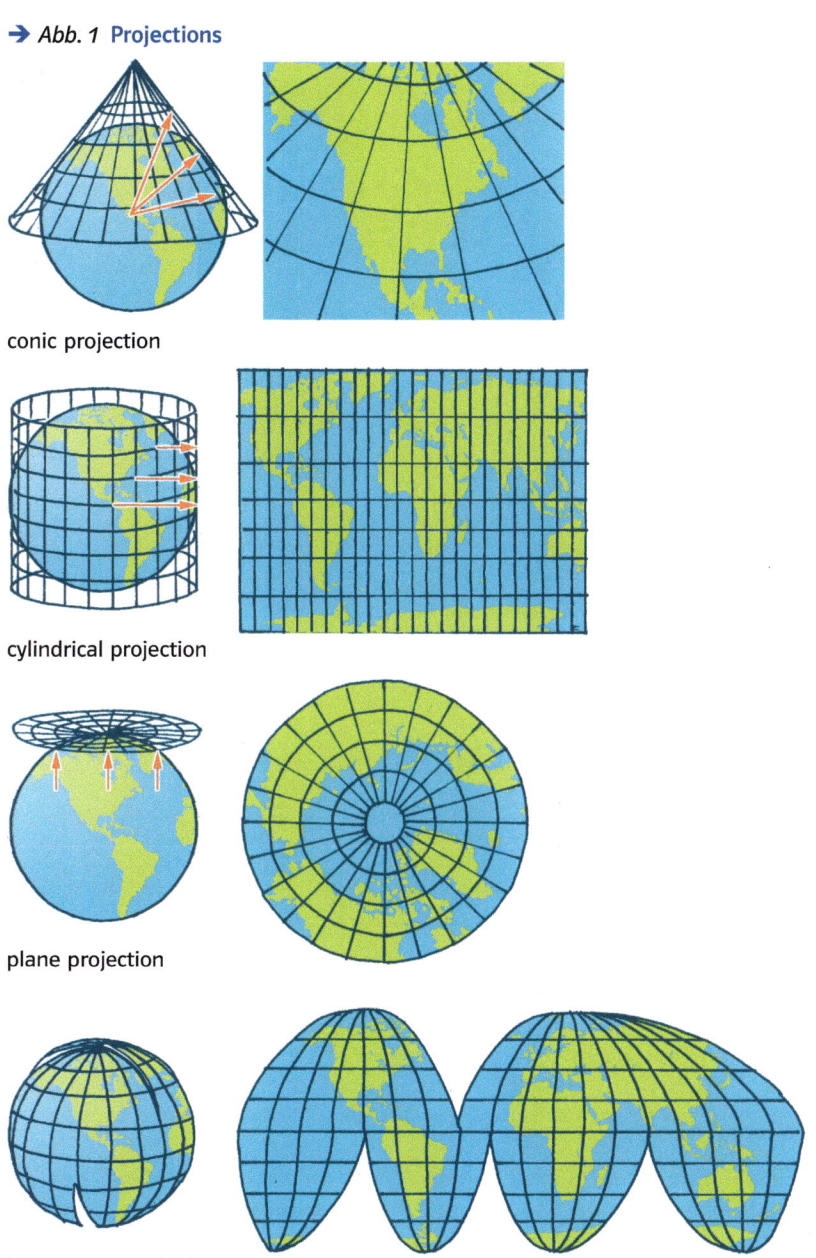

conic projection

cylindrical projection

plane projection

interrupted projection

Projektionen S. 16 + 34

➜ *Abb. 2* **Working with maps**

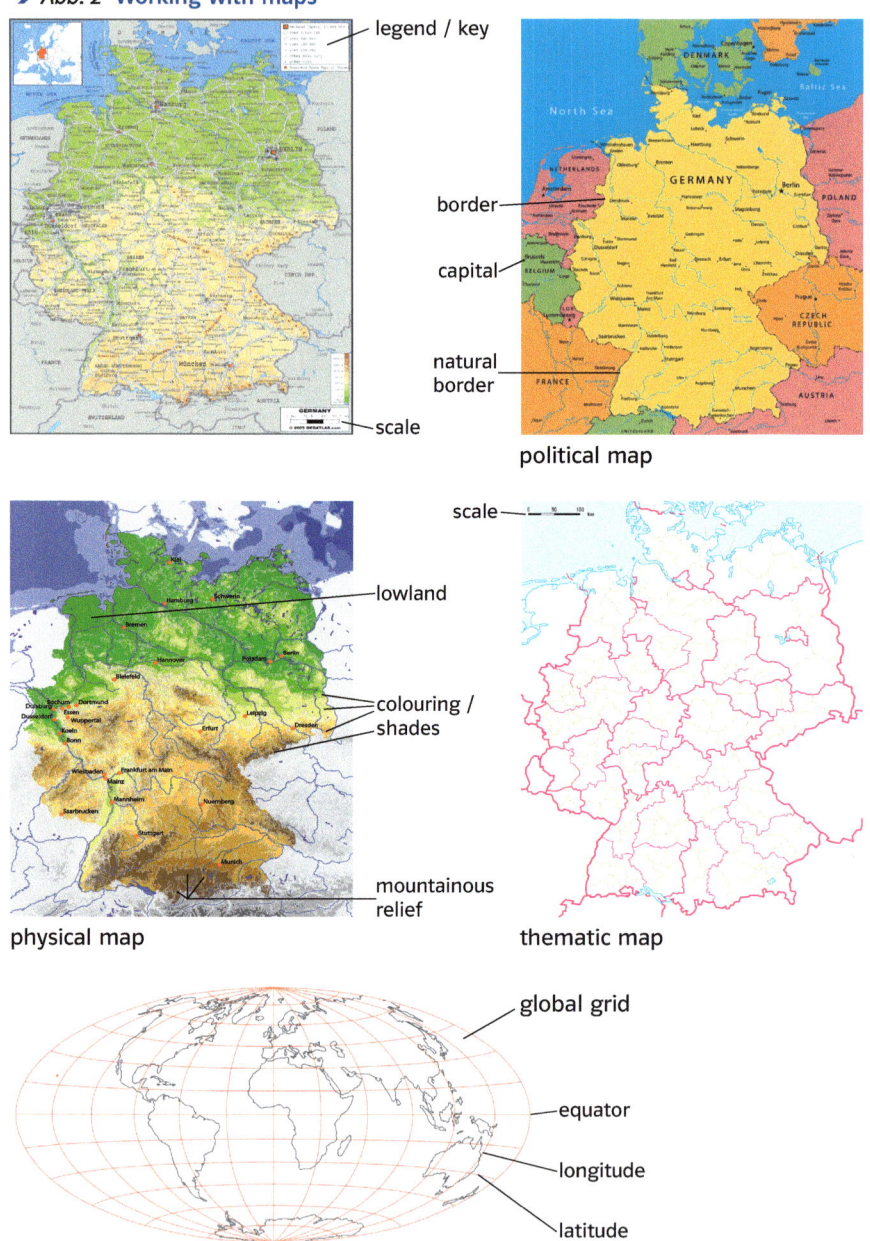

Karten S. 16–21

→ Abb. 3 Working with illustrations and visuals

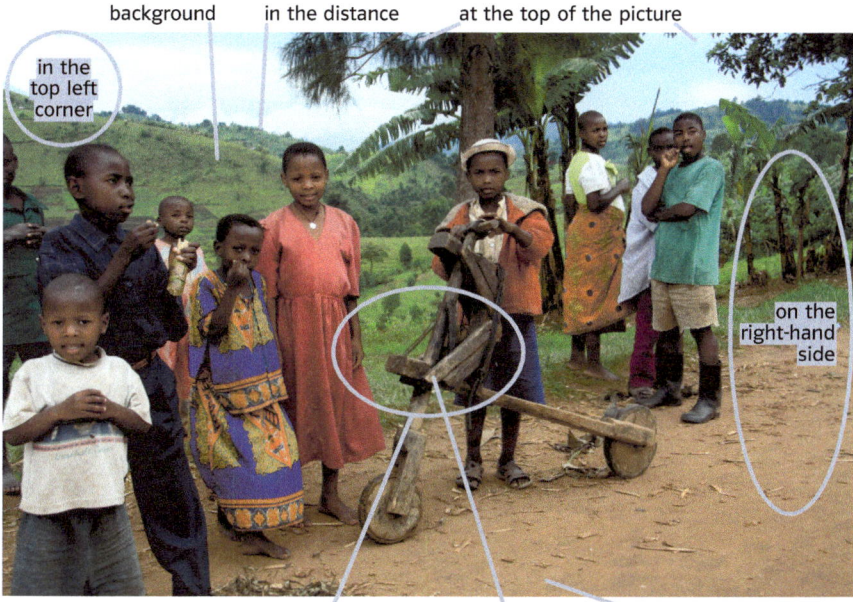

background · in the distance · at the top of the picture · in the top left corner · on the right-hand side · photograph · in the centre · foreground · bottom

aerial photograph
(oblique aerial)

satellite image

Illustrationen und Bildmaterial S. 21–25

→ *Abb. 4* **Working with graphs and charts**

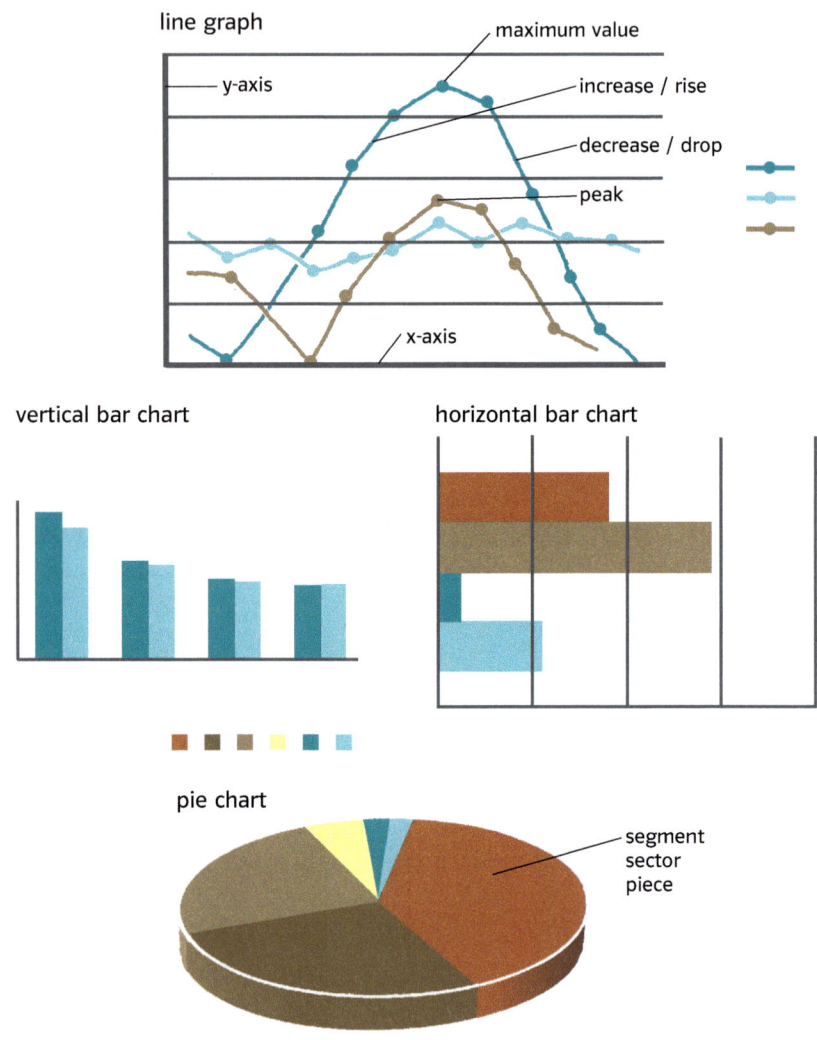

Diagramme S. 26–30

→ *Abb. 5* Working with GIS

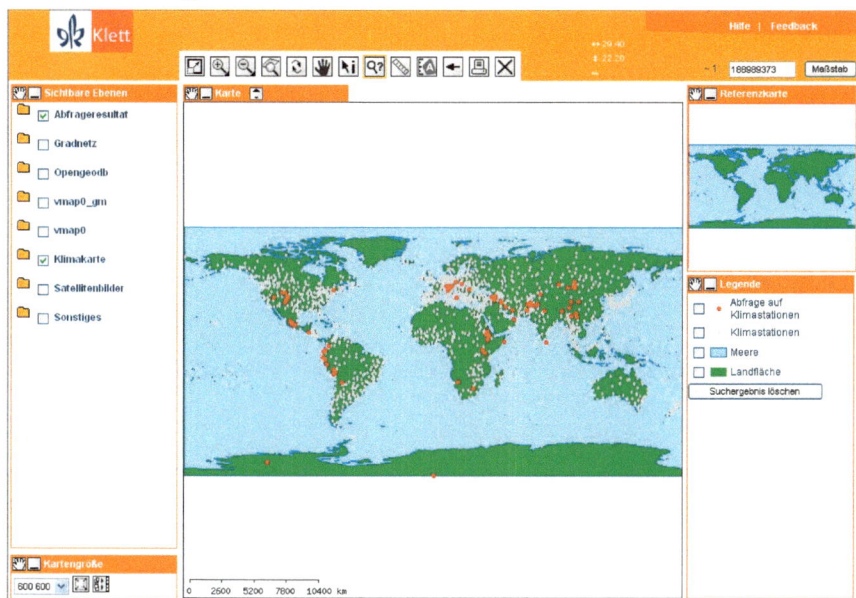

GIS S. 31–32

→ *Abb. 6* Protractor

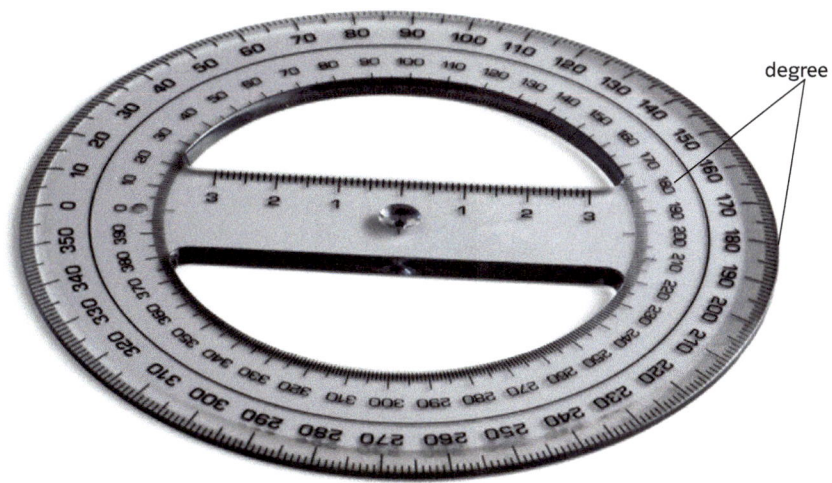

Winkelmesser S. 29

➔ *Abb. 7* **River**

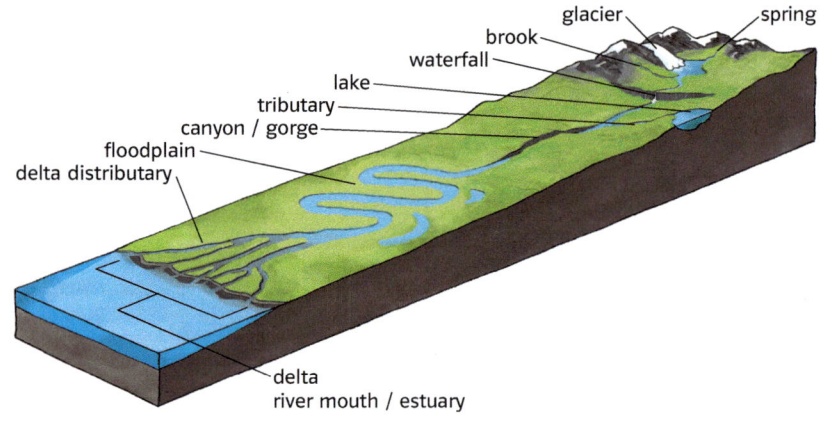

Fluss S. 34 + 78 + 81

➔ *Abb. 8* **Lakes**

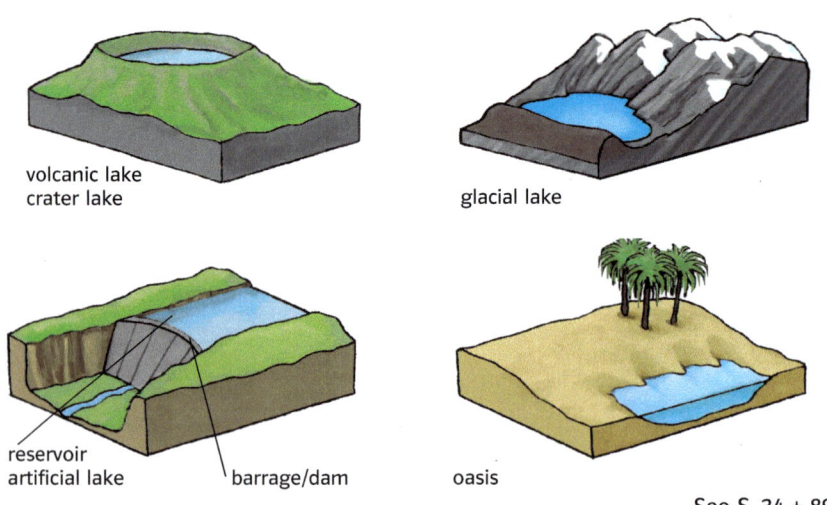

See S. 34 + 89

→ *Abb. 9* **Mountains**

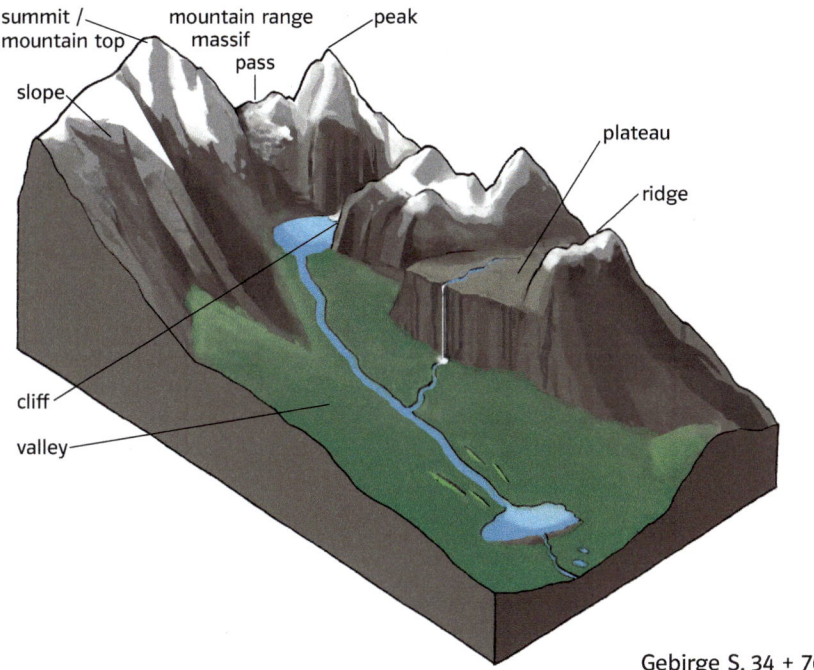

Gebirge S. 34 + 76

→ *Abb. 10* **Glacier**

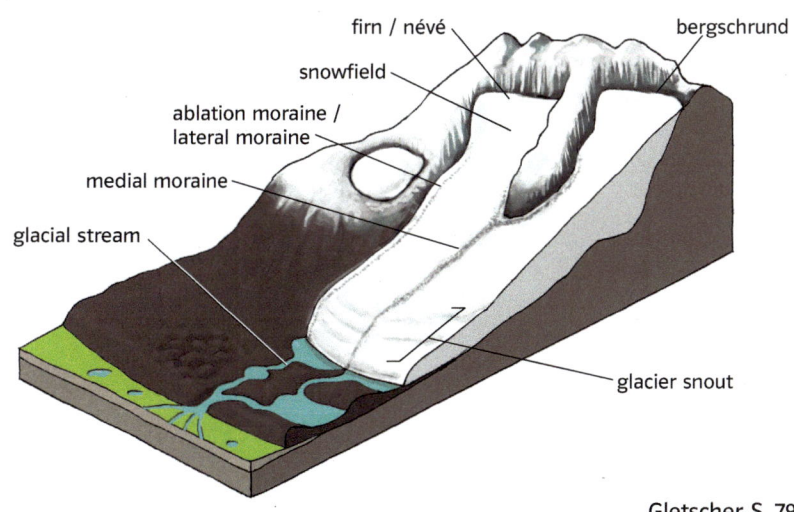

Gletscher S. 79

→ *Abb. 11* Coast

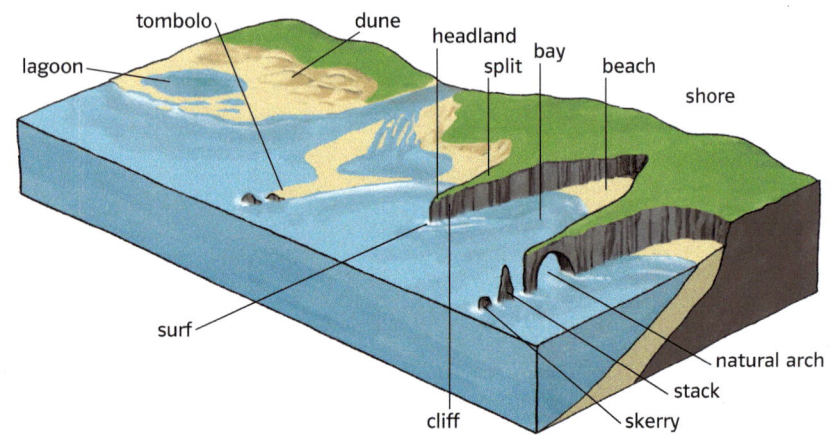

Küste S. 35 + 84

→ *Abb. 12* Islands

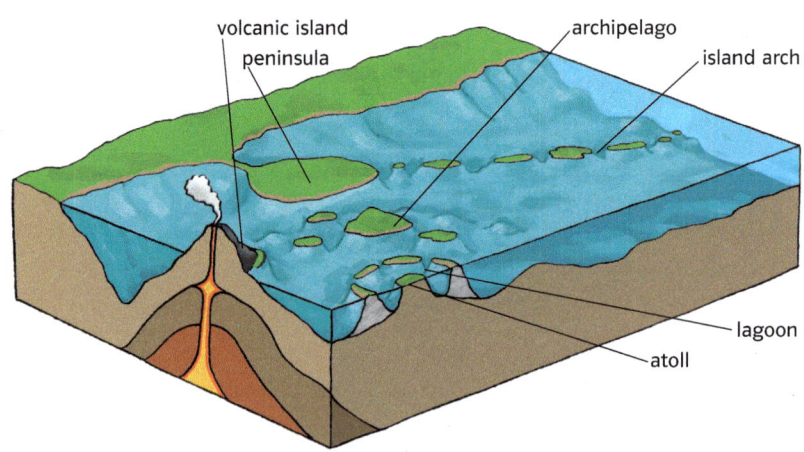

Inseln S. 35

258

→ *Abb. 13* **Earth's interior**

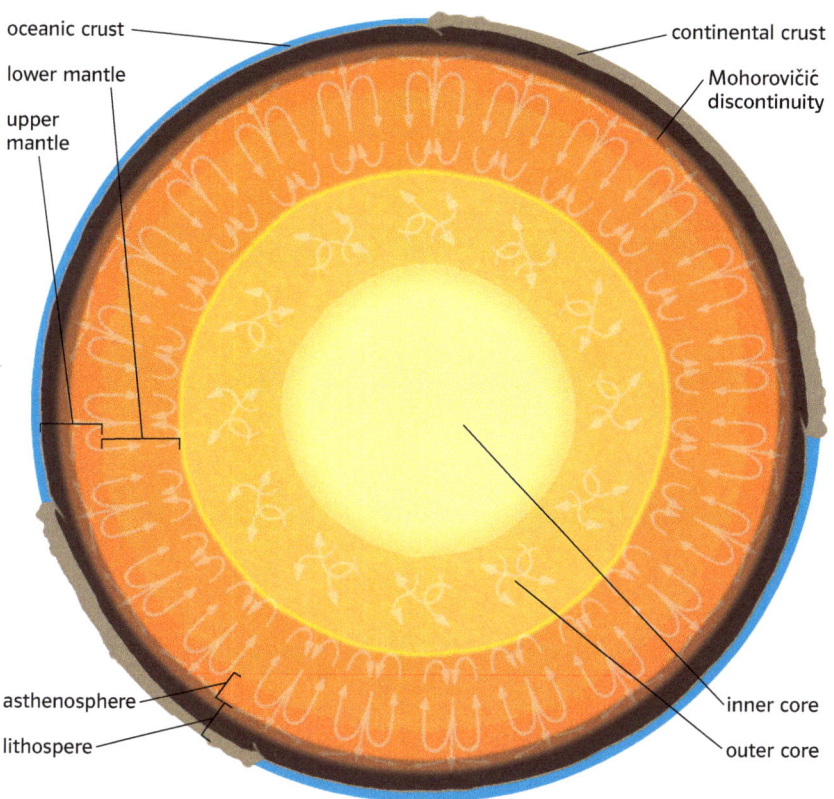

Das Innere der Erde S. 51

→ *Abb. 14* **Volcanoes**

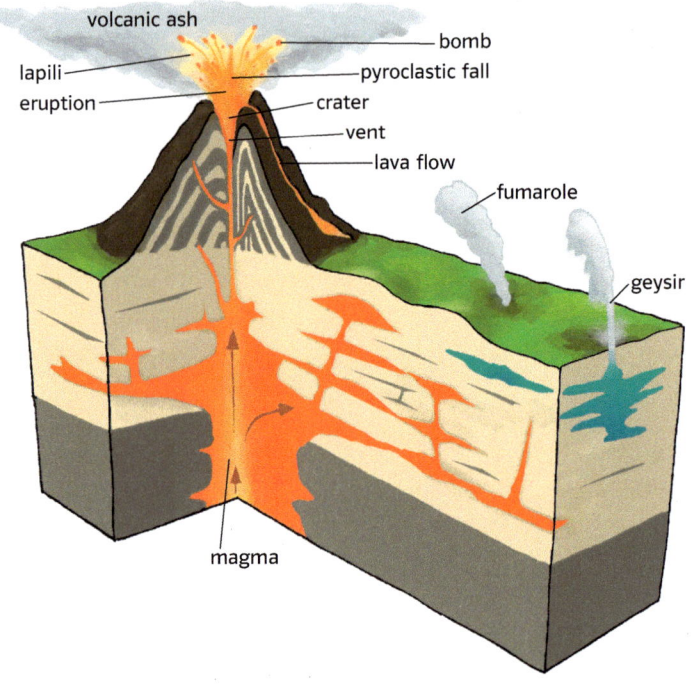

Vulkane S. 53

osphere of the Earth

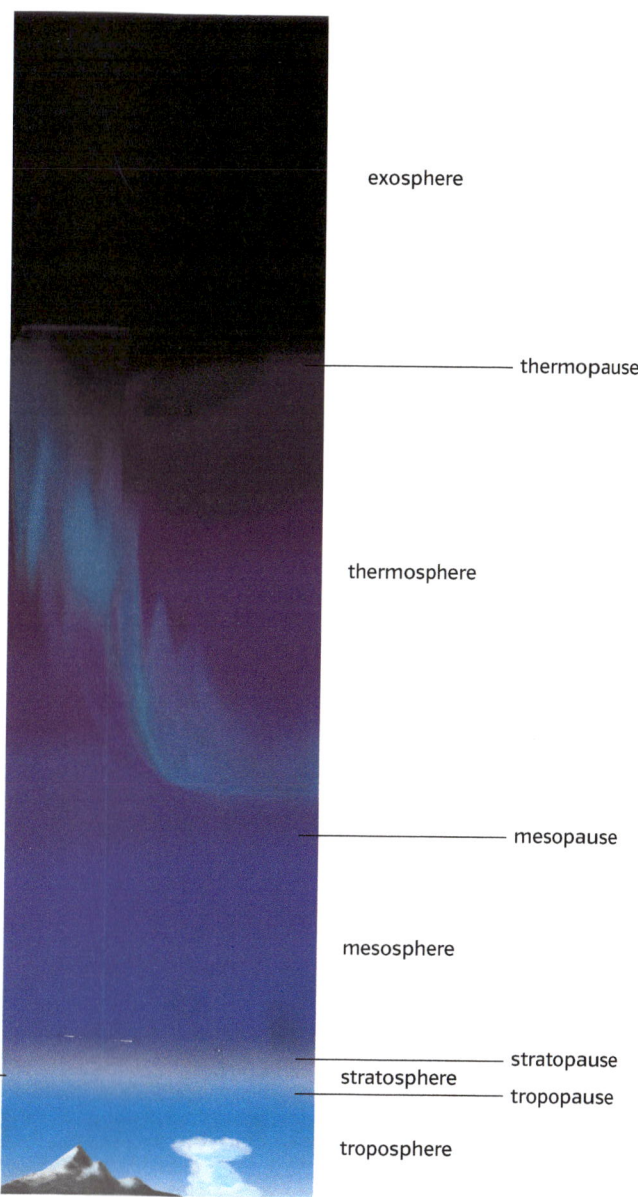

exosphere

thermopause

thermosphere

mesopause

mesosphere

stratopause
stratosphere
tropopause

troposphere

Erdathmosphäre S. 66

→ *Abb. 15* Plate tectonics

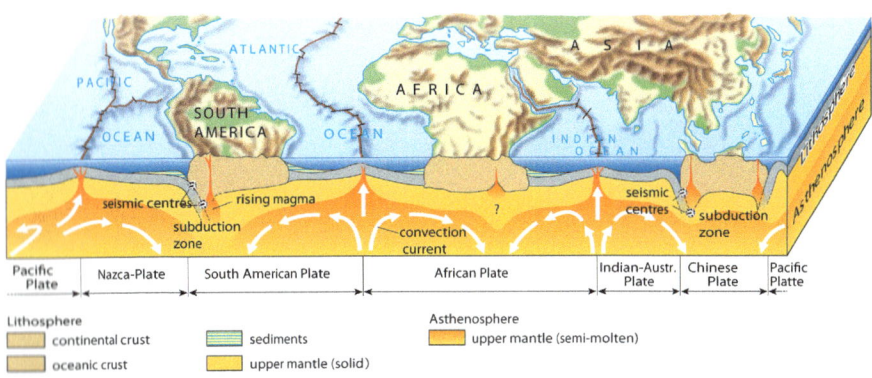

Plattentektonik S. 52

→ *Abb. 16* Continental drift

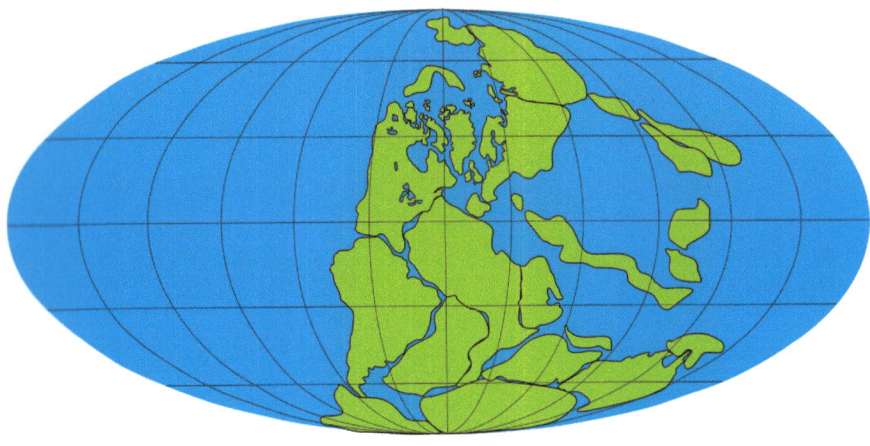

Urkontinente S. 37 + 53

→ *Abb. 17* **Rocktypes**

basalt

gneiss

feldspar

tuff

sandstone

shale / shist

quartz

lignite / brown coal

marl

mica

coal

marble

Gesteinsarten S. 57

→ *Abb. 18* **Soil horizons**

A

B

C

→ *Abb. 19* **Altitudinal vegetation zone**

tierra nevada

tierra helada

tierra fria

tierra templada

tierra caliente

andine

→ *Abb. 20* Atm

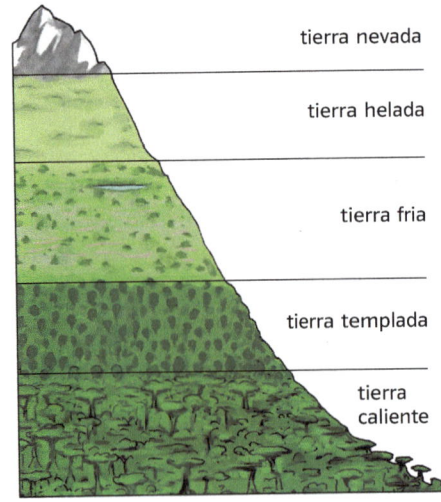

ozone layer

➔ *Abb. 15* **Plate tectonics**

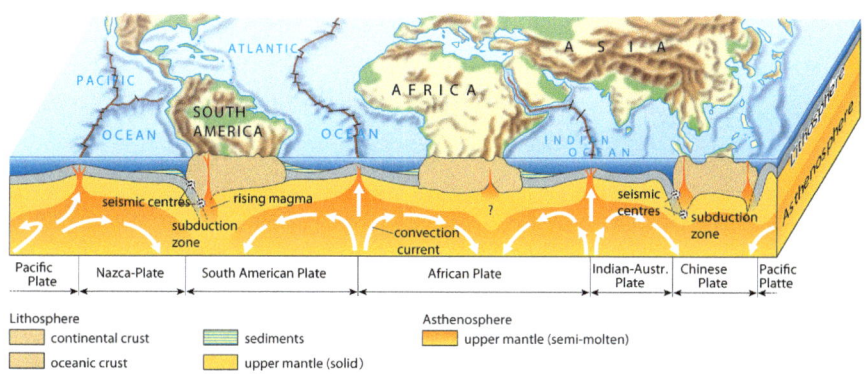

Plattentektonik S. 52

➔ *Abb. 16* **Continental drift**

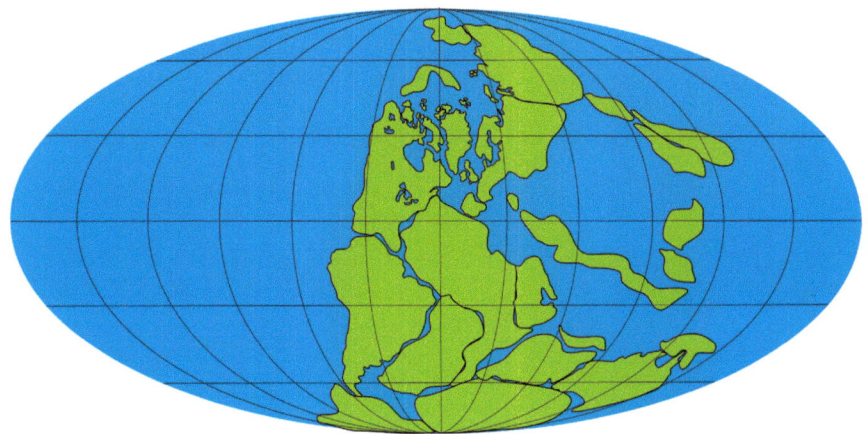

Urkontinente S. 37 + 53

→ *Abb. 17* **Rocktypes**

basalt gneiss feldspar
tuff sandstone shale / shist
quartz lignite / brown coal marl
mica coal marble

Gesteinsarten S. 57

→ *Abb. 18* **Soil horizons**

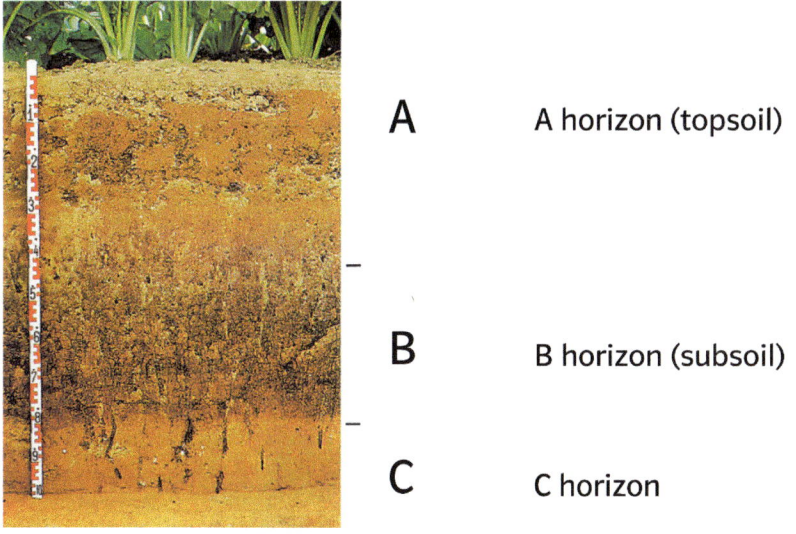

A — A horizon (topsoil)

B — B horizon (subsoil)

C — C horizon

Bodenhorizonte S. 62

→ *Abb. 19* **Altitudinal vegetation zone**

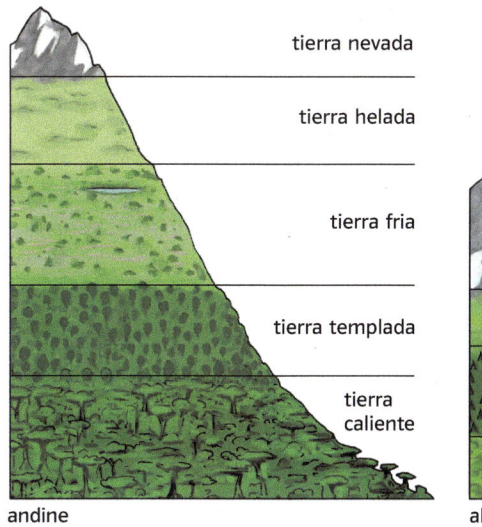

Höhen- und Vegetationsstufen S. 76

263

→ *Abb. 20* **Atmosphere of the Earth**

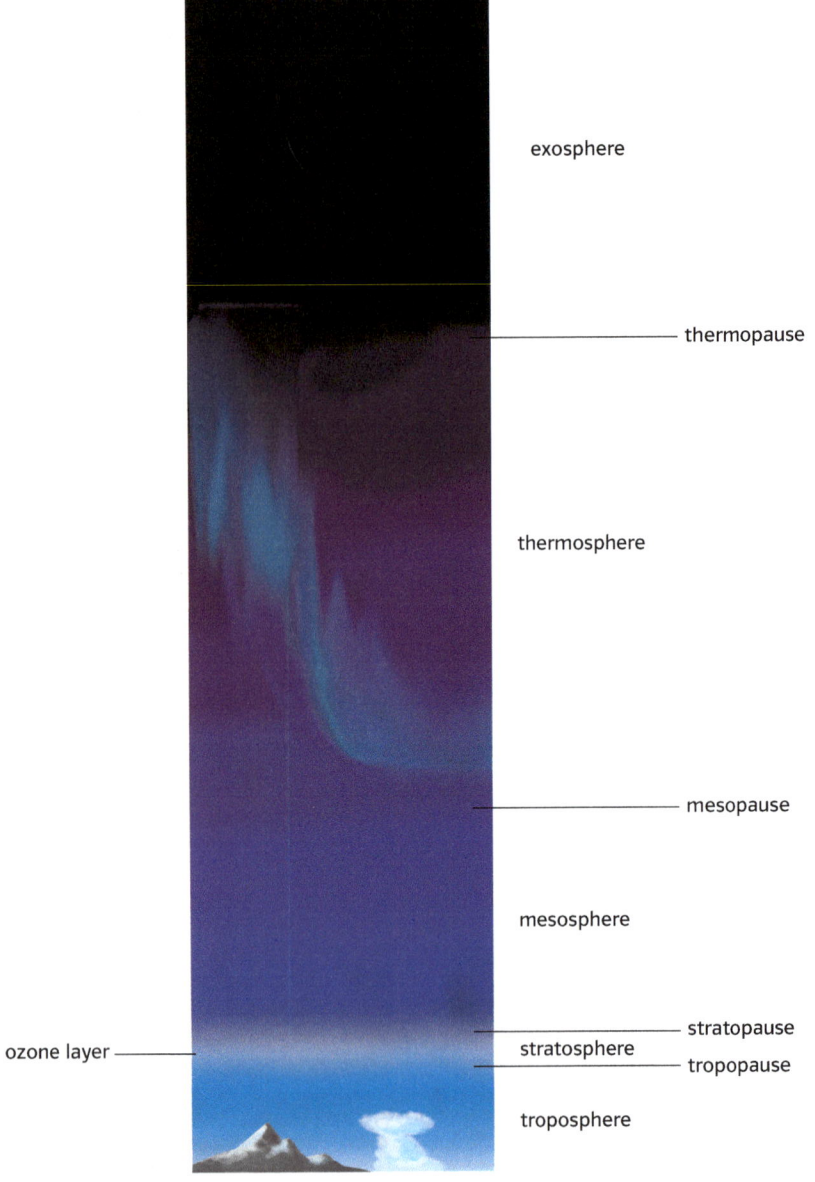

Erdathmosphäre S. 66